# UNSTRUCTURED GROUP THERAPY

## creating contact
## choosing relationship

Revised and updated edition of the book previously published in
the United States as
*Creating Contact, Choosing Relationship:*
*The Dynamics of Unstructured Group Therapy*

## Richard C Page and Daniel N Berkow

***PCCS BOOKS***
Ross-on-Wye

This revised edition first published in 2005

First edition published in 1994 by Jossey-Bass under the title
*Creating Contact, Choosing Relationship: The Dynamics of Unstructured Group Therapy*

BOOKS Ltd
1omas Row
lton Road
ss-on-Wye
IR9 5LB
UK
(0)1989 763 900
ccs-books.co.uk

© Richard C Page and Daniel N Berkow 2005

**Unstructured Group Therapy:
Creating contact, choosing
relationship**

A CIP catalogue record for this book is available from the British Library

ISBN 1 898059 67 5

*Cover design by Old Dog Graphics
Printed by Bath Press, Bath, UK*

# CONTENTS

## THE AUTHORS

RICHARD C. PAGE is a Professor Emeritus of Counselor Education and Counseling Psychology at the University of Georgia, Athens. He received his PhD degree (1976) from the University of Florida in Counselor Education. He is a former Fulbright Scholar; having been awarded two Fulbright Scholarships in 1988–1989 and 1994–1995 and both times taught and performed research at the Department of Applied Psychology, University College Cork, Ireland. He also currently is a Visiting Professor at ISMAI University, Porto, Portugal.

Richard C Page's main research activities have been in group counseling and therapy, drug and alcohol treatment and multicultural counseling and therapy. He has done extensive research on the effectiveness of unstructured therapy groups with drug and alcohol abusers, high school students, university students, physically and emotionally disabled individuals and persons who live in different countries. He has published over 80 articles in professional journals and at least 20 articles on the effects of unstructured therapy groups on different client populations.

He has had much work experience with illicit drug abusers; he set up the first therapeutic community to be established in a prison setting for female inmates with drug abuse problems in the state of Florida and he worked for three years as a Counseling Psychologist at a therapeutic community for illicit drug abusers in Atlanta, Georgia. He was the editor of the *Journal of Addictions and Offender Counseling* for six years and served as the President of the International Association for Addictions and Offender Counselors and as the Chair of the National Board for Certified Counselors.

DANIEL N. BERKOW is currently working as Associate Director of the Counseling Center at the University of North Carolina, Wilmington. He provides individual therapy and leads process-oriented therapy groups for college students. He received his PhD (1995) from the University of Georgia in Counseling Psychology. He is currently a member of the American Psychological Association. In addition to twelve years of experience in university counseling centers, he practiced three years in a community mental health center and has conducted unstructured therapy groups with a variety of populations. His publications and professional presentations cover a wide area of interests, including group therapy, intercultural understandings of therapy, and integrating Asian wisdom traditions with Western models of therapy.

# FOREWORD

This is a rare book. The authors have offered a mixture of timeless philosophical constructs and practical advice about unstructured groups. The universal themes of love, power, and justice are considered central concepts in the relationship processes that form the 'heart and soul' of unstructured group therapy.

Substantive components of the ontological focus have been derived from Paul Tillich's explanation of the dynamics of love, power, and justice. Martin Buber's philosophy of I-Thou relations, and interpretations in Gestalt and Person-Centered theories, are offered as rationale for group therapy that facilitates growth in individuals.

The authors have managed to concretize the concepts of love, power, and justice in a way that provides functional meaning for such macro-conceptions in relation to the foundation of practical and functional forces in unstructured therapeutic group work. Likewise, they have identified a process that allows a cognitive guideline for facilitators of 'unstructured' groups. The specific structure of any given group is developed from the interaction process and from the non-interventive, yet subtle facilitation of the group facilitators.

The authors draw from their studies of philosophers, group dynamics, and practice of group psychotherapy. Dr Page's experience with and research of unstructured groups with women in prison and with substance abusers in a halfway house are notably present in the discourse of a theoretical stance on unstructured groups. Dr Berkow's work as a therapist brings even greater practical significance to their theory.

I had the privilege of observing and periodically being involved in the process and deliberation of the authors in the development and implementation of this book. I was chair of the Department of Counseling, Counseling Psychology, and Human Development in which the authors were involved during this process. They separately delved into the literature and their own experiences while they pursued their inquiries. They met regularly in offices and libraries to buttress their thoughts. Most intriguing to me was their weekly afternoon lunches where they brainstormed their thoughts and beliefs, resolved their differences, and questioned their considerations. Later, a few beers and non-linear speculations added to the fullness of their final explorations. Their effort was a human and personal as well as scholarly venture.

Specifically, the book offers the essential dynamics that the authors believe occur in unstructured group interactions. It focuses on both the communication processes and relationships among participants. The universal themes of love, power, and justice are herein delineated as relationship processes that form the heart and soul of group therapy.

The book is not designed to provide recipes for successful therapy. It provides an analysis of the dynamics of therapeutic groups in relation to modes of communication and justice that explains interpersonal healing in human groups. It is sprinkled with examples from group encounters.

A principle assumption in their conceptual scheme is that meaning is simultaneously created through interpersonal interactions and perceptual processes within persons. 'I' and 'We' are considered to be mutually involved in a co-creative process that develops human identities, lives, and meanings.

My reactions to several aspects of the book are that the discourse offers an overall delineation of what amounts to a participant-friendly approach to group work. It also offers readers the opportunity to focus separately, if they so desire, on the conceptual 'macro-concepts' (Love, Power, and Justice) or on the practical operations of unstructured groups. The 'ontological dignity' of *Love, Power, and Justice* (Tillich, 1954: 21) that reflects an ongoing dynamic within the field of interpersonal interaction is integral to the conceptual scheme of the book but not actually necessary for the pragmatic reader.

The group process, group stages, and communication aspects of the practice provide solid direction for clinical practice. The relational context for human awareness wherein group members can integrate awareness and extend it to others based on mutual caring and responsibility is enough of a theoretical guide in and of itself.

As a Client-Centered/Person-Centered advocate, I find the authors' ideas generally congenial to my beliefs. Their definition of Unstructured Group Therapy might be loosely applicable to Person-Centered Group Therapy. Their definition is the following:

> *Unstructured Group Therapy* . . .[is] an organized human activity in which individuals meet with the intention to share their resources for mutual growth and healing without imposing a preconceived structure on the process, dynamics, and outcome. (p. 6)

The authors add an aspect of free will indicating that '. . . the essential theoretical position is that responsibility is a central factor in psychological health and well-being' (p. 6). The term implies that the person is to some extent:

> ... an agent, who can be aware of consequences, and who can be viewed as a being who makes choices ...
>
> ... a creator of his or her perceptions rather than being a passive recipient of them. A person may be responsible for interpreting a

situation in a particular manner, for setting certain goals, for acting in a specific manner, or for maintaining a system of values that affects interactions. (p. 6)

Person-centered groups often meet the same unstructured criteria of not having preconceived structure on the process, dynamics, and outcome. Client-centered therapists generally have a similar focus on the phenomenological perceptions of the participants. The client-centered assumption is not apt to be quite so specific as that of creating '... opportunities for the members to have choices, and to make decisions about interactions, relationships, and the direction of the group ...' (p. 6). The client-centered assumption is that individuals become more responsible as they become more congruent; i.e., as the individual's self-concept becomes more integrated with her organismic experiences. Client-centered theory assumes that the individual becomes more responsible (including more self-aware and free) as self-actualization progresses from the presence of a particular atmosphere. Otherwise, the authors are proposing a theory that is theoretically comparable to client-centered theory in many ways.

First, they assume a therapeutic climate of Unstructured Group Theory (UGT) in the triad of Love, Power, and Justice (LPJ). This is developed with the interactions of the members and the facilitator.

Second, the triad promotes 'Self-Actualization' (which is the combination of Awareness, Freedom, and Responsibility). The facilitator's level of self-actualization affects the group climate, the development of the balanced operation of LPJ. The increased self-actualization of the leaders and members promotes the balanced operation of LPJ.

A similar theoretical format for CCT is possible. Client-centered theory (CCT) assumes that the triad of therapist congruence, unconditional positive regard, and empathic understanding promotes a process. Simply put, CCT assumes that therapist congruency (included with that congruence is unconditional positive regard and empathic understanding) enhances the possibility of client congruency.

Examination of and speculation about unstructured group therapy is close to the practice of client-centered group therapy. Generally, the group participants are likely to create their own direction, in their own way (mostly), and at their own pace. The basic process 'goals' are also reflective of client-centered groups. I do not consider the term 'goals' as useful in client-centered formulations and I believe the term might be somewhat misleading of the intention of the book. Nevertheless, these 'goals' are noted in Chapter 2 as follows:

1. the development of a climate that promotes disclosure of individual concerns and that is supportive of members who work on personal problems and

2. the emergence of meaningful interpersonal learning focused on present relationships between members. (p. 18)

This characteristically describes the client-centered process as often developed by group members.

Both theories assume the group process to be a natural occurrence that is accelerated when the appropriate psychological atmosphere is provided. In client-centered therapy, the psychological atmosphere refers to the congruent therapist's experiencing of unconditional positive regard and empathic understanding of the therapist towards the client. In unstructured group therapy, the balance of Love, Power, and Justice can be considered the psychological atmosphere.

Part of the subtle difference between the framework of the unstructured group offered in this book and Rogers' theory is the different view of self-actualization. The authors' define *self-actualization* as 'a process through which a person becomes simultaneously more independent and more aware of and involved in relationships' (p. 9). Rogers' definition of *self-actualization* is that of the relative congruence between the self-structure and the total experience of the organism (Rogers, 1959: 196–7). Ultimately, Page and Berkow's definition reflects several of the probable characteristics and behavior of high levels of congruence between the organism and the self.

It is not the intent of the authors (nor this Foreword) to identify with or compare the concepts in the book to client-centered therapy. However, many readers are apt to have an interest in the commonalities and differences between these two theoretical frames. The unstructured group is often identified with client-centered therapy, probably rightly so. However, such a group is not necessarily client-centered. The inherent non-directivity of client-centered therapy is not necessarily present in an unstructured group. The unstructured group is not necessarily non-directive. That is, the extent in which the focus is upon the participants directing their own way, pace, and direction without therapist intervention is more dependent upon the particular facilitators than upon the therapy model.

For example, these particular authors seem more inclined to defer to the individual phenomenological directions of the participants within the context that the facilitator also influences the direction of the group.

Given some differences between the postulated dynamics of unstructured group therapy and the assumptions of non-directive person-centered groups, there is a great deal of commonality. The authors offer a stimulating dialogue on the values of the unstructured group. Their work promises to be a meaningful reflection on theoretical premises and a pragmatic way of proceeding in clinical group practice.

Jerold D. Bozarth PhD
Professor Emeritus
University of Georgia

# PREFACE

This text is written to address the need for an integrated theory of group therapy. The authors have observed that existing group therapy theory tends to focus either on psychodynamics of group functioning, or a here-and-now experiential focus for group interactions, but has not been able to integrate both. We provide an explanation of how psychodynamics and here-and-now processes of relating are interconnected. Additionally, we show the connection of social, family, and group structuring through the dynamics of love and power, with the natural desire for relationship that is just, that is open and inclusive.

Theories of therapy either involve ways to provide structuring that supports the therapist as authority, or negate structure in ways that make the group a kind of communal being that doesn't require leadership. Because we view the structure versus no-structure dichotomy as artificial, we present a theory that shows that the dynamics of unstructured relationship are involved in any kind of human group— simply in a less overt way when a focus on externally required structuring is provided. With this understanding, a therapist can adapt to the needs of a setting with regard to providing external structuring, and yet work with the unstructured aspects of relationship dynamics. We investigate these dynamics in terms of love, power, and justice because these key aspects of relationships are found not only within diverse cultures, but are involved when cultures interact with one another. Thus, we have formed a theory that addresses not only group therapy, but in addition the ways that human beings form groups, and interact within and through groups.

As an integrated theory, the model we propose in this text shows how phases unfold as group members allow defenses to function permeably, how and why past relationship patterns unfold in a group setting, and how here-and-now interactions form the basis of change. We not only integrate key aspects of person-centered, existential, and psychodynamic theories but include ways that cognitions and relational behaviors can change as a result of group participation. The theory of group work presented herein shows that personal integrity and integration of interpersonal dynamics at the levels of group, community, and culture are mutually interactive and supporting of each other.

The theory we present in this text integrates core constructs from person-centered and existential therapy and philosophy with psychodynamic insights. We also show how shifting relationship dynamics change the processing of feeling-level responses, as well cognitively based beliefs about self and others. Thirdly, we integrate a perspective on interpersonal relationships that emphasizes that effective personal wholeness requires balanced relating within an inclusive arena beyond the individual. This balance within self and through interpersonal relating requires that the natural inclination toward a sense of power be co-aligned with an awareness of love. Such balance can allow a person to learn that power as an individual results when one is able to hear and include others as integral to one's sense of self and being. Group therapy is an ideal format for such learning, which embraces creative justice. A creatively just group is able to allow each member to experience being heard, valued, and to contribute according to his or her proclivities and awareness of involvement.

In order to understand the meaning that love, power, and justice have for group dynamics, a group leader must be aware within moment-to-moment interactions, and be able to encourage recognition of responsibility. The theory we present in this text values freedom as the basis for growth in awareness, and shows that responsibility can never be considered as divorced from an open and acute awareness within the process of being with self and others. Thus, freedom, responsibility, and awareness mutually imply one another, and enhance each other's functioning. Clarity about these principles—particularly when considered with respect to the integration of love, power, and justice—informs effective group leadership, as well as an understanding about relationships people form within communities and cultures.

The authors use this approach to understanding human groups in a variety of settings, and have supervised therapists in diverse settings in the use of this theory. These settings include group therapy for university students, in prison and drug abuse treatment settings, for adults in the community, and in various countries. Additionally, we use this theory in understanding supervision, and the behavior of psychologists, counselors and other helping professionals functioning in a team perspective. As this theory is applicable to formation of modes for communicating, establishing social norms, and developing roles for interpersonal behaviors, the scope of this theory potentially extends well beyond therapy to understanding diverse groups that human beings form. Issues of justice, freedom, responsibility, and power are relevant to understanding how societies form relationships. Group therapy, in this sense, is work on society by members of society who have suffered from injustice in one form or another, abuse of power, and/or withholding of love.

# CHAPTER 1

# INTRODUCTION

The term 'unstructured' group therapy seems to have gained popular acceptance because these groups appear to lack formal structure and systematic organization. Why then write a formally and systematically organized work about this kind of activity? One answer is that if we examine what occurs in unstructured therapy groups, we find that there is indeed meaningfulness and hence orderliness to the proceedings. This organization is not imposed by authority and may not be initially apparent. However, a great deal of the therapeutic value of these groups results from the intrinsic human activity of meaning-making; this activity affects interactions if there is an environment that provides the freedom for this dynamic to be expressed.

Amoebas and rivers may initially appear shapeless and lacking in formal organization. However, if a person investigates these phenomena with care, a definite organization appears. We become aware of it as we learn to observe the role that amoebas play in a larger whole, in an ecology of living beings. A river plays an important role in an environmental ecology. In the same way, we can learn to observe how interactions in an unstructured group relate to a larger whole, an organization formed by the lives and relationships of participants. The apparent looseness and freedom that characterize interactions in an unstructured group form a basis for communications that have specific purposes and meanings. These link specific interactions with each member's ongoing experience and pattern of relationship and with the pattern of interactions that is formed by the group as a whole. What initially appears to be an unstructured form of relationship, if examined with care, thus reveals itself to be an organized and meaningful activity.

The interactions that occur in unstructured group therapy can be considered aspects of an organized form of activity—namely, the activity of human relationship. Unstructured group therapy therefore reflects the structures that human beings give to their interactions. Unstructured therapy respects the intrinsic structuring involved in human communication *without* imposing external structure upon members' communications. Some external structure is always involved in therapy groups—for example the temporal limits of the group and the physical setting in which interactions take place. However, every attempt is made in these groups to optimize the atmosphere of freedom that allows members to create their own process and to discover the intrinsic structures and patterns that affect their communications.

1

## RATIONALE FOR A THEORY OF UNSTRUCTURED GROUP THERAPY

This book has grown from the authors' attempts to clarify how best to understand and conceptualize the intrinsic organization involved in human relationship insofar as that organization affects the process of therapy. We had both observed the powerful healing process that can be released through interpersonal communication in a group setting. Yet we found that existing theories of group process had not really met our needs for understanding various aspects of the therapeutic process. Some that we felt had not been adequately addressed in previous theories included adequate descriptions of the interpersonal tensions and connections that members create as they interact in a group, analysis of the modes of communication that affect therapeutic process, and the rationale for members' frequent use of their group to deal with past relationships as they work on present relationships.

We have attempted to address behavior, affect, and cognition within a perspective that views the person as potentially whole. This perspective is a holistic view of the person. The person is seen as functioning most effectively when thinking, feeling, and acting are integrated and are mutually influencing. No one aspect of people needs to control the other aspects if there is harmony in their interactions. The integration of various aspects of being occurs through creating a whole that is more than the sum of its parts. Personhood can be considered human awareness in developing experiential meanings—that is, meanings anchored in living perceptions and feelings. Therapy therefore encourages persons to create and experience meaning within the actions of ongoing encounters.

The key aspects of communication and relationship that influence therapeutic process must be understood and integrated to form a coherent theory of group therapy. These key aspects are, of course, defined in part through subjective experiences and perceptions of human behavior in groups and other relationships. We have observed that treating individuals as potentially responsible beings who are essentially free to make choices leads to the most effective results in therapy. Freedom needs to be assumed to be a reality in a theory of group therapy based on the actual perceptual dynamics that lead to constructive change. (The truth of freedom does not negate the fact that people are conditioned by past relationships and are limited by various physical factors and conditions.)

Human freedom is essentially the freedom to choose awareness or to avoid it. The choice to be aware leads to the recognition of responsibility; the avoidance of awareness leads to irresponsibility. Thus, in our view, the experience of freedom and the recognition of responsibility are inevitably linked, both in theory and in its application to therapeutic interactions. The movement of individuals towards healing and growth always involves awareness and cannot occur if individuals choose to avoid freedom and responsibility. The activity of being aware in organizing perceptions is the basis of the dynamics through which interactions are structured in an unstructured therapy process.

# Introduction

## THE NATURE OF UNSTRUCTURED THERAPY IN GROUP SETTINGS

The self can be understood as an interactive whole that forms and is formed by relationship (O'Hara, 1984). The self is created through contact and relationship and generates contact and chooses relationship. The self does not exist separately from relationship, and relationships are a manifestation of the nature of the self. The self is an 'I' that is simultaneously a 'we'. It is formed through dialogue and interaction (Friedman, 1992). Even the most rugged of rugged individualists would have no identity apart from the social and cultural relationships through which the individualist identity was formed. Unstructured group therapy is an ideal setting for learning how 'I' and 'we' are aspects of one process of being and becoming. Although valuing 'I-ness' may seem to preclude valuing 'we-ness', unstructured group therapy can often promote what Arnett (1989) has termed 'the dialogic reality that much of life rests in our creative search for the unity of opposites of seemingly separate camps' (p. 58). The apparently opposite vectors of force created by I-ness and we-ness are reconciled if unstructured processes in human groups lead to the establishment of healing and creative dialogue.

In unstructured therapy, leaders of groups tend to assist members in struggling with their own uncertainty about how to communicate clearly, find answers or directions, and relate to others. Unstructured group therapy becomes structured through participants' choices of modes of communication, attention to specific themes, and movement toward certain roles in relationships. An unstructured format allows participants to confront how their own choices have affected the forms of communication employed in interactions, the topics of concern upon which they focus, and their use of roles. Participants in these groups can potentially learn a great deal about who they are being and becoming with others because they draw upon their own sense of themselves, and on their own established patterns of interaction as they confront the ambiguity and uncertainty of unstructured situations.

Individual recognition of responsibility, mutual influence, and mutual assumption of responsibility are the process through which group members create their therapy. In this process, a leader's non-direction is not necessarily a good thing and being directive is not necessarily a bad one. However, it is important for the leader to maintain awareness and an open and accepting attitude toward members. To set up rules which say that certain forms of interaction are good or bad would undermine the group's sense of freedom and members' mutual responsibility for forming group process.

## AN ONTOLOGY OF RELATIONSHIP WITHIN AWARENESS

An analysis of the leader's communications in terms of their being directive or non-directive is not sufficient to understand how healing groups operate. It would be possible to analyze members' interactions using their cognitions and concepts; yet such an analysis would minimize the effects that members' feeling states and nonverbal communications have on one another. Members mutually influence not only cognitions and perceptions but each other's basic relatedness in being with others (or process of being). It is, of course, difficult to define and analyze aspects of a construct that is as global as a 'process of being'. This construct is abstract and is only partially within the realm of empirically based science (it is also involved in such realms as art, literature, religion, and philosophy). A person's process of being involves aspects that are immediate and nonverbal as well as aspects that are mediated by cognition and perception. Nonetheless, we felt that it was necessary to base our observations on such a global and abstract construct because we needed to address the immediate and nonverbal aspects of relationship as well as those aspects that are cognitively mediated.

A basic 'map' for conceptualizing the process of being and relationship that proved to be of great value for an analysis of therapeutic groups was that provided by Paul Tillich (1954) in his book *Love, Power, and Justice*. Tillich was an influential existential philosopher and theologian whose works, such as *The New Being* (1955), had an impact on twentieth century philosophy and theology. Tillich's interest in psychotherapy and the concepts that he presented in his book *The Courage to Be* (1952) have influenced psychological theorists such as May and Yalom (1984).

Love, power, and justice are universal elements of the process of being that have relevance in a variety of cultures and contexts. These elements can be seen to be active (in different proportions and with varying degrees of integration) in any human relationship. We decided to use love, power, and justice as ontological categories to discuss the intrinsic dynamics of relationship and communication. In this text, being includes interpersonal relationship, the relationship of persons to nature, and that of individuals to the potential depth of their own process of being.

The basic ontological elements of love, power, and justice are useful as constructs that can help explain how individuals' world views are integrated with a process of relationship, and vice versa. In principle, the integration of love, power, and justice indicates how group members can operate without interfering with one another. If love, power, and justice are operating in disharmony in a group, its members are likely to interfere with one another's integrity, possibly by being judgmental or by selectively disengaging. If power is emphasized in a manner that infringes on love, participants may create norms that encourage autonomy without respecting needs for supportive caring. If love is emphasized in a manner that infringes on power, norms may be created that encourage interpersonal closeness and reliance without respecting needs for differentiation and assertiveness. Justice can be rigid and infringe on expressions of love or power, or can be balanced, in which case members feel heard and are free to define relationships through their participation rather than external dictates. If love, power, and justice interact in a harmonious fashion, participants in a relationship will experience themselves as able to enhance one another's experience of growth and well-being, to accept differences creatively, and to understand the feelings of others.

Disharmony between love, power, and justice within an individual's perceptual field can lead to barriers in awareness such as denial, repression and compartmentalization. If the ontological elements are united, an individual's perceptual field will function as an integrated whole, and all aspects of experience will be accessible to awareness. Thus, an individual's willingness to be aware can influence patterns of love, power, and justice in a way that increases integration in perception and relationship. Similarly, if an integrated dynamic of love, power, and justice is created in a group or relationship, participants are encouraged to accept and exercise their potential to be aware. We have attempted to conceptualize basic ontological integration through relatedness so we can (1) account for the role that awareness and self-actualization play in the integration of love, power, and justice and (2) account for those relationship dynamics that we have subjectively experienced to be most effectively therapeutic. We did not want to treat our subjective experience of therapy in isolation, and we have made efforts to draw connections between our own observations and relevant theory and research in this field.

We have constructed a theory that can account for a process wherein individuals build groups at the same time that these enhance members' individuality. Although individuals construct relationships, they cannot become individuals without participating in relationship. Relationships construct individuals as much as individuals construct relationships. We have met with a common misconception among clinicians that for persons to work on themselves as individuals, they need to seek individual therapy; group participation is conceptualized as merely a means to enhance social skills. On the contrary, however, we have found that participation in a group allows members to address two central process goals that have the potential to enhance individuality. These are (1) engagement in communication that provides feedback about individuals' concerns and problems, and (2) enhancement of awareness of self through learning that occurs in the development of interpersonal relationships.

Although we value the therapeutic power of individual therapy, we do not believe that group therapy has any less potential power for enhancing individuals' awareness and expression of their uniqueness. Philosophically stated, this belief in the power of a group to enhance individuality is based on the principle that through the universal the particular comes to be and through the particular the universal exists. In psychological terms, through the collective the individual comes to be, and through the individual the collective has its existence—ideas that we will discuss later.

## THE PROCESS OF UNSTRUCTURED GROUP THERAPY

*Unstructured group therapy* can be defined as an organized human activity in which individuals meet with the intention to share their resources for mutual growth and healing without imposing a preconceived structure on the process, dynamics, and outcome. Unstructured group therapy is an organized human activity, and as such, is an intentional activity. The structure of these groups is the result of collective responsibility, is fluid rather than static, and is subject to change when individuals in the group decide to redirect their focus of attention.

Unstructured groups, during the initial stages of group development, may be anxiety provoking. The process of unstructured therapy therefore needs to encourage members to use their anxiety and uncertainty as a means to enhance awareness. Anxiety and uncertainty represent opportunities for decision-making and for the recognition of responsibility. The cohesion of such groups must develop from within the group through actual relatedness, as there is no external authority dictating a theme or goal. If members feel free to express feelings of anxiety, this communication has the potential to build cohesion.

As implied earlier, the essential theoretical position supporting unstructured group therapy is that responsibility is a central factor in psychological health and well-being. Opportunities for members to have choices and to make decisions about interactions, relationships, and the direction of the group are viewed as environmental conditions that allow experiential learning. The leader of such groups is responsible for helping to create an atmosphere that is conducive to members' acceptance of an unstructured situation that provides such opportunities.

The construct of responsibility is obviously important to an understanding of how unstructured groups can facilitate growth, health, and worthwhile relationships. *Responsibility* can be defined behaviorally, cognitively, socially, legally, morally, or on an individual basis. All of these levels of interpretation imply the existence of a person who is an agent, who can be aware of consequences, and who can be viewed as a being who makes choices. Responsibility implies that, to some extent, the person is a creator of his or her perceptions rather than being a passive recipient of perceptions. A person may be responsible for interpreting a situation in a particular manner, for setting certain goals, for acting in a specific manner, or for maintaining a system of values that affects interactions.

A group situation is an especially relevant setting for individuals to confront how their values and attitudes affect their relatedness to other individuals. Some individuals may suffer from an inability to recognize themselves as responsible agents involved in a relational process with others. An unstructured therapy group can provide them with feedback and opportunities to observe themselves in this process. By developing responsible relationships in a therapy situation, an individual can gain experiential learning that can be generalized to situations outside the group, thus increasing adaptability and enhancing the individual's sense of engagement.

Other individuals may already experience themselves as responsible beings but may believe that an unstructured therapy setting can enhance self-awareness and can challenge their creativity and openness. They may wish to participate in an unstructured therapy group that is organized as a vehicle for exploring styles of relationship or as an occasion for experiential learning and personal growth.

There are some problems that affect the suitability of unstructured group therapy for individuals. This form of therapy may not be appropriate for those who have specific behavioral goals that they wish to work on or who experience excessive anxiety in groups or in unstructured situations. Usually, such persons will choose another form of therapy when they have been advised of the nature and demands of an unstructured situation. It is desirable that unstructured therapy groups be attended on a voluntary basis. If individuals have the opportunity to make an informed choice about participation, this choice in itself supports their ability to recognize themselves as responsible beings.

Members who exhibit compulsive attention seeking, who show frequent outbursts of hostility, or who are dealing with an imminent crisis can be disruptive to a group. Unstructured groups are, however, well suited for helping such members receive constructive feedback that might not be available in an individual therapy setting. Therefore, it would be a limitation to view the goal of unstructured therapy as gaining cohesion by excluding potentially disruptive members. There may, of course, be situational or institutional factors that affect the composition of the group, and leaders may sometimes limit membership to those persons who are less likely to be exceedingly disruptive or for other reasons.

It is rare that a member becomes so disruptive that expulsion becomes necessary. How the members respond to such circumstances can indicate their willingness to recognize responsibility for the direction of the group. These events in the life of a group can be part of the group's coming to terms with fears of deviant modes of expression and behavior. Sometimes apparently disruptive behavior can be a prelude to discussions of feelings that are difficult for members to express or to own.

It is most consistent with the theory of unstructured group therapy to view clients as individuals who suffer from problems in living, rather than to view particular clients as unsuitable because of a diagnosis or some other label. The purpose of an unstructured group is to allow members to determine their own values and norms. It would be inconsistent with this purpose to have predetermined ways of judging the value of members. The theoretical views of existential-humanistic therapists such as Maslow (1962), Perls (1969), Rogers (1961), Bozarth (1998), and Szasz (1961) support our premise that all human beings are potentially valuable participants in the human community.

Because we focus on the interactions through which individual and collective decisions form a process of being, we do not concern ourselves with questions about the essential nature of human beings. Thus, human problems are not viewed as evidence of a negative essential nature or as proof that the environment has distorted an essentially positive human nature. Problems are viewed as opportunities to enhance awareness by learning about the nature of interactions and choices that are involved in problems. Psychological problems often reflect difficulties that people have in dealing with conflict in relationships, barriers in awareness, and anxiety concerning the recognition of responsibility. These kinds of problems, no matter how severe, are (at least theoretically) capable of being improved. Psychological problems may be intertwined with genetics, the environment, and neurology, but cannot be completely attributed to their effects. Psychological problems also stem from conscious and unconscious decisions that have led a person to diminish his or her own potential awareness.

Clients who benefit from unstructured therapy view themselves as having at least one and typically all of the following characteristics. (1) They believe they would be likely to respond positively to an opportunity for interactional learning. (2) They see themselves as having life problems that can be explored in a relational context. (3) They would like to increase their perception that intimacy with others is possible. (4) They want to experience a sense of involvement with others or to have an experience of communing with others. (5) They believe they would benefit from being in a supportive and democratic group atmosphere. (6) They would like a chance to give and to receive honest feedback, or would like to learn to do so. Individuals who are informed about the process goals of group therapy may decide that individual therapy is more suited to their needs. A combination of group therapy and individual therapy is sometimes highly beneficial for individuals who are capable of working on their concerns in a setting where they share attention as well as where they are continually in the center of attention.

## PATTERNS OF RELATIONSHIP

The concerns of unstructured therapy are in many ways analogous to those of a democratic society; the value and worth of every participant is emphasized. The unstructured therapeutic group encourages the acceptance and enjoyment of diversity; these groups promote a form of learning that acknowledges persons' divergent abilities, values, and subjective experiences. Unstructured group therapy seeks to create an atmosphere of freedom where individuals can explore their abilities to trust others, discover self-worth and worthiness of others, and to communicate clearly.

A basic theme of this book is that our *patterns* in relationships have an impact on our lives and on those of others. These patterns can be discussed in terms of the interaction of love, power, and justice in relationships. Previous patterns of love, power, and justice can represent unfinished business from families of origin, peer groups, or other intimate relationships. Members often recognize and wish to confront the patterns of relationship that they have previously established, especially if they experience a dynamic in the group that is different from that of their past relationships.

# Introduction

Successful unstructured group therapy is assisted by the leader's (and other members') willingness to proceed without relying heavily on preconceived strategies or expectations. If a group leader enters the therapeutic situation with an attitude of openness and with a willingness to share authority and control, he or she will be more able to creatively deal with the unique dynamics that unfold. A group leader intent on controlling or directing the process can miss aspects of interactions that do not fit his or her preconceived goals.

Writers have at times differentiated the concerns of counseling from those of psychotherapy. This text, however, does not distinguish between group counseling and group psychotherapy, preferring to address a ground that is common to both of these fields. This common ground is the context and process of group relationships and their impact on the process of each member's self-actualization.

For our purposes, *self-actualization* can be thought of as a process through which a person becomes simultaneously more independent and more aware of and involved in relationships. Because we view self-actualization to be of interest to both counseling and psychotherapy, we have used the generic term *group therapy* to describe the activity wherein people meet collectively to further their own healing and growth. Self-actualization can occur in personal growth, counseling, or psychotherapeutic groups.

The term *leader* has been used to designate the individual who conducts therapeutic groups. This usage should not be misconstrued as an indication that group therapy simply consists of a leader and his or her followers. Rather, the initial responsibility for organizing and introducing the group, as well as for determining basic ground rules (such as confidentiality, the duration of the group, and limits for emotional and physical coercion), involves a leadership role. The individual who performs this role inevitably is perceived by members, at least initially, as the group's leader. He or she thus has a specific significance in the development of a group. It is difficult to understand the developing pattern of relationships in a therapeutic group if the activities that differentiate the role of a group's leader are not considered. A successful group evolves through developing a decreasing sense of psychological distance between the leader and members and a lessening of the perceived power differential between the leader and other participants.

## EXISTENTIAL VALUES AND THERAPEUTIC PROCESS

Therapy cannot be meaningfully considered as free of values, or as limited to dealing with concretely observable behaviors. Persons' feelings, perceptions, and values interact to produce change throughout the life of individuals and that of a group. Some aspects of change can be meaningfully considered the result of observable overt behaviors. However, a great deal of the impact that members have upon one another results from nuances of verbal and nonverbal communication that are experienced on emotional and intuitive levels of awareness. The leader of unstructured therapy groups can function most effectively if he or she can be aware of how a group atmosphere develops an almost tangible quality of harmony or discord. To the degree that ontological elements are functioning as a balanced and integrated process, a therapeutic environment is being created.

One of the authors had an experience during a 16-hour-long therapy group conducted with illicit drug abusers that taught him how member's feelings, perceptions and values interact to influence a group's atmosphere. The group was being held in a residential drug treatment center with men who had been released from prison to receive treatment. The author, a counseling psychologist, acted as a consultant to this program; the other group leader was not a staff member of the program but a volunteer who had worked with the author in many other groups.

The residents had been in groups in this drug treatment program prior to participating in this group; they typically took part in what were called Synanon-Transactional Analysis groups every week that they were in the program. These were highly confrontive and emphasized forcing the residents to change attitudes and behaviors. Peer pressure and negative labels were used as a means to change attitudes. By contrast, the leaders who were conducting the therapy group placed much more emphasis on helping residents to become self-aware and to examine and change their own attitudes and behaviors.

During the first eight hours of this group, the members avoided examining anything personal and refused to provide feedback that was specific and focused. During the break, the leaders talked privately and agreed that they felt disappointed by what had happened in this group up until this time. After the break was over, however, and the interaction started again, the atmosphere was completely different. The members gave one another specific feedback in a concerned way and were also willing to express their feelings about the problems and situations that they faced.

This change appeared to the leaders to be dramatic and illustrated the ways that the values and perceptions of the leaders and members combined to produce a change in atmosphere that was therapeutically significant. The group atmosphere changed during this 16-hour-long group primarily because of the nonverbal interactions that occurred during the first eight hours. Both the leaders and the members indicated that the group had been personally meaningful once it was finished. Members gained sufficient trust to allow for direct expressions of how they saw each other. The result was a new alignment of love and power in the group. Members then became free to work toward a form of justice that allowed them to give to and receive from each other.

An existential value system underlies our view of the person as a being who is continually formed through a process of encounter and relationship. We have portrayed the person as a participatory being involved in a life process that allows for the expression of both creative and destructive capabilities. Creativity becomes ever more apparent as we are able to comprehend peoples' unique phenomenological realities, the worlds that they construct through the activities of perception and association. These worlds reveal various meanings and perceptions of beauty or threat as individuals respond to their encounters with others. Although persons are able to create, they are also able to be receptive and responsive. They not only create meaning actively but their ability to be open and passive allows them to receive impressions and meanings from nature and from others. If members engage and are open to one another, their interactions can help them to balance their abilities to be interpersonally active and passive; they can learn how to use these interactions to enhance the process of relationship.

An ontological analysis is not antirational, but it is an attempt to understand persons as they exist prior to the application of categories that fragment what can be a whole experience. A person's sense of meaning is originally a pre-eminently experiential sense of reality. Experientially unified meaning can be split by various polarities that develop as conceptual thinking is used to set one aspect of experience against another (for example, controlling self and controlled self, ideal self and real self, love and hate, good thoughts and bad thoughts, or good feelings and bad feelings). Polarities impede self-actualization if the person is not able to realize that he or she is simultaneously the creator and container of these polarities. The ability to engage in relationship is diminished if people project unwanted aspects of polarities onto others (Perls, Hefferline and Goodman, 1951/1980). For this reason, we have attempted to minimize the application of polarizing conceptual categories to our understanding of group members' experiences.

## CREATION OF MEANING BY INDIVIDUALS AND GROUPS

Individuals can creatively integrate the polarities of which they are aware into new forms of being and expression (Perls, 1973). The person is capable of living as a creative being because actualization has creative potentials. Thus, the person does *not* create a separate sense of meaning out of an existential void, contrary to the writings of such theorists as Becker (1973), Sartre (1956), and Yalom (1980). Forming personal meaning within a meaningless void would turn out to be self-defeating even if it were possible.

The person makes meaning through actively participating in interactions, and through actively receiving or rejecting what is given in these. He or she thus becomes aware of meanings that are 'created' and 'given' through the ongoing process of being. These meanings are experiential wholes that connect a person, through an ongoing subjective experience, with others, with nature, and with the process of being. The person can choose to invest energy and awareness in what occurs in encounters with others, and this choice leads to the discovery of new meanings. The person therefore lives in an intuitively perceived universe of meaning rather than in a meaningless universe. Theorists who have written about the relationship between individual experience and a universal meaningful process include Buber (1970), Fromm, Suzuki and DeMartino (1960), Jung (1958), Maslow (1962), Rogers (1961) and Tillich (1954). These theorists portray persons as unique creators of meaning who may have to move through meaninglessness to come to terms with an inherent meaning within the process of living, one that is not personally created. The meaning within life and experience that is not personally formed is of potentially greater depth than one that is.

The proposition that all meaning is not created individually is an important concept for a theory of group therapy. This concept paves the way for an understanding of the group itself as a potentially healing force. The power of the group as a whole does not come about at the expense of members' individuality. In fact, this power is diminished if members create norms that require a sacrifice of individuality for the sake of group belongingness. The power of a therapeutic group is at its maximal potential when group norms encourage and accept full individuality and when the group itself can assist individuals to create meanings from within their unique experience of encounters.

The group can be considered as a gestalt—that is, as a whole that is more than simply the sum of its parts. Similarly, throughout this book, we consider love, power, and justice as a gestalt. When these elements function in an integrated manner, they take on a unique quality of wholeness that is more than the sum of parts. This wholeness can affect an individual, a relationship, or a group. Perls, Hefferline and Goodman (1951/1980) write, 'Meaningful wholes exist throughout nature ... they are meaningful in the sense that the whole explains the parts; they are purposive in that a tendency can be shown in the parts to complete the wholes' (p. 302). This gestalt orientation helps form our frame of reference toward human groups and toward the function of the ontological elements.

The tendency to form meaningful wholes from within experience is a basic quality of human awareness. (There may be an equivalent tendency in nature to form meaningful organizations within the movement of energy.) We have viewed persons as aware beings who can choose to form a more comprehensive and whole experience by coming into contact with and integrating aspects of experience that are uncomfortable or threatening. People can also choose to retreat from increased awareness. Environments that restrict personal freedoms are ones that tend to generate impositions on the movement of awareness. Psychological maneuvers to avoid awareness by constricting and distorting contact in the present or by unnecessarily focusing energy on the past or future also restrict freedom and awareness. Given a willingness to be open and a free environment, awareness tends to increase in intensity and extensity. The more members and the leader are willing to encourage freedom for exploring feelings and perceptions, for maintaining authenticity in communication, the more healing and growth are fostered.

If preconceived directions or artificial limitations on persons' explorations of self and others are imposed, a constrained atmosphere results. Members of a restrictive or avoidant group environment are likely to experience greater difficulty in making the necessary choices to move toward personal and interpersonal integration (McClure, 1990). In an unfree environment, members may be rewarded for moving toward a prescribed form of wholeness that is an imposed and artificial solution to personal problems. This form of wholeness is a barrier to the wholeness that persons can create within their own perceptions of ongoing experience.

## INDIVIDUALITY AND INTERDEPENDENCE

People who meet in a free environment for the purpose of promoting their own growth often use their group as an opportunity for experimentation with new interpersonal behaviors and new ways of perceiving experience. They give and receive honest feedback about their feelings and observations as they become willing to trust others and to trust the group environment. If a group promotes authentic communication, members learn about their individuality—how they perceive themselves and how others perceive them. They learn how their choices affect their relationships with others and how they either accept or avoid responsibility for various aspects of their life process. Although a group setting can provide an excellent atmosphere for learning what it means to be an individual, this environment can also promote an awareness of interdependence. Members learn about the value of interdependence as they discover that the therapeutic process in a group is a collaborative process.

If interdependence is to be established on genuineness and choice, then independence must not be sacrificed for the sake of cohesion. As a person's unique and independent movement toward wholeness unfolds within group process, that individual simultaneously connects with specific others and with the larger group. The individual movement toward wholeness and integration is simultaneously a personal concern and a collective one.

Individuality grows from persons' awareness of distinctness. People learn how they are different from others and how others are different from each other. This understanding can grow only through relationship and interaction. The interactive process that is necessary to form individuality is an essentially universal human process. Human growth and self-actualization occur through a creative synthesis of the polarity of self and other. A self develops from contact with others, and the distinctness of others is increasingly recognized and accepted as the self becomes strong and healthy. If self-actualization is a process that is simultaneously individual and universal, there should be a great potential for a group setting to enhance self-actualization.

Members can interact in ways that encourage awareness of individuality and universality or they can avoid such interactions. They can enhance their consciousness of individuality by acknowledging and accepting differences in participants' perspectives and experiences. Members can grow in their awareness of universality as they discover some common ground in their life experiences and as they recognize a common purpose and a shared process for which they need each other's cooperation and involvement. They also may take options to avoid awareness of universality and cling to the view of themselves as separate and needing separation.

The group members generally benefit from learning that exploration of conflicts within and between persons can provide experiences that enhance growth and individuality. Moving toward wholeness does not mean denial of differences or conflicts, although this denial can be used as a defense against anxiety (Agazarian, 1992). Group members can create a growth-promoting group culture without requiring that everyone like each other. However, if members experience a common bond of affection and concern they are more likely to be able to assist each other's healing and growth.

Unstructured groups have the advantage of providing an atmosphere where uncontrived intimacy can potentially be experienced. Intimacy develops as members can enjoy differences. Successfully therapeutic groups provide an atmosphere wherein members can identify with the experiences and feelings of others without losing their perception of their own and others' uniqueness.

Educational or structured forms of therapy may be helpful for some clients who wish to understand how to develop worthwhile relationships, how to express needs assertively, how to communicate empathically, and so on. Yet an unstructured setting has the unique potential of allowing ontological dynamics to be confronted in a direct and open manner; it can permit examination of these dynamics within ongoing interactions because there is no set agenda to which members must adhere. Persons are free to develop their own forms and structures for examining themselves and their relationship dynamics. They are free to establish intimacy or to move away from connections with others.

If experiences of intimacy do occur in an unstructured group, participants are likely to fully own responsibility for them. They are less likely to misperceive that an educator or a leader providing structure is 'really' responsible for any feelings of closeness. Individuality is enhanced in unstructured groups because members are encouraged to recognize they are creating the patterns of their interactions. If intimacy occurs in a relationship between members, they are able to identify themselves as the initiators of this intimacy. Participants can also benefit from discovering a universal aspect to their experience that was not the result of a teaching that was simply handed to them.

## INTERDEPENDENCE OF INDIVIDUAL AND GROUP GESTALTS

One of the dilemmas of many theorists who have previously developed theories of group therapy was to explain how individual growth is possible in a group setting. It seems paradoxical that people can become stronger individuals because of group experiences. Some personality theorists, including Freud (1948), expressed extreme skepticism about the overall beneficial effects of most groups on personality development and value formation. It will be emphasized throughout this book that individuals can benefit from (or be hurt by) their group involvement and that they in turn can influence the type and quality of the atmosphere that evolves. This kind of mutual influence can best be addressed by conceptualizing group activities in terms of gestalts or integrated configurations of meaning.

We believe that individual and group development are interrelated and that the ingredients central to the formation of a helpful atmosphere in a therapy group affect individual development; in turn individual growth influences the creation of a therapeutic group atmosphere. The development of groups and individuals who make up these groups cannot be discussed in a meaningful way in isolation from one another. We have explained the bipolar function of groups on an individual basis (focused on awareness, freedom, and responsibility) and an interactive basis (focused on love, power, and justice). We have discussed the importance of awareness along with its concomitants, freedom and responsibility, and shown how these function as a gestalt to influence the values and self-actualization of an individual.

We have also emphasized that the interaction of love, power, and justice affect the atmosphere and relationships that form in a therapy group. Thus, we believe that love, power, and justice exist as a gestalt or dynamic in a therapy group and influence its development. As has already been stated, awareness, freedom, and responsibility operate as a gestalt or dynamic in individuals and influence individual development or self-actualization. We further view these two gestalts as interrelated. Their mutual influence occurs during any human interaction. For this reason, awareness, freedom, responsibility, love, power, justice, and self-actualization are all relevant constructs that need to be discussed when an ontological theory of group therapy is developed. These constructs explain the gestalt function of group activities as each individual interacts with others and with the group as a whole.

## RELATIONSHIP DYNAMICS AND STRUCTURED THERAPY GROUPS

Structured therapy groups can be more appropriate in certain situations than unstructured ones. If there is a set agenda for information that participants need to receive, then it is often helpful for a leader to facilitate a structured group (by using exercises or by having a defined focus). Sometimes members have specific reasons for joining a counseling group, such as learning job seeking skills, which make a structured group appropriate. Even in structured groups, however, it is wise for the group facilitator to focus on the relationship dynamics that affect what is being learned. These dynamics can interfere with what is being taught or can facilitate learning.

One question that the readers might ask is how the dynamics of an unstructured therapy group compare with those of structured groups. For instance, if the group leader uses exercises to facilitate the group process, how does this affect the relationship dynamics of a group? If a group is set up to achieve certain goals, such as teaching the participants assertiveness or job skills, do the same dynamics occur that operate in an unstructured therapy group? The answer to these questions is that relationship dynamics that affect the atmosphere and interpersonal learning that occurs in unstructured therapy groups also affect the dynamics of structured groups.

Even in a counseling group that is established around a particular theme or objective, the ways that the members respond to what is taught depends to a large degree on the relationship dynamics that occur in these groups. If a group leader helps members to feel accepted and respected, then these members will be more likely to respond in an open and positive way to what is being taught in the group. People who feel affirmed as persons in a learning situation are more able to take full advantage of what is being taught and to realize their full potential as learners. Additionally, they are more likely to find creative ways to apply their learning to their individual life circumstances. It is important to remember that both structured and unstructured groups can help members to develop more healthy relationship styles and to become stronger individuals. These objectives are more likely to be realized in any group setting when love, power, and justice operate as a unified gestalt.

## RELATIONSHIP DYNAMICS AND THE LARGER SOCIETY

The dynamics of members' interactions in group therapy reflect their dynamics in other social groups. Thus, the theoretical issues that are explored herein are relevant not only for practitioners of group therapy but also for anyone who is attempting to understand how patterns of relationship affect human growth and development. Ontological dynamics apply to all relationships because they all involve some assertion of power, some desire for connection, and some form of justice that mediates the effect of one participant on another. Any relationship will be created through mutual awareness and will be affected by how participants recognize and define their responsibility toward themselves and the others involved. Readers are therefore likely to find that the dynamics that have been discussed in terms of members' interactions in a therapy group apply to other interactions as well.

Because unstructured therapy groups allow members to confront universal aspects of being with others, there can be applications for unstructured groups in a variety of settings. Specific settings and specific populations can create unique challenges for practitioners. Each setting and culture gives different forms to the activities of love, power, and justice. Individuality and interdependence are defined differently in different cultures and subcultures. Yet the creative dynamic that evolves from the relationship of the individual to the group and of the group to the individual takes place in every culture. The dynamics of ontological integration can be considered universal in nature and integrated on both individual levels and collective levels of perception.

The dynamics of relationship can be considered from a range of perspectives: individual, family, group and community, cultural, and global. These levels are different perspectives related to a gestalt that can be considered universal in nature, reflecting the reality that the whole is more than the sum of parts. There is no one true perspective about the dynamics of being and human relationship; nevertheless, the more that it can include the diverse forms of relationship that people create, the more useful that perspective will be for conducting groups that can involve members with different backgrounds, personal perspectives, and cultural conditioning. A comprehensive and integrated view of reality that allows flexibility is probably more useful for conducting therapy groups than a narrow view based on knowledge of 'the truth'.

We invite the reader to explore his or her own dynamics of love, power, and justice while reading this book. Readers can relate these forces to their own experience of becoming an individual and their own learning about how interdependence plays a part in that process. One can extend an understanding of one's own process of relationship to include the processes of others whom one has observed in families and groups. Each individual represents an intertwining of the personal and universal aspects of love, power, and justice. Each individual is affected by past relationships, family interactions, and cultural patterns that have conditioned thought and feeling. Each individual is capable of confronting his or her own pattern of being and able to relate this learning to interactions with others and with groups. We therefore invite the reader to consider not only how ontological dynamics affect the course of therapeutic groups but also how they affect the construction of their own lives and lives of significant others, relationships in which they are involved, and social systems in which they participate. Therapists who conduct individual or group therapy can only become more effective as they learn to be aware of dynamics that influence individuals and social systems in a universal sense, as well as the specific dynamics arising from particular events and life histories.

CHAPTER 2

# PROCESS GOALS IN UNSTRUCTURED GROUP THERAPY

Analysis of the dynamics that affect group process can lead to recognizing that complexity and ambiguity are characteristic of many of the communications between participants. Members sometimes communicate on different levels simultaneously—for example, on a direct level, on a symbolic or metaphorical level, and on a nonverbal level. Complexities that occur in communications between members can be simplified by defining certain core concerns, focal points that form a common center around which multiple levels of communication occur. We can make the task of conceptualizing unstructured group therapy easier by relating various forms of interpersonal communication to the basic focal points of therapeutic process. We have referred to these focal points as process goals because they form directions for meaningful explorations of experience.

## TWO GOALS WITHIN GROUP PROCESS

Process goals are not end products that a group strives to achieve or create. Rather, they serve as anchors within a group's process that allow members to invest energy in their group and to experience it as more than a collection of separate individuals. These goals focus energy within the group and within the present, rather than outside the group's spatial and temporal context. We have defined two basic process goals that can be observed consistently to anchor the process of therapeutic groups. These goals arise naturally (and almost inevitably) within the process of unstructured group therapy.

The basic process goals are (1) the development of a climate that promotes disclosure of individual concerns and that is supportive of members who work on personal problems, and (2) the emergence of meaningful interpersonal learning focused on present relationships between members. We can define process goals rather easily, but understanding the emotions and communications that develop around them is often far from simple. Participants may struggle to appreciate how one another's unique personal perspectives, values, and assumptions are affecting their work on problems and their interpersonal learning. However, it is generally when members simply accept one another's differences that the most effective work on process goals occurs.

18

Leaf approximately 2/3 life size

**Elder** / *Sambucus nigra*

# Elder / *Sambucus nigra*

### Native shrub

### Where
Very common on wasteland, scrub, hedges and woodland edges. It tends to creep in and flourish in disused areas.

### Description
In spring the elder has huge clusters of tiny white flowers which smell unpleasant. In autumn these flowers have turned into purply-black round berries which the birds love.

### Fact
Folklore has it that bunches of elder leaves keep flies away, whether that's from us, horses or our food!

Group members, including the leader, are likely to benefit from clarifying their personal assumptions and values. Understanding the effects of one's own personal history is also helpful, especially insofar as this history affects awareness of others. If members assist each other in clarifying personal values and the effects of personal history, they can gain mutual understanding that assists their movement towards constructive work together. A member's values and history play a part in expectations and hopes and help determine what each participant believes would be meaningful or therapeutic in interacting with others.

A group is most likely to facilitate therapeutic directions within ongoing interactions if members collectively perceive the value of addressing process goals and accept responsibility for moving toward them. Members can have a constructive impact on their group's process if they disclose thoughts and feelings that demonstrate an awareness of others as persons and an awareness of self as a participant involved with others. These kinds of disclosures help to create an atmosphere wherein it becomes possible to explore problems and acknowledge present relationships as real.

The two process goals tend to arise within group process as members acknowledge involvement with one another and awareness of each other as persons. However, members can form resistances towards the process goals as these goals begin to become apparent. *Resistance* can be evidenced by retreating from problems that are disclosed, minimizing the significance of problems, and minimizing or avoiding meaningful interpersonal contact. Resistance is sometimes expressed as an unwillingness to invest one's full energy of awareness in a group's process, as a lack of respect for the personhood of others, or as avoidance of responsibility for determining directions for growth. These kinds of resistant interactions can create a group climate that reflects interpersonal defensiveness and restricts open communication (Agazarian, 1992). Group members cannot be forced to deal with resistance, since attempts to force awareness usually increase it. If, however, members work through the anxieties involved in resistance, they may choose to make their group a place where it is safe to discuss problems openly and to acknowledge interpersonal relatedness as meaningful.

Members' perceptions of the role of the group leader are often based on their assumptions that the leader has theoretical and experiential knowledge that will help facilitate movement towards these two goals. Members often assume, or would like to assume, that the leader is a person who can promote a group atmosphere wherein members can be comfortable in sharing problems. Participants often view their group leader as a person who they believe can assist them in learning from present relationships.

A leader's effectiveness in addressing the process goals is enhanced by the development of sensitivity to a variety of communication styles and personal needs and problems. If a leader lacks this sensitivity, he or she may encourage group members to avoid dealing with their different ways of communication; the members may adopt the leader's ideas about defining the nature of valid problems for discussion and valid styles for interpersonal relationship. Members may then covertly or overtly strive for approval, recognition, and attention in a manner that undermines genuine communication and honest expression of feeling. Those who most closely approximate the norms of the leader may then dominate group interactions. If members feel that goals are being imposed on them, they may 'revolt' at some point in the group's process or they may terminate their involvement. Therapeutic use of the two process goals can also be diminished if the leader or other members seek harmony at the expense of individual differences. Members may then avoid expressing disagreement, may ignore uncomfortable feelings, or may become detached observers who avoid expression of divergent views to maintain acceptance.

Members may not always perceive themselves as being in a group to learn about responsibility in communication and interaction. Participants may also not see themselves as being in a group to discuss personal problems and concerns or to learn about interpersonal relationship processes. Some members may simply want to experience being with others or may arrive with little awareness of how such groups can contribute to integration and growth. Participants may be unsure about what problems (if any) they want to discuss and may be quite uncertain about how (and whether) to form relationships with other members. If their group's process begins to be perceived as trustworthy by these members, they are likely to choose how they can disclose concerns and how they can form relationships with others. An atmosphere of trust tends to facilitate the emergence of the process goals even if members are naïve about the process of therapy and do not know what to expect.

Members who have expectations for their group based on previous group experiences will come to recognize that their current group presents unique dynamics that affect the disclosure of concerns and the development of relationships. The present group will never have exactly the same dynamics as other groups. Comparisons with previous experiences or unrealistic expectations based on other groups' dynamics can be used to avoid dealing with the process goals within the context of a present group (Leszcz, 1992). Similarly, unfavorable comparisons of present relationships with past ones can have the effect of suppressing current opportunities for communication. Each group is a unique event, and therapeutic interactions occur as members are able to express themselves as unique individuals and to accept other members in the same way.

The importance of the two process goals in unstructured group therapy is not limited to any particular theory. For example, the study of psychoanalytic groups, existential groups, and person-centered groups leads to the conclusion that the two basic process goals are addressed in each theory. Psychoanalytic groups move toward an atmosphere where members are comfortable discussing problems and current relationships by encouraging *free association* (Wolf and Schwartz, 1962). Free association is a process of the uncensored sharing of thoughts and feelings in a nonjudgmental environment. Existential therapy groups move toward the process goals by emphasizing self-awareness and responsibility issues for participants (Corey, 1990). Person-centered groups are based on the philosophy that participants can be trusted to know how they can best use their group to enhance their own self-actualization (Rogers, 1970). The process goals can be identified as aspects of self-actualization if we note that as people learn to live fully and effectively (as they self-actualize), they learn how to develop worthwhile relationships with others and how to confront problems creatively and constructively.

Therapists often align themselves with schools of therapy according to their congruence with the relationship style. Within the context provided by a theoretical frame of reference, individual group leaders will define an orientation toward interpersonal learning. Leaders also develop a personal style that helps facilitate an atmosphere wherein members can feel comfortable to work on personal problems, difficulties, or unfinished business. Developing an awareness of process goals contributes to our understanding of how leaders and members develop interactions in a group setting in a therapeutic or nontherapeutic manner. An effective group leader respects and encourages individuals' intrinsic motivation toward therapeutic use of their group. This leader does not attempt to instill motivation through an authoritarian stance. Such a stance tends to foster resistance and to generate an environment of dependency or mistrust.

Members of various types of unstructured therapy groups (e.g., person-centered, existential, and psychoanalytic) often choose to use their time together to develop relationships and to discuss concerns and problems. We assume that if a group develops an open and therapeutic atmosphere, members are likely to choose to move toward the process goals. These goals are not the property of any particular theory but emerge within group process as members define for themselves how to use their time together constructively.

## THE PRINCIPLE OF INCLUSIVITY IN UNSTRUCTURED THERAPY GROUPS

A leader who organizes a therapeutic group often has the option of selecting members who are either relatively heterogeneous or homogeneous (according to various more or less overt characteristics). A group leader who believes that creativity is important may well believe that heterogeneous membership is desirable. Members' ability to relate creatively and empathically is likely to be stimulated and challenged in a heterogeneous group. The capacity to accept divergent views and experiences of problems is also likely to be challenged if membership is heterogeneous. If people are excluded because they do not fit a certain profile, a leader may be organizing a group according to principles that inhibit the development of creativity and lessen opportunities for members to learn to accept diversity.

Of course, communication can be facilitated if members initially 'speak the same language'. Moreover, groups are often organized around a shared problem, such as drug addiction or issues of loss. Members may have certain similarities in world-views. Yet they are likely to discover that there are important differences in their perspectives. An atmosphere of freedom is a central factor that affects members' opportunities to learn about aspects of experience that are divergent from norms that have been adopted by members outside or inside the group.

One reason that groups are often developed around specific initial concerns is practicality—that is, certain settings are often oriented towards specific concerns. Another reason is that anxiety about meeting with strangers can be diminished if participants believe that others in their group will be like them. A policy that encourages diversity in views and backgrounds of members may heighten the initial anxiety of an unstructured situation. However, members of such groups often discover that they learn a great deal about who they are and how they are with people simply by being with others who initially seem different. People who are uncomfortable with individual differences may not choose to attend a heterogeneous group. However, if participants choose to attend in spite of anxiety about the inclusion of others with divergent problems or social status, they are likely to find that they can accept these differences, and can grow from exercising their ability to accept.

Members of therapy groups which are homogeneous in such categories as social status and cultural background and that isolate themselves from conflicting feedback from others behave like certain social or political groups. Such groups are likely unquestioningly to accept mutually shared prejudices and defenses, may develop a kind of 'groupthink' based on common assumptions, may deny awareness of events that do not fit prejudices, and may develop a sense of identity based on their 'exclusive' group characteristics (see Janis, 1982). Members may develop a rationale for maintaining one pattern of relating to others in their group and another pattern for relating to people outside it. However, all the aforementioned problems that can occur in homogeneous groups are only likely to arise if they are encouraged by the leader. If that person initiates a 'flight from freedom' in a homogeneous group, members can be induced to adopt norms that assist each other to avoid anxiety. Group leaders may also encourage members to adopt restrictive norms to maintain a position of prestige or to avoid personal anxiety about unstructured situations. By contrast, if a group's leader is comfortable with open discussion and the exploration of experience, members are likely to move through an initial tendency to want to be the same as others to an increased awareness of each other's unique concerns and individual perspectives.

One potential benefit of an unstructured group is the opportunity to help participants to develop a less exclusive and more open approach toward interpersonal relationships. When individuals are able to accept varied aspects of other people's experience, they not only develop an attitude of openness to others but may also develop an acceptance of divergent aspects of their own experience. Members who become open to other participants do not *necessarily* become more open toward their own experience, but they often realize that valuing the first thing implies value in the other. Typically, a member must explore his or her own feelings in a free manner to be able to extend self toward another member seen as 'different'.

Some groups may gain cohesion by accepting members with diverse concerns but may demand a common degree of 'ego-strength', or ability to cope with anxiety, from members (Yalom, 1995). The drawback to the strategy of excluding members who lack ego strength is that participants will not have a chance to learn there is no unbridgeable gap between the strong and the weak. A person who is evidently strong can learn about his or her own hidden weaknesses by learning to accept a member who seems weaker, more unbalanced, or more fragile. Similarly, a person who is convinced that he or she is inherently weak or unstable may find that he or she has been denying strengths. Sometimes individuals suppress their abilities to cope constructively or creatively with anxiety because they are used to feeling victimized or out of control. Creative abilities can be evoked within the context of relationships formed with other members who can encourage the recognition of strengths. This recognition can occur if individuals are willing to share their life problems with others and are able to get feedback from others concerning how they handle stress and difficulties.

Heterogeneity may not be useful if participants are included who are likely to experience ongoing discomfort or hostility in a group setting (Korda and Pancrazio, 1989). Nevertheless, the more heterogeneity that is acceptable within a group, the broader the base becomes for interpersonal learning and mutual work on personal problems or unfinished business (Wolf and Schwartz, 1962). Initially, the degree of heterogeneity is defined by differences in overt characteristics such as nature of presenting problem, age, income, education, religion, ethnicity, and skin color. As a group develops, heterogeneity is defined by differences in less overt characteristics, such as life themes, emotional concerns, attitudes, perspectives, and values. This subtle evidence of heterogeneity is likely to emerge even if overt characteristics initially appear to be similar. Heterogeneity becomes increasingly tolerable in a group as norms are established that allow the norms themselves to be challenged and as these norms provide acceptance of divergent views, perspectives, and feelings.

## AUTHENTICITY IN THE GROUP THERAPY SETTING

What group members do to move toward the two process goals is work that requires authentic communication. If members are not honest about their concerns, they will minimize the potential of their group to assist them to deal with these issues. Similarly, if members communicate in a manner that is not authentic, they will develop relationships that are distorted rather than healing. They also limit their ability to develop open communication in their relationships. Thus, working on problems has the potential to enhance relationships, and developing relationships allows members to feel free to discuss problems.

People generally avoid disclosing their concerns and difficulties as a result of past learning or to protect their self-image (Egan, 1970). The images that individuals project to others may involve conscious decisions about which attitudes and feelings a person will express. These decisions are the result of an intention to influence the perceptions of others. A projected self-image can also be the result of habituated patterns of behavior that involve very little conscious attention. In either case, the self-image that people project to others can play an important part in their overall sense of identity. *Identity*, one's sense of oneself, includes self-perceptions that have formed into a coherent image over time. Perceptions of self generally include an image of how one believes one has been seen by others and one's hopes or expectations of how one will be viewed. The self-image is therefore not the portion of one's sense of self that arises from immediate awareness or from present sensory experience; it results from the processing of past experiences and projections into the unknown future. People generally learn that the image of self that is shown to others will influence their success at work and can have a powerful effect on personal relationships, especially insofar as certain roles are involved in these relationships.

Sometimes people can develop a strong attachment to negative self-images that have influenced their survival. One of the authors once worked as a counseling psychologist in a drug treatment center, and one responsibility of this consulting job was to lead therapy groups. For about a year, a client named 'Larry' attended an unstructured therapy group at the center. Larry had been a heroin addict for at least ten years prior to being imprisoned for armed robbery. Larry described a lifestyle that he had on the streets that was completely at variance with the way he acted in his group. On the streets, there were several people who wanted to kill Larry because he had stolen drugs or money from them. Larry described himself as being a 'bad' actor when he was a member of the drug culture prior to entering the treatment center. He had developed a strong identity as a 'bad guy who people should not mess with'. This author had the impression that Larry developed this type of self-image when he was a drug addict because having a negative self-identity was better than having no identity; also, of course, showing others in the drug culture that he was dangerous was related to his own survival and to his ability to get money to support a drug habit.

People often have a great emotional investment in their projected self-image. Because the two process goals require authentic communication, movement toward them provides a challenge to manipulative or habitual attempts to project a certain image. Members are likely to confront their emotional investment in their self-image as they move toward the process goals, regardless of whether this image is positive or negative or is consciously chosen or unconsciously habitual. It is not uncommon for members to find that their consciously chosen image is only projected

24

to a limited extent, whereas unconscious patterns of behavior affect others' perceptions to a greater extent than was imagined. As members learn about their investment in a self-image, they may assume responsibility for meeting needs that contradict that image. These unmet needs have an impact on relationships, although people may choose not to be aware of it. As members learn how they affect others, they can use this learning to change patterns; they can disinvest themselves in the past or future orientation and can reinvest themselves in present-centered communication. Their interpersonal process can become self-actualizing rather than 'image-actualizing' or 'role-actualizing'.

People tend to devalue spontaneity as they learn that society (beginning with the family and extending through various other social institutions) rewards consistent enactment of certain images. As people learn that performing a role can be essential for their social identity, they can come to believe that individuals *are completely defined* by their roles. They may believe that 'who one is' is identical to the role that one plays (Jourard, 1971). If people identify with a role, they have inevitably disowned aspects of self that do not conform to it. People can, for example, disown their childish aspects to play the role of an adult or can disown their adult aspects to play the role of a helpless child. People frequently repudiate feelings and thoughts that they have learned to perceive as negative.

People can disown aspects of their experience by minimizing the intensity or importance of feelings, by attributing their own rejected thoughts and feelings to others rather than to themselves, or by diverting attention from uncomfortable feelings or perceptions within ongoing encounters. Other members in an unstructured group are often able to see the aspects of self that an individual is attempting to disown. These members can provide reactions concerning the nature of thoughts or feelings that a participant is denying and can show this participant how repudiating these affects who and how he or she is with others. This type of authentic feedback can help members to move toward the two process goals. If they can be aware of feelings or behaviors that they have denied, members can become more honest about problematic historical events (for example, family relationships or sexual and romantic concerns) and can develop relationships with others that are not based on image projection.

It has already been said that the client named Larry was able to develop new roles in the unstructured therapy group that was conducted by one of the authors. These new forms of relationship were at variance with the types of roles and images he had projected while living as a heroin addict. When Larry was a member of the therapy group he consistently displayed concern with the welfare of the other members who also had drug abuse problems. He was one of the members who could be counted on to support and empathize with other members who were experiencing distress in their lives.

Being in the unstructured therapy group enabled Larry to experiment with roles that were dissimilar to the roles that he normally assumed as a member of the drug culture. Larry was able to gain new perspectives about human relationships from being in this unstructured therapy group. Of course, learning new roles and perspectives is not a guarantee of permanent change. When Larry left the drug treatment program, he became involved in some injurious relationships with other addicts and eventually started using heroin again. He did re-enter another drug treatment program voluntarily at a later time. Once he re-entered this program, this author lost contact with him.

## DENIAL AND SELF-IMAGE PROTECTION

Members may discover that they have denied certain problems to feel secure and comfortable about themselves. If they have learned that others will respond positively to their self-control and competence, participants probably learned to deny those feelings and experiences that led them to feel out of control or incompetent. If their group leads them to communicate authentically about their experience, members often discover the existence of 'unacceptable' memories, attitudes, thoughts, or feelings. They also may discover that they have avoided awareness of the price that they had to pay for their denial of unacceptable feelings or realizations. This price is often found to include one or more of the following: emotional deadness, occasional experiences of panic or dread, recurrent anxiety, persistent feelings of frustration, uncomfortable internalized tension, and estranged relations with significant others.

Patterns created in past relationships are carried into present relationships when these patterns affect present perceptions, modes of communication, and strategies for dealing with needs and feelings. Perls (1973) refers to these patterns that originate in the past as 'unfinished business' because individuals' awareness and energy can be bound up in uncompleted transactions from significant past relationships. The present and past become intertwined as people repeat past patterns of emotion and communication. Unfinished business can become finished only when members find a new form of relationship in the present that allows them to feel finished with a past form. However, individuals can generally grow from acknowledging the power of unfinished past relationships and dealing with whatever feelings and perceptions they have denied. Others in their group can facilitate a member's confrontation with unfinished business if they are able to be honest about how they react to that person.

The self-image that interferes with authentic present encounter has been described as arising from an accumulation of experiences over time that affects how a person attempts to survive, to gain rewards, and to avoid punishment (Berne, 1964). Social conditioning and introjected values can be seen as central to the formation of the self-image (O'Leary, 1992; Perls, Hefferline and Goodman, 1951/1980; Rogers, 1961). One aspect of this conditioning process is that people may learn to keep thoughts and feelings to themselves. Over time they may well have learned to discount their own feelings and perceptions and to misrepresent to *themselves* what they have felt, experienced, and thought in the past.

Maintenance of the self-image therefore is a central factor in many individuals' personal and interpersonal problems, as well as in the difficulties that they have in disclosing these problems to others. The self-image is a construct that will become reified insofar as an individual identifies this image with continued survival. The self-image will then be protected against feelings or thoughts that threaten its cohesion. Group members can help each other to learn that they can survive together and accept one another without relying on rigidly maintained self-images.

## THE IMPORTANCE OF FEEDBACK

As members discuss problems and participate in interpersonal encounters, they invite feedback from others in their group. *Feedback* is a key aspect of the process by which group members can take advantage of the therapeutic potential of their interactions. As members share problems, they demonstrate trust that there will be value to the feedback that other members may contribute. Without this trust, members would hesitate to disclose problems that might reveal some of their inadequacies, questions about themselves, and difficulties in relationships. If members believe in the value of the feedback of others, they are far more likely to move toward the two process goals.

Although the term 'feedback' is useful, it tends to minimize the multileveled nature of interpersonal communications. At the same time that a member is receiving information in the form of feedback, the person is sensing whether the other member genuinely cares and understands. The member who appears to be providing the feedback may simultaneously be sensing whether the other member is trustworthy. On one level of communication, there is a process of information exchange; on another level, there is nonverbal interaction of an intuitive and emotional nature whereby members learn whether they can trust one another and be open with one another. Members are not always looking for information that will help them to correct ineffective patterns of relating to others; they are often looking for experiential awareness that others are 'with them' and can understand and care (Leszcz, 1992; Rogers, 1970; Yalom, 1995).

Some aspects of nonverbal communication are subtle, and the impact of these communications may be distorted or diminished if they are made the focus of verbal exchange. For example, subtle nonverbal signals may indicate the beginnings of friendship; however, to focus on these messages verbally would create unnecessary anxiety and inhibit the development of the friendship. If there is a contradiction between verbal content and nonverbal cues in communication, members can become uncomfortable with one another without clearly understanding how their discomfort has arisen. At the same time, members may feel accepting of one another in spite of apparently critical exchanges if there is an experience of mutual understanding based on congruence between verbal and nonverbal messages.

The full nature of an interaction cannot be comprehended if an interaction is judged by the exchange of content alone. One member may appear to be providing feedback, but may actually be seeking to gain information from the other during the exchange. Additionally, the member who is offering feedback may simply be communicating in a nonverbal way, 'I care about you', or 'You're someone worth knowing'. Often, the nonverbal interpersonal awareness that members explore during interactions is more important to them (and more difficult to address at the time it occurs) than is the surface content. Nonverbal messages may generate a cumulative impact that develops over several interactions, and these messages may need to be addressed verbally at that moment when their impact has become noticeable.

Feedback is essential to the process by which the two basic process goals are approached and developed. According to Corey (1990), 'feedback that is specific and descriptive rather than global and judgmental is the most helpful' (p. 67). When information is accurate and specific, it allows members to focus on problems in a direct manner and to understand clearly how other members see them. Feedback can also help participants to question the labels or stereotypes that they may use to evaluate themselves and others.

Members who disclose problems often value the unexpected perspectives that other members may bring to their awareness through the process of feedback. Learning about others' points of view can help members consider options for forming values and behaviors that they had not previously considered. People outside the group who are closest to members may hesitate to be direct or may present their perspectives in a controlling manner, simply because they are being personally affected by the problem with which the member is dealing. Group members may have become habituated to a view of reality that is reinforced by others with whom they have formed close relationships. Participants in a therapy group engage themselves in a situation that allows them to receive new information from others outside their problem situations or relationships; an unstructured group thus becomes a source of potential change in members' perceptual maps of reality.

## PROBLEM SOLVING AND AWARENESS

A leader's recognition that group members use the therapeutic setting to disclose and discuss personal problems can lead to different conclusions about treatment. One possible conclusion is that groups should be oriented around one specific central and shared problem. The members of such groups might be expected to have a degree of prior consensus in their evaluation of life circumstances and their concepts of desirable and undesirable life goals. Another possible conclusion is that groups should focus on how members process information and perhaps assist these members in developing needed problem-solving skills. This conclusion would lead to organizing groups that are cognitively oriented, with the goal of improving members' effectiveness in dealing with their life problems. A third possible conclusion, which relates specifically to any theory of unstructured therapy groups, is that people can individually find ways and means to use their group constructively. A group setting that has not been specifically structured to address certain problems or problem-solving processes can still be useful for these purposes.

If predetermined structures are imposed on the manner in which problems or problem solving will be addressed, members may miss out on some of the resources potentially available in their group. On the one hand, if problem solving is defined as a cognitive activity, members might only focus on cognitions *about* relationships and miss opportunities for experiencing present emotional relatedness. On the other hand, a cognitive focus might be appropriate for a member who is capable of being involved emotionally with others but who has problems understanding the patterns involved in these involvements. Because unstructured groups do not have a predetermined focus, members learn that they can help each other in ways that are individually appropriate.

Another difficulty that can arise from predetermined structures is that 'problem areas' can be defined beforehand in a manner that restricts self-explorations and that may inhibit disclosures of problems that do not fit the agenda. Members may feel 'steered' toward certain preconceived forms of interaction and thus will not assume responsibility for discovering their own unique mode of interacting authentically, helpfully, or caringly. An unstructured setting thus requires that members experience relatively equal and mutual responsibility to determine how to address problems together.

Unstructured groups allow members to learn about ontological dynamics that are often addressed only covertly, and sometimes not at all in other situations. An unstructured group can move what is 'background' in most groups into the 'foreground'. Many families, businesses, and social interactions are governed by unspoken rules that regulate what can be said, who can speak, and to whom it is appropriate to speak. Members can use the freedom of an unstructured setting to address personal problems in a manner that helps them to see how their own awareness (and lack of awareness) of these issues affects them.

Some problems are situational in nature and simply require new information and skills. Problems that are more psychological generally require a new perspective along with new information or new skills. In reality, of course, there are many occasions when psychological and situational factors are joined in an ambiguous manner. Because there is no authority who has decided for group members whether their problems are situational or psychological, participants learn to rely on their own judgment whether new information, skills, attitudes, or awareness of self would be most useful. Members often use their observations of how each participant forms relationships in their group to help determine whether psychological factors may be influencing that person's problems. Members can use feedback from others, but ultimately they have to decide whether they are creating unnecessary problems for themselves or whether they simply lack necessary skills.

## MEMBERS AND THE GROUP AS FIELDS

The unstructured group becomes therapeutic by creating an atmosphere wherein members feel free to reveal themselves, their struggles, their achievements, their mistakes, their joys, and their problems to others. Problems and distress within an individual's life generally should not be considered in isolation; often having a particular problem (such as a family problem) affects the person's life in multiple areas. If the individual is considered as a field of activity, then disharmony in one area of this field affects other areas. Thus, a difficulty that a member has in a present romantic relationship can involve unfinished business with a family member. A group setting can provide evidence to participants that they exist as fields since difficulties that they encounter with others in their group often relate to other concerns and problems that members bring with them to their group experience.

Members may observe that their group itself functions as a field. For example, problems between two particular members usually affect other participants. The influential theoretical perspective that persons and groups function as a dynamic field of interacting forces (rather than as a collection of separate elements), can be traced back to the theory of individual and group functioning developed by Kurt Lewin in the 1940s (see Agazarian, 1992; Yalom, 1995). If a group is viewed as a field, then as one person works on a problem, other individuals and the group as a whole will be affected. Conversely, others' reactions and changes in the group atmosphere will affect how an individual continues to work on and perceive a particular problem.

A common means of coping with a perceived problem is to compartmentalize the problem, to keep it outside awareness, and to avoid relating the problem to other events and perceptions. Metaphorically speaking, people treat problems the way that organisms treat noxious internal substances; people separate problems from the rest of themselves. This strategy can assist adaptation and survival to a degree. However, just as organisms can benefit by expelling a noxious substance or by breaking it down and assimilating it in a manner that allows the development of immunity, people can expel introjects that distort perceptions and can assimilate problematic feelings and experiences that have interfered with an integrated process of being. By compartmentalizing or encapsulating unhappy feelings and experiences, people construct rigid structures of being that render them vulnerable to stress and unpredictable life events.

Thus problems often exist as collections of elements in perceptual fields that have not been successfully assimilated and integrated into experience and ongoing encounter. For example, a person may think, 'If I have experienced being sexually molested in the past, then I cannot be a good person'. This person may strive to feel like a good person by denying the feelings associated with being molested. By keeping experience separate from self-concept, integration is prevented, and the person never truly feels good about self. A variety of life problems can be created as a result. He or she may undermine relationships at work or at home, take unnecessary risks, hurt others to gain revenge, and so on. If members change their behaviors, values, and assumptions about who they are in relationship to others (which means changing who they are within their own perceptual field), these changes tend to arise primarily from ongoing experiential learning. The verbal content that is learned in discussions is far less important than how one sees oneself, others, and one's self being with others as these discussions take place. Members may learn to relate differently than they have in the past, and this experience often opens new possibilities and alternatives. In unstructured groups, epistemological changes are not construed to occur separately from ontological changes. People therefore alter their beliefs, attitudes, and perceptions as there are changes in their ongoing experiencing of being.

There are several key questions that are raised in an unstructured group context. What is the relationship of I and we? What do I learn from being with you? How does it feel to be with you? Who are you being with me? To what extent do I perceive myself with other members becoming we? Do I and you assist each other's strengths, becoming, and well-being? A person's attitudes towards having problems can sometimes change due to the development of a new awareness of the import of the interpersonal field. The person's self-understanding can shift from the seeing of oneself as an isolated entity who 'has' (in other words, carries) problems to the viewing of oneself as a more engaged individual whose past problems do not interfere with relationships.


## PERSONAL PROBLEMS AND GROUP PROCESS

Because members are unique individuals, it is difficult to generalize about which types of interaction are most empowering for members who are dealing with problems. Hill (1965) performed research on unstructured group therapy with the intention of discovering which interactions are most therapeutic. He has devised a scale to measure group process and has concluded that therapy can be viewed as a continuum wherein members fluctuate in their commitment to therapeutic work and to developing relationships. The most significant therapeutic work of groups, according to Hill, is to establish and deepen present-oriented relationships with other group members. Personal problems are therefore assumed by Hill to be addressed most therapeutically if they are shared in the context of an ongoing relationship with one or more other group members. Problems can be shared less therapeutically when they are expressed in a manner that avoids or diminishes a member's awareness of current relationship with other participants (Hill, 1969).

31

Hill also indicates that disclosure of problems can be used to create unequal relationships wherein one participant becomes an identified patient. He refers to these interactions as speculative because members tend to speculate about causes and solutions (Hill, 1965). Additionally, Hill observed that problems can be shared to draw attention to oneself, to draw focus away from the emotional impact of immediate events within group relationships, or to use intellectualization to distance oneself from immediate experience and feelings. Problems can be revealed in a manner that invites others to become helpers and problem-solvers, thus providing roles that allow the person being helped to avoid responsibility and the helpers to be distracted from revealing themselves to others. Hill (1965) also notes that members can disclose problems in a manner that connects one participant to others and promotes constructive interpersonal interaction. To be therapeutic, the sharing of problems must occur in an atmosphere of equality, as well as in the context of a meaningful interpersonal relationship between members (Hill, 1965).

If problems are being discussed in a manner that promotes interpersonal contact and mutual respect, then finding a solution to them tends to become secondary to the enhancement of mutual awareness within the context of present communication. Members may become aware that their deepest psychological problems are in some way being acted out within ongoing group relationships. In fact, one sign that trust is developing in a group is that members will be willing to expose the difficulties that they have in contacting others. Group participants may not be able to resolve long-term problems that affect being with other people, but openness about these issues may itself be an important change. Members are likely to find that being honest helps them to feel accepted, and to accept who they are able to be with others. Acceptance leads to changes in patterns of relationship, and members may then view their problems from a new perspective—a perspective from which the existence of problems is less 'problematic'.

## INTERPERSONAL LEARNING
## IN UNSTRUCTURED GROUP THERAPY

Much of the significant learning that takes place during therapeutic groups has been observed to have an interpersonal focus based on present relationships (Agazarian, 1992; Foulkes, 1957; Leszcz, 1992; Rogers, 1970; Yalom, 1995). The interpersonal aspect of learning becomes more prominent as members find that they experience growth and healing within the process of revealing who they are to others, revealing how they respond to others, and discovering how others respond to them. Interpersonal learning that is likely to be constructive and meaningful can be differentiated from interpersonal learning that has less impact or is even potentially damaging.

Therapeutic communication is likely to be oriented toward personal experience within the present. The nature of the perceived impact of communications and the meanings that participants draw from the act of communication (verbal and nonverbal) determine whether interactions contribute to growth. Rogers (1967a) notes that although a therapist might feel and communicate empathy, this may not be healing if a client feels threatened or intruded upon. No form of communication in and of itself can be considered as essentially therapeutic. To know if a communication is therapeutic, one must have an understanding of the relational and perceptual context in which it is offered and interpreted (Barrett-Lennard, 1985).

Understanding the interpersonal context in which communication occurs is necessary to understand how effective therapeutic relationships develop (Bozarth, 1984, 1998; Bozarth, Zimring and Tausch, 2002; Friedman, 1992). Empathy seems to grow from a mutually interactive form of dialogue and cannot be considered as a commodity that is provided by one person (the therapist) to another (the client) (O'Hara, 1984). The experience of empathy can be seen as an important aspect of interpersonal learning that occurs through a context that is mutually constructed by participants in unstructured therapy groups.

As group members come to value the interpersonal learning that is possible in a therapy group, they begin to explore how they relate to others and may initiate personally untried or unusual ways of relating to people. (Page, 1984; Page, Weiss and Lietaer, 2002). Explorations of new forms of communication and relationship arise naturally if trust and openness are established between members in a group. There seems to be an innate curiosity that leads people to be interested in how others see them, to want to find out what others may have to contribute to their experience, and to discover what they may have to contribute to others.

Beyond the factor of curiosity, people also have an understanding that it is through others that they learn who they are and how they are. The self is formed in relation to others and to an environment. The exploration of relationships in a group is one aspect of individual member's lifelong endeavor to create themselves, an exploration that begins in infancy and ends only with death. Interpersonal learning is therefore a form of joint co-creation. If members explore unfinished business from past relationships, this process is often an adjunct to the learning they gain about co-creation within present relationships. Members who experientially realize how their sense of self involves others are likely to form new understandings and interpretations of past as well as present relationships.

## THE THEME OF ESTRANGEMENT VERSUS INTEGRATION

A broad range of therapists from various orientations have noted that clients in group therapy benefit from the interpersonal learning that is gained by developing relationships with other members. Generally, theorists acknowledge that it is valuable for members to work toward communicating authentically and learning about their self-limiting patterns of interaction. One way that people can affect others is by assisting each other to become aware that being together can be meaningful. As people grow in awareness, they change.

Sometimes people can be fearful about becoming more aware of their problems and the ways they relate to others. Anxiety about revealing oneself and learning how others experience oneself can lead to estrangement—that is, distance from others and avoidance of authentic interaction. Tillich (1954) used the term *estrangement* to refer to the process of separation that can lead in particular interactions to alienation of a person from others and ultimately to separation from the 'ground of being'. The development of barriers within individual awareness can be viewed as a process of estrangement. The potential to move toward either an estranged position or one of relatedness is always present within interpersonal encounters, either overtly or covertly. The work done in this area affects the degree to which members make contact with one another and the degree of cohesion they experience as a group.

Members can either use or avoid using their ability to assist one another to move beyond estrangement. An individual can be helped by others to learn about his or her own dynamic process of being and to understand what it means to be a person who exists with others. Group participants often feel estrangement as they encounter others. To experience estrangement is to feel blocked from contact and inhibited from full utilization of one's resources. If estrangement is experienced in its larger sense, members may feel separated from the ground of being, however they individually understand this ground.

Individuals sometimes perceive themselves as separated from reality, God, humanity, nature and all that is beautiful in life. One of the authors worked in a hospital where he conducted an unstructured therapy group. One of the members of this group was a person named 'Joan'. Joan was extremely bright, but she had a difficult time completing even the simplest of tasks. She could not make herself get up for work because she felt that others were laughing at her. Joan would not go out with boys because she felt extremely ugly in spite of assurances from others that she was quite pretty. Joan literally thought that God had created the universe solely to make a mockery of her. Although Joan may have thought that she was significant in God's scheme of things, she felt doomed to a life of failure no matter what she did because she thought that God was out to get her. Joan was trapped by her avoidance of the meaning of her feelings of aloneness and insignificance to others. The nature of this trap was endlessly repeated fantasies and feelings of persecution.

Estrangement is a reaction to the anxiety that is experienced if awareness itself is perceived as threatening to self. Awareness and self are essentially one, and it is through awareness that the self recognizes unity with 'other'. The self can attempt to disown awareness to escape relationship and responsibility. However, attempts to divorce self from awareness create an inescapable bind. Estrangement is evidence that the self is in a bind, that attempts to avoid relationship have depleted the self, and that awareness has become split in a manner that interferes with recognition of relatedness.

Thus the estranged person suffers from disconnection with others and even with nature, but typically repudiates the act of awareness that created the disconnection. The awareness of an individual can be enhanced when this person recognizes that blocks or barriers have been created towards aspects of experience that were uncomfortable or threatening. If these barriers can be recognized, a person can begin moving into the blocked area and start to integrate split-off aspects of experience.

If interactions in a group enhance awareness, members may experience a pull toward greater integration. The act of integration is motivated by the attraction of awareness. This attraction can be experienced as love or courage and motivates people to move through barriers to reconnect with others and with disowned aspects of experience. Thus, integration can be considered as a movement into and through anxiety that opens a person to the experience of relatedness with others and existence.

## THE HEALING OF ESTRANGEMENT IN THERAPEUTIC GROUPS

Therapeutic process encourages members to experiment with boundaries—to allow in more of who others are and let out more of who one is. To create this process, members must risk accepting that which previously was viewed as unacceptable and to question assumptions about the unacceptability of certain feelings and persons. Therapeutic process occurs, not when participants eliminate all boundaries regulating expressions of feeling, but when a boundary is determined by mutual awareness of what is valuable in a situation. Openness allows people to construct flexible boundaries, whereas judgments based on acceptability versus unacceptability are often rigid and lack adaptability to various challenges in life.

All human beings feel estrangement at one time or another, especially at times that involve significant losses and heightened perceptions of vulnerability. These experiences lead people to create a basic polarity in the way they react, a polarity between what they can tolerate and what they cannot. Some examples of estrangement that often appear in problems that members share are the separation of self from experience, thought from feeling, intention from action, person from person, and self from the larger society. Unstructured group therapy is designed to allow members to encounter and express estrangement and to move toward reintegration of elements that have been separated. The essential learning that members gain through interpersonal encounters and relationships concerns both their own estrangement and their own potential for integration.

Although past history, family relationships, and personal characteristics play a part in estrangement, it would be incorrect to blame its existence on these factors. To be estranged may be perceived as an evil or aberration, and this perception and its attending anxiety can lead people to attempt to find a cause for these feelings. Anxiety that can be explained is instantly under more control than inexplicable anxiety, which has no possibility of being understood or controlled (Frank, 1963). Estrangement, in a sense, is a fall from grace. One might want to blame this fall on a 'serpent in the garden'—for example, a family member, a group of people viewed as destructive, or certain historical conditions. However, although family members and historical events often contribute to it, estrangement can also be considered an inescapable aspect of human lives. Although we may want to create environments that help ameliorate and heal estrangement, we recognize as absurd any attempts to eliminate it from life experiences.

The image of the T'ai Chi figure, in which yin and yang intertwine, helps explain why estrangement is an inevitable aspect of human life. The Taoist philosophers invented the image of T'ai Chi to represent the psychological awareness of a dynamic interplay and balance of opposing forces, a perception that polar opposites gain their existence in relation to one another (Suler, 1991). Because persons can be aware of closeness, they can be aware of losing it. Because trust can be established, it can be broken. Estrangement and reintegration are aspects of a spiral of human growth generated through the development and transformation of relationships. In a group setting, rhythms of contact and withdrawal, closeness and distancing, form the context for communications and relationships.

Attempts to deny and escape estrangement create a great deal of psychological stress, so the simple willingness to encounter these feelings honestly can reduce the sense of being overwhelmed. As has been stated, much of the persistence of estrangement comes from a split in awareness that is based on avoidance of feelings and relationship patterns. Thus, individuals and groups of people grow in awareness and personal power as they come to terms with patterns of estrangement and assimilate related feelings, and move toward reintegration. Growth of awareness can lead to new learning and growth, to new life within relationships, ethnic groups, and cultural and political systems. Estrangement can be a challenge rather than an evil.

A client named Joan was described earlier in this chapter. After an initial period of individual counseling, Joan expressed some interest in becoming a member of an unstructured therapy group led by one of the writers. Joan came to the group regularly and gradually began to think of herself as making a contribution there. Joan also began to like some of the group members and even began to think that they were showing some acceptance of her as a person. Joan never completely abandoned the idea that God had created her as a joke on life itself, but she did begin to develop some constructive relationships with the other group members. While Joan did continue to experience personal and interpersonal difficulties during and after the group, she considered this unstructured therapy group to be a personally meaningful experience. Her awareness of self had enlarged to include others to a greater extent than before. She had somewhat relaxed her restricting perception of self as contemptible and worthless.

People generally enter therapy groups as initially estranged. These individuals usually have had no previous experience with each other. How they confront their estrangement and use their group to create forms for relationship will depend on their individual resourcefulness, the cooperation of other group members, and perceptions of responsibility. As members move toward mutual responsibility and authenticity, they move from estrangement to integration. They move from seeing themselves as separated strangers whose processes of being are disconnected from one another to viewing themselves as having increased their personal and interpersonal connections within the group. Members can extend their sense of being and of self to include others and the experiences of others as their group progresses. This extension is expressed by changes in the nature of their relationships with others in the group. These changes move in the direction of greater self-disclosure and openness in giving and receiving feedback. Members may find that they are capable of mutual confirmation, of moving from I-It relationships towards I-Thou relationships (Friedman, 1963, 1992).

## INTERPERSONAL LEARNING AND I-THOU RELATIONSHIP

In conducting a psychoanalytically oriented version of unstructured group therapy, Wolf and Schwartz (1962) were focused around helping members to move from seeing each other as objects to experiencing each other as persons. These concerns were similar to Martin Buber's (1970) philosophical observations about the nature of worthwhile human relationships. Buber was an existential philosopher and theologian whose views on human relationship affected Rogers (Friedman, 1986; Perls, Hefferline, and Goodman, 1951/1980; and Yalom, 1980). Buber believed that a central life issue for each person was whether to relate to the other as a *Thou* or as an *It*. To experience one other person as a Thou makes it possible to experience anyone in that way.

The qualities that characterize an I-Thou relationship have to do with perceptions of mutual involvement. This form of relationship is therefore the basis for dialogue in which there is listening and understanding, mutual respect, and perception of the other as a being who is unique and yet shares the same qualities of humanity and awareness that one feels are basic to oneself. I-Thou dialogue is a mutually creative act.

The I-It relationship is based on inequality (Buber, 1970). The world is not sensed as a living environment, but rather as a world of objects that may have their uses. Other people are not perceived as fully alive or real. Since others are viewed in a manner that objectifies them, I-It dialogue lacks the qualities of listening, caring, and empathizing.

Buber's discussion of human relatedness and dialogue points to the recognition that there is a common basis for relationships that can arise from therapy, friendship, and love. These may take place differently in these diverse kinds of relationships, but each serves as a way through which people can learn about the fundamental qualities of I-Thou relatedness. Though unique boundaries and limits pertain to each form of relationship, the dynamics of each can assist participants to move toward I-Thou relatedness.

One way to understand how roles affect therapy is to view interactions in terms of overt dynamics and covert dynamics. The *overt* dynamics of interaction revolve around the differences in participants' perceptions of the responsibilities they have within the relationship. Essentially, roles reflect the assumption that the therapist is there to offer help and the client is there to seek and receive it. In a group setting, participants may take on certain parts that revolve around a script, just as an actor in a play knows her role and script. Such roles have been analyzed in terms of facilitation (i.e., initiator, elaborator, or evaluator), maintenance (encourager, harmonizer, or compromiser), and anti-group (aggressor, recognition-seeker, or monopolist) (Vander Kolk, 1985). Anti-group roles can apparently be very useful for the development of therapeutic dialogue if new learning can be gained through interaction, confrontation, and acceptance (Gans,1989; Unger, 1990). These roles may reflect past learning and present interpersonal dynamics.

The *covert* dynamics of interactions do not concern projected images and roles but rather participants' awareness or lack of awareness of others as persons. Although the overt dynamics of a therapeutic group are likely always to show some evidence of differentials in power or status, the covert dynamics can increasingly move toward mutual acceptance and confirmation. Thus, within the situational limits that affect unstructured therapy, participants in effective groups can move towards a more full awareness, acceptance, and inclusion of one another (Cohen and Smith, 1976; Rogers, 1970).

Because much of the interaction in a group is between participants other than the leader, the overt dynamics that accompany the therapeutic role of the leader are less likely to have a constant influence on ongoing interactions. Group therapy settings can provide rich learning about the covert dynamics that affect members' perceptions of each other as objects or as persons. Since the status barrier between a therapist and client is not present in many interactions, group members can encounter their own dynamics in establishing relations with others with whom they are on an equal initial footing. In individual therapy, covert relationship dynamics may not be as clearly observable or may take longer to become apparent.

The I-Thou relationship is most congruent and powerful when overt relationship dynamics are not inconsistent with covert relationship dynamics—that is, when participants' roles do not interfere with their perception of each other's humanness. Although many psychological theorists have valued the potential for therapy to lead to I-Thou communication, there is much variation among theorists' descriptions of the nature of this communication. For example, Van De Riet, Korb and Gorrell (1980) have written 'The essence of Gestalt therapy is I and Thou, Here and Now' (p. 95). Gestalt therapists follow Buber, according to these authors, by differentiating between 'using' (I-It relations) and 'experiencing' (I-Thou relations). Experiencing is a form of relationship in which an 'I' encounters another 'I' (p. 32). In Gestalt therapy, it is also traditional for the therapist to provide direction and focus for clients in a manner designed to assist clients to come to greater awareness.

Van De Riet, Korb, and Gorrell (1980) believe that it is possible to have an I-Thou form of relationship in spite of roles that develop from the therapist's use of methods and techniques that are designed to lead clients in a certain direction. The therapist facilitates I-Thou relatedness by making direct contact with the client and working on a shared task that has the goal of increasing her or his awareness (p. 99). Korb, Gorrell and Van De Riet (1989) have described I-Thou contact as a process in which participants 'become unmediated presences *to each other* through an act of faith' (italics in original), participants' conscious processes of cognitive control may be temporarily suspended, and a loving experience is created that is a 'healthful, healing, and contactful state of confluence' (pp. 113–14). This description indicates that participants in an I-Thou relationship experience sufficient distinctness for contact as well as a merging of boundaries (confluence).

James Simkin, another Gestalt therapist, has depicted the 'I-Thou' relationship as a 'horizontal' relationship (1976: 79). A 'vertical' relationship in which the therapist maintains a 'superior' role as director or expert can discourage the confluence that can occur in a horizontal relationship. A horizontal relationship is described by Simkin as one in which the therapist can share of self and can allow the client access to the world of the therapist. The therapist encourages the client to ask to 'invade the privacy' of the therapist if the client wishes to learn something, just as participants often assume that therapy will invade their privacy. Although participants, including the therapist, always have the right to refuse to answer questions, a therapist who insists on retaining a vertical position remains emotionally hidden and may encourage dependency by projecting the image of an authority figure.

In unstructured group therapy, members can move toward awareness of themselves within a group that supports the personal expression of meaning and feelings. To begin this movement, they make authentic contact with one another and gradually relax self-protective modes of interaction. They may then begin to perceive that they are not separate from others. Of course, interpersonal learning does not necessarily or automatically move people toward this perception.

## ALONENESS AND I-THOU RELATIONSHIP

Members may continue to perceive themselves as isolated beings throughout a group, especially if they do not feel sufficient trust and openness to relax habitual modes of defense. They may need to learn to trust their defenses before they can allow themselves to extend themselves to others. They may need to learn that they can say no to others who want closeness so that their yes can have meaning and can affirm a spirit of freedom. The ability to say no is necessary for people to learn that they can differentiate their own perspective from that of others. Introjects from early childhood are powerful because parents project values and experiences at a time when children are not yet able fully to say no. Therefore, human development depends as much on learning how to say no and to exclude as it does on learning to say yes and include. A person whose relationships are based on introjects is not able to say yes in a way that fully expresses personal choice and power.

The realization of individual uniqueness does not necessarily lead to an isolating sense of separation from others. If participants accept and integrate feelings of aloneness, they may recognize that these can be a basis for contacting others. The experience of aloneness that often accompanies recognition of what cannot be shared also often leads to an understanding that distinctness leads to relationships. If a person communicates vaguely, never meaningfully declares feelings or thoughts, and avoids a distinct presence with others, the person will also avoid relationship. The recognition that 'I am I and you are you' is therefore vital. Of course, some sameness of feelings and perceptions is necessary for communication and is indicative of universality of being human, but distinctness is equally essential.

Members often initially experience their individuality in a group as aloneness. They are especially likely to feel that way if their distinctness arises through expression of feelings or thoughts that others do not support. Members may feel lonely because they have reached out to others and have been rebuffed or misunderstood. They may also experience existential aloneness if they realize that being with others means being distinct from as well as sharing with others.

The experience of existential aloneness can arise through emotional and cognitive awareness of limits inherent in the process of being (May and Yalom, 1984; Walsh and McElwain, 2002; Yalom, 1980). Anything that comes into being can, and eventually will, cease to exist. Therefore, individuals must contend with the physical and emotional consequences of limitations such as illness, loss, and death. Perls (1969) has found that clients in therapy need to move into and through aloneness as they encounter an impasse. The impasse typically involves the realization that environmental support is not available and self-support is not currently sufficient (Perls, 1969). An individual moves through an impasse into new growth by creatively forming a new gestalt, a new awareness of meaning, within an experience of meaninglessness and emptiness (Perls, 1969; Tillich, 1952).

Thus, awareness of aloneness can attend the recognition that no one can completely accompany one through the dilemmas that are encountered in the process of personal growth. Individuals may also encounter aloneness if they are aware of needing to define personal ethical values to guide and limit their behavior in certain situations or if they feel the limits of language and communicative abilities that restrict the degree to which experiences can be shared. Any of the previously discussed limits may initially be experienced as isolating or constricting. If, however, they are viewed as necessary aspects of human existence, they may paradoxically become liberating (May, 1981).

This realization is part of the basic learning that can be gained from participation in a therapeutic group. For example, when members struggle to manage time so that different people get to share the attention, they may recognize that they are helping to create a unified field for interaction. If members recognize differences in their wants and needs, this recognition becomes basic to their awareness of individuality and differentiation. Similarly, as members struggle to define norms for interpersonal behavior and communication, they learn that these form the basis for expressing self and forming relationships. Limits are definitions, definitions are distinctions, and distinctness is a basis for relationship. Persons as individuals and as members of a group grow through recognition of differences that form distinctions and awareness of similarities that form connections within distinctions (Agazarian, 1992).

If members retreat from the experience of existential aloneness they are simultaneously (and usually unconsciously) retreating from being. Members can retreat from aloneness by setting up the leader or another member as an authority figure, by forming group norms that stress cohesiveness through conformity, or by pursuing contact with others in a manner that avoids disclosure of self. In the last case, I-It dialogue is likely to result. A person who is using contact with others to escape aloneness is likely to feel uncomfortable simply to be with others. Such a person is likely to use these others as a way to escape unwanted feelings of aloneness and therefore will have difficulty responding to others receptively.

Members who examine those patterns of relationship in which they may have sought to dominate others, have sought to be dominated by others, or have experienced being addicted to others, often find that they were using their interactions with these others to avoid confronting themselves. People avoid confronting self when they fear the sense of aloneness and emptiness they may find within themselves. If I-Thou dialogue is established, this dialogue will inevitably bring the person into awareness of the very aloneness he or she is attempting to avoid. When I-It dialogue is used by individuals to avoid awareness, their communications may seem anxious or even desperate to others. I-It interactions will, at least temporarily, distract these individuals from experiences of aloneness but the lack of interpersonal communication in these relations will eventually make itself apparent.

A person can understand and accept the aloneness of others if he or she understands and accepts his or her own. At the same time, this acceptance creates a basis for understanding the most shared aspects of human existence and awareness. For example, if one has struggled through the feelings of loneliness involved in the ending of a close relationship or in the loss of a loved one, one can respect and understand the grieving process of another person. As group members learn to sense when and how others need space and contact, a sense of connection develops that includes an appreciation of aloneness as well as an appreciation of the process of sharing.

The dynamics of unstructured therapy groups often form a kind of rhythm. Members tend to seek contact at times when they perceive value in contributing, gaining support, learning by interacting. If they complete this kind of contact, or if they feel unable to establish connection, participants will withdraw from interaction. Members may move toward I-Thou connectedness and then move toward a more distant posture. If members disconnect from interactions that form the center of a group's attention, they may want to learn from observation or they may want time to process what they have experienced previously. It is necessary that members move from expression of self to silence. This movement creates spaces within the process of a group that allow freedom for other members to communicate and for the group as a whole to form new foci for attention.

The rhythms of a group's process can contain many levels of intensity and many themes and subthemes. One theme may be explored, then dropped, and then picked up again later. A group may move from a theme that involves all members to a concern of one particular member and then back to a more universal concern. Members may focus on here-and-now encounters, may move toward exploring relationships outside the group or past family relationships, and then may go back to a discussion that reflects present relationships. The intensity of I-Thou relatedness varies throughout the life of a group. The complexity of the rhythms and patterns of relationship that occur in an unstructured group allows members to seek the degree of contact with others that they need and to create the degree of emotional space that they also require.

The interpersonal learning that occurs in a therapy group allows participants to recognize the value of I-Thou communication, but it also permits them to see that timing is an aspect of intimate communication. Members come to terms with perceptions of existential aloneness as they realize that it is impossible to hold onto moments of I-Thou relatedness and to force intimacy to occur on demand. There are times during the life of a group, and the life of a relationship, when I-Thou communication emerges spontaneously and naturally. There are other times when such communication is absent, and to attempt to force such a level of intimacy into being would undermine whatever genuine contact is available. I-Thou relatedness can occur between members during a given interaction or within a given period of their relationship and may then recede.

## THE CREATION OF SHARED PSYCHOLOGICAL SPACE

Thus the ebb and flow of I-Thou contact is part of the overall ebb and flow of closeness in interactions. Closeness and distance are both essential aspects of relationship and the process of living. Members can grow from confronting and accepting feelings of distance as well as feelings of communion with others. Acceptance of individual uniqueness and difference allows a person to establish a 'space' from which to form connections.

*Psychological space*, unlike physical space, is not possessed or owned (as physical territory is). Psychological space is established as individuals explore experience and use this exploration to enhance their awareness. This kind of personal space is the ground in which various aspects of experience can be integrated. The ground can be extended to include others and can become shared. The perception of shared psychological space enhances the richness and meaning of communications. This space enables people to use awareness mutually to develop gestalts of meaning within experience. Because a sense of shared space is constructed by extending personal space, the former depends on the latter. If people lack a sense of personal space, they may be greedy for new experiences and sensations but may not be able to appreciate what they already have or what others are offering. They may unconsciously discount aspects of experience that another brings to communication because they have not established a basis for learning from what is presented.

The establishment of psychological space does not require any particular kind of activity. In fact, certain mental activities can distract from the openness that establishes psychological space. People can use mental or physical activities, chemicals, or excessive verbiage to fill up their psychological space. People who have truly established a sense of psychological space, however, do not need to fill it up because they appreciate the openness that exists when one is simply receptive and 'there'. Developing comfort within psychological space is an antidote for addictions and compulsive mental activities. There are many ways that people can develop this sense of existing as a receptive space as well as a physical body. For example, people can enhance their sense of psychological space as they go fishing or hiking, listen attentively to music, learn to listen to their 'inner voice' and their feelings in therapy, participate in various forms of meditation and contemplation, or silently view works of art at a museum. All of these activities offer opportunities to empty oneself of preoccupations and internal chatter, to listen and observe, and to enhance appreciation of events within present awareness.

The key factor in the development of this personal sense of space is that individuals learn to value the simple act of being silently aware. No activity per se is necessary; the person may release any sense of striving to get 'somewhere else' and is likely to be open *to* experience without demanding things *from* it. Maslow (1962) refers to this kind of openness as a part of 'peak experience', but in less dramatic fashion, silent awareness can become a part of everyday activity and being. Group members who can relax and be open within experience can also relax and be open with others.

Members who have a sense of personal psychological space can demonstrate for others how people can interact in ways that communicate respect for one another's space. This respect is an aspect of the development of loving contact that underlies I-Thou relatedness (Korb, Gorrell and Van De Riet, 1989; Simkin, 1976). Group participants who are dealing with patterns of being developed in families that were enmeshed or rejecting can benefit when other members communicate respect for and caring about one another's space. Members will feel and be affected by a sense of inclusivity and acceptance. A group then begins to function as a whole that is more than the sum of individual parts. Members can then experience cohesion and belonging with others, as well as support for their uniqueness and individuality.

Receptivity and acceptance are attitudes that are essential for the generation of psychological space. Within a shared physical space, two people can be considered as separate 'objects'. Within a shared psychological space, people can be within each other. The presence of one person enables another to disclose who he or she is, and vice versa. Shared psychological space is created as people begin to accept each other's presence without judgment and to disclose thoughts and feelings. People then become comfortable with themselves being with others and with experience as it unfolds.

Shared psychological space allows all members to feel that they are actively involved with one another, even when certain members are temporarily 'center stage'. This kind of space allows the focus of attention in a group to shift as needed and enables members to assist one another and view each other as equals within a shared process. Participants are not using their group to provide drama, except insofar as genuinely helping one another to enhance awareness can sometimes be dramatic. Members can become comfortable with silence as well as speech. They can enjoy simply being together as well as sharing thoughts and feelings. As they create psychological space, group members are not pressured to reveal thoughts or feelings but offer these naturally. Natural sharing occurs as members use communication to increase understanding of self and others. Members are not trying to *make* something happen when they communicate in this manner but are communicating something that *is* happening. Communication within shared psychological space can creatively heighten awareness of what is happening and of the fact that their shared experience is rich with possibilities for exploration.

CHAPTER 3

# SELF-ACTUALIZATION
# AS A CENTRAL THEME

Theorists have ideas about the nature of human beings that affect their assumptions about human behavior in groups. Assumptions lead theorists to focus on various aspects of group process, to diverge in their interpretations of observations, and to vary in their descriptions of typical occurrences and themes in unstructured therapy groups. Theorists' descriptions of events in therapy vary in part because they are oriented toward different central themes. It is worthwhile to review some of the concepts that influential theorists have used to focus their observations. An underlying or basic theme involved in unstructured therapy groups may be found within the divergent themes that theorists have observed and described.

One concept that certain theorists have viewed as an underlying or basic theme is self-actualization (for example, Bozarth, 1998; Maslow, 1962; Patterson, 1980, 1985; Rogers, 1951). Although some have hoped that self-actualization could serve as a unifying construct for understanding healing and growth (see Patterson, 1985), others have observed that self-actualization has not lived up to its promise to become a truly integrative concept (see Daniels, 1988; Geller, 1984). One persistent criticism of self-actualization theory has been its reliance on a biological metaphor for human growth that does not fully address the impact of dialogue and the mutual construction of experiential realities between partners in dialogue (Arnett, 1989; Friedman, 1986; Geller, 1984). Recent attempts to revitalize the concept of self-actualization have attempted to move toward a process-oriented view that can integrate awareness of biological aspects of personhood with dialogical, experiential, and social aspects of personhood (Daniels, 1988; Frick, 1990). Using a process-oriented and integrative conceptualization, self-actualization can be a useful term for describing self-directed human movement toward growth. From this perspective, growth harmonizes personal and interpersonal realities (Daniels, 1988). Thus, to achieve a viable conceptualization of self-actualization, we must move beyond either-or thinking in which individual is pitted against group, self against other, inside against outside. Instead, opposites can be viewed as arising in mutual definition (Suler, 1991).

Individuals develop with and within groups, and groups are defined by their members. Self arises with and is enhanced by others (Watts, 1961). Self-actualization can therefore be understood as a process, a resonating movement that harmonizes polar forces, which allows these forces to work together harmoniously and with

45

mutual benefit. The perceptually conflicting forces of 'I' and 'them' can become the mutually enhancing forces of 'I' and 'we' as movement toward self-actualization occurs between persons in a group.

The frequently criticized idea that an '*a priori*', 'essential', or 'core' entity is being actualized (see Geller, 1984; Smith, 1973), is not necessary for a useful conceptualization of self-actualization. Following the lead of Wilson (1988), we view the 'real self' or 'core self' experientially, as an integrative unity of mind-body and social and physical awareness of being. We propose that individual movement toward wholeness occurs within awareness, as a resonance of intrapersonal and interpersonal forces that may sometimes clash but which yet can be experientially integrated. The self can become a stronger self by giving itself to others, by including more of others, and by experiencing itself with others. This self that becomes stronger is not an entity that exists separately from experience, from others, and from nature. Rather, the self can be conceptualized as an integrative potential that arises as relationship and that potentially includes all of experience, all others, and all of nature (Tillich, 1954). This kind of conceptualization of the self can be enhanced by the integration of Eastern and Western psychology (Berkow and Page, 2000; Daniels, 1988; Page and Berkow, 1991; Watts, 1961). One purpose for such an integration is to provide a workable framework (an effective 'myth') that can coherently reconcile human experiences of self-expansion and self-transcendence (see Daniels, 1988).

The movement of the self between polar conditions (for example, aloneness and contact, estrangement and communion) is a process by which relationship is developed and enhanced (Perls, Hefferline and Goodman, 1951/1980); Schnieder, 1990). Thus, the self uses experiencing to integrate and differentiate (Frick, 1990). The self does not exist as an entity apart from experiencing and relationship. Thus, an individual's self-actualization inevitably includes others. Mythically, self-actualization can be viewed as a 'quest' that is a 'shared adventure' (Daniels, 1988: 35). Variations of this mythic theme can be found in various theories that attempt to explain how human growth can be enhanced through group therapy.

## INTEGRATION OF THEORIES OF SELF-ACTUALIZATION

Eastern perspectives about psychological well-being have portrayed awareness of one's original nature as consistent with a harmonious integration of self with the world of nature (Berkow and Page, 2000; Page and Chang, 1989; Page et al., 1998). Individuation, if it includes integration of self and nature, will also include the possibility of communion with others. The uniqueness of personhood does not separate the individual from others because awareness of harmony with nature and others is part of realizing one's self. A theory of self-actualization can evolve that is compatible with both Eastern as well as psychodynamic perspectives. Such a theory would view potentials that are actualized as uniquely individual and universally human. Self-actualization can be defined as an activity that resolves self-other tensions and polarities; therefore, self-actualization can occur within activities that people use to communicate with one another. Group therapy then becomes understandable as one of the human activities through which a potential process of self-actualization can be enhanced.

Participants in therapeutic groups often ask questions that refer to themes of identity, direction, and experience. Directly or indirectly, people ask, 'Who am I, where have I been, where am I going, who am I going with, and what is my experience of being here and moving there?' These ontological themes continually surface and resurface, revealing self-actualization to be a process, a movement, a creation of self within the act of relating oneself to others. As the individual relates self to others, the individual also relates ongoing experiences and aspects of experience within the act of being.

Self-actualization is expressed in different ways in various cultures. Because self-actualization is creative, it is never completely defined by any person's or any culture's myths and symbols. Individuals can become excessively invested in cultural symbols that provide positive self-representations if these people have become creatively blocked in their self-actualizing use of encounters. Cultures themselves can be viewed in terms of collective self-actualization. Cultures define themselves in relation to other cultures. If a culture is insecure, it may affirm itself aggressively against other cultures or may become isolationistic. A self-actualizing culture, according to the definition used in this text, is willing to form constructive and confirmatory relations with other cultures. A therapy group's culture can also form constructive relations with the other cultures in which members may participate. In a group therapy setting, members' self-definitions include those that these participants have achieved in other groups in which they have been involved. By defining oneself in relation to others in a group, one tends to use past definitions of self that are present within one's ongoing acts of relationship.

## THEORIES OF GROUP PSYCHOTHERAPY AND SELF-ACTUALIZATION

To be understood as an underlying theme in human activity, self-actualization must be conceptualized in a manner that can account for the negative as well as the positive aspects of human self-direction. Some psychological theorists have focused on ideas such as unfinished business (Perls, Hefferline and Goodman, 1951/1980), compulsive repetition (Freud, 1920/1955), games that people play in relationships (Berne, 1964, 1966) and communication (Bateson, Jackson, Haley and Weakland, 1956). Persons' acceptance of unsatisfying or self-limiting patterns in relationships, even when other options are available, is a factor in therapy (and life) that is difficult to deny.

The movement toward self-actualization can be severely distorted, although never totally negated (it is too basic to the process of being). Some relationships can be seen to lead to diminishment of participants' self-esteem and self-efficacy and to tragedy and hurt. Others strengthen and enliven the participants. A valid theory of self-actualization should account for people's willingness to engage in destructive game-playing as well as mutual affirmation. Psychoanalytic thinkers have been among those theorists who have attempted to understand how people create and maintain self-defeating patterns in relationship. It is useful to examine how these thinkers have viewed group therapy.

### PSYCHOANALYTIC INFLUENCE ON THEORIES OF GROUP THERAPY

The views conceptualized by psychoanalytic theorists have played an important role in many therapists' views of unstructured therapy. The influence of psychoanalytic thought is due in large part to the impact of certain key theorists, trained in psychoanalysis, who were pioneers in the use of unstructured groups to promote improved social and personal functioning. Though they have thought critically about many of the central issues involved in conducting therapy groups, psychoanalysts have placed certain limitations on the themes on which they have generally focused. These assumptions lead to reductionistic and negativistic descriptions of human motives for interacting with others. Negativistic descriptions of people maintain a core focus on the potential of people to hurt themselves or each other through pleasure-seeking behaviors or through unchanneled aggression.

The psychoanalytic view of human beings invites us to look at ourselves and others without illusions and to be suspicious of our innate ability to organize our thinking around palatable self-deceptions. At the same time, it tends to minimize persons' constructive potentials to help each other to grow and succeed. Of course, a viable explanation of self-actualization needs to account for destructive interpersonal patterns of relationship without being naïve and without placing all responsibility for destructiveness outside the person. Yet, we would like to be able to recognize and to account for destructive behavior without necessarily *expecting* negative behavior and without seeing interpersonal destructiveness as inevitable and inherent in human nature.

For Freud (1926/1953a; 1934/1953b), the id was the basis and origin of human personality. The *id*, as described by Freud, is an essential driving force in human nature that is fundamentally instinctual and that strives for immediate satisfaction and relief of tension. The structure of identity, which Freud termed the *ego*, and the structure of moral conscience or guilt, termed the *superego*, arise because external reality frustrates the desires of the id for immediate satisfaction of its drives for pleasure and destruction. The ego and superego can be viewed as portions of the id whose functions have become differentiated to cope with aspects of reality external to the person (Alexander, 1961).

# Self-Actualization as a Central Theme

One implication of Freud's view of the person is that the psychoanalytic therapist needs to represent a somewhat authoritarian image. This image is necessary insofar as the therapist represents the impingement of 'external reality' on clients. The therapist needs to exert control on the process of therapy to strengthen the egos of clients (Freud 1940/1964). Within the context of Freudian theory, we do not find explanations of how clients can move toward greater integration without direction from a leader or authority figure. The therapist is required to encourage the appropriate channeling and expression of needs, so that the ego of the client does not become overwhelmed by denied and repressed impulses from the id.

Because repressed life energies are thought to be related to past experiences that have not been integrated, the psychoanalytic therapist helps patients recover memories that have been buried or denied (Greenson, 1967). At the right time, the therapist can interpret for the client how her or his present relationship with the therapist is a re-enactment of themes connected with the forgotten past (Greenson, 1967). If therapy is successful, the client will release previously bound-up energy, and will become freer to choose modes for self-expression and directions in relationships that are not a compulsive acting-out of past patterns.

Psychoanalytic therapy emphasizes a causal relationship between the past and the present; it therefore becomes necessary to discover 'the truth' about the past. However, in reality, the only truth that is available in the therapy session is the client's reconstruction and memory of past events and the therapist's guesses and opinions about these memories. The importance of past events in the process of therapy is therefore a matter of subjectively experienced meanings rather than objectively verifiable ones. The client's present mode of being affects how he or she focuses on certain past events and how these are remembered and reconstructed. The effect of past patterns on present encounters is a matter of the personal meaning attached to previous events. Whether a person is reacting inappropriately to current relationships because of unfinished business is ultimately determined by the person's own present awareness, although feedback from others can be helpful.

## GROUP WORK AND THE LEGACY OF FREUD'S THEORY

Psychoanalytic theory can, perhaps, be differentiated from psychoanalytic therapy (Hawkins, 1997). The latter offers clients opportunities to explore experiences freely and openly. It is believed that people can use this self-exploration to become more effective and more fulfilled in work and in love. Clients are encouraged to relate aspects of experience (especially the present to the past) in ways that they have previously not been able to do. They are asked to reflect on themselves, their feelings, and their patterns of being with others. This form of therapy implies that people can become more aware, more self-reliant, and more effective (in other words, more self-actualizing) by exploring who they are in an atmosphere of freedom. The theory of psychoanalysis seems to be far more pessimistic about the basic nature of human beings than is the actual therapy employed. Psychoanalytic theory presents human beings formed by the past, and motivated by greedy and hostile feelings that make other people into objects for individuals' desires and aggressions. Although the therapy pursues the idea of awareness in an atmosphere of freedom, the theory negates it by conceiving of it only as a device to allow people to delay gratification and to redirect drives.

In application to groups, psychoanalytic theory generally indicates that members are not likely to assist each other's growth unless the leader maintains a strong presence. Freud's pessimism about human nature was based in part on his observations concerning human behavior in groups. If people are in an unstructured group that lacks direction from a leader, they would likely act out unresolved feelings of aggression or sexuality that are prevented expression in other social situations (Bion, 1959). Even if there is the presence of a strong leader, the group members are expected to have deeply conflicting feelings about that person. Freud was in fact pessimistic about the long-term ability of humans to survive collectively. He feared human beings' tendencies to unleash aggression as a group activity (Freud, 1930/1961). Increased technological abilities for destruction, combined with the regressive instincts of people that Freud observed emerging in group situations, led him to take a dim view of the future survival of the human race.

Freud (1921/1948) observed that people in groups may regress to a disinhibited mob psychology. A human mob tends to find a leader with whom they can obtain power through identification. They may compete for the leader's affection or may wish to view the leader as loving everyone equally. The expressed desire for the leader's love is largely an illusion to reverse the phylogenetically inherited murderousness of the primal horde (Freud, 1921/1948). This theory is an attempt to explain how mobs of people can be fused into a unified group through identification with a leader who is able to rouse their hatred and channel their aggression towards an outside enemy, an occurrence that has not been historically uncommon.

Human psychology in unstructured groups tends toward regression, according to much of psychoanalytic theory, and is therefore a problematic environment to assist individuals to establish ego strength. The phenomenon of regression in group situations leads to such human inventions as carnivals and orgies, which can temporarily ease the tension between ego and ego ideal and may thus have an anxiety reducing effect (Scheidlinger, 1980a, 1980b). Freud did not advocate the practice of psychoanalysis in group settings, a view that is consistent with his theoretical beliefs. However, later psychoanalytic therapists made various attempts to modify Freudian theory in a manner conducive to treatment in a group situation (Scheidlinger, 1980b).

As previously noted, some of the earliest and most significant authors who wrote about therapy in an unstructured situation were trained in psychoanalysis. S. R. Slavson, S. H. Foulkes, W. Bion, A. Wolf, and E. K. Schwartz were some of the pioneers. These theorists had to reinterpret facets of Freudian theory and had to explain the nature of group identity in a manner that was consistent with their observation that groups have a potential to assist members to become strong and healthy individuals. These theorists also had to contend with the diminished control of the therapist over the therapeutic process that is inherent in a group situation. These theorists varied in their allegiance to Freud's view that the central themes of human groups revolve around the control of aggression, individuals' desires to regress, and the need for the leader to provide direction and channeling for the instincts of group members. In coming to terms with Freud's hypotheses about human nature in groups, these authors addressed basic concerns about conducting group therapy that are relevant for group leaders of any theoretical persuasion. These psychoanalytic group leaders saw opportunities for individuals to grow through interacting with others in a group, although they had considerable differences concerning how growth might take place. Though none of these theorists used the term *self-actualization*, their work implied that an individual needs interactions with other people to become more individual and more whole.

Conceptualization of the themes around which growth-producing interactions occur in a group evolves from assumptions about the basic nature of a human group. A group may be characterized as a collection of separate individuals or as a whole that has unique qualities that cannot be described solely as the sum of separate parts. Foulkes (1953, 1957) and Bion (1959) have taken the latter position and have gone so far as to characterize the group as having an identity or personality. They both spoke of the group personality in a manner that is identical to references made to individual personalities. Therefore, the group personality is viewed either as being expressed consciously or as manifesting itself on unconscious levels. This personality is said to arise whenever individuals join together. The group personality is said to arise as an entity that is more than a conglomeration of the separate identities of individuals.

Though agreeing that the group could be considered a personality, Foulkes and Bion disagree about the nature of this hypothesized group personality. Bion's (1959) view was closer to Freud's pessimism concerning the potentially destructive nature of the human unconscious. He expects the group's unconscious motives to become evident in expressions of dependence, in acts of overt rebellion against the leader, or through covert noncooperation with the leader. Bion believes the leader will have to confront and interpret the resistance of the group as an entity. The group as a whole will resist working together to solve problems. In addition, there is also the resistence of individuals who interfere with growth toward their functioning as conscious and aware persons. Bion foresees the likelihood that individuals will use the group as a means to flee from the demand to work on problems or to fight the leader or each other rather than work together. Members could imagine external or internal enemies that were nonexistent or feel themselves as dependent on the leader or on the group for survival. Individuals could also attempt to form pairs with each other or with the leader and thus resist cooperation and unity with the group (Bion, 1959).

Bion (1959) believes that the leader should function as the ego of the group, regulating the destructive capacities of its unconscious. The leader can forge the group into a work group by preventing any one of the basic unconscious assumptions (fight-flight, dependency, and pairing) from becoming dominant in the group's functioning. The leader, as described by Bion, does not involve himself or herself in the mutuality of group relationships. This approach allows the leader to function as an objective observer who can interpret the activities of the group and who can maintain control of the group process against the unconscious forces that threaten to promote regression. Bion's theory suggests that any kind of self-actualization that is possible must use a perspective dissociated from emotional trends in the group.

Foulkes (1951), also influenced by Freud, takes a much more positive stance towards the personality of human groups. Foulkes believes that the group unconscious can move in constructive directions without the imposition of controls by an external source. The leader is viewed as more of a guide than an authority. The leader can function as a participant who guides the group toward constructive work and does not need to function as an emotionally removed commentator on group process. The conductor, as Foulkes refers to the leader, can accept a leadership position but actually desires to surrender this role as members assume more responsibility. The leader does not concern himself or herself with setting goals that would make the group efficient and is instead interested in generating a free-floating discussion (Foulkes, 1948).

Within this discussion, the therapist might notice conscious and unconscious levels of meaning, called *resonances* (Foulkes, 1975). Although it is important for the conductor to interpret meanings within the context of the group matrix, such interpretations should not have the effect of moving the group away from its present interaction or from an atmosphere of free-floating discussion. The therapeutic group that functions as a healing group becomes a matrix for the development of the identities of its members. The members begin to sense themselves as part of a whole and are not threatened by group dynamics in the manner suggested by Bion. In fact, the group that is functioning most therapeutically is one where the leader exerts little overt control on the direction of group process (Foulkes, 1951). Foulkes is far more confident than Bion that human self-actualization can arise from the emotional and cognitive matrix of the group process itself.

Wolf and Schwartz (1962) agree with Foulkes and Lewis (1944) that group treatment has therapeutic potentials that are not available in individual treatment. Wolf and Schwartz (1962) also agree that the leader's proper role is to exert little control on group process; they advocate the use of alternate sessions where the members meet without the leader. However, Wolf and Schwartz emphatically deny the existence of a group personality or group mind. Although they acknowledge the importance of understanding group dynamics and group process, they view concepts of a group personality as mystical and countertherapeutic. The group personality is seen as an illusion that could be perpetuated to promote conformity and mediocrity at the expense of autonomy and genuine I-Thou relationships (Wolf and Schwartz, 1962).

Foulkes (1951) finds a healing power in the group itself that transcends its individual members. It is therefore conceivable that individuals who function pathologically elsewhere could create a healthy group norm that reinforces their ability to relate and that corrects their neurotic reactions. This idea of Foulkes' is regarded by Wolf and Schwartz (1962) as a 'deification of the group' (p. 20). They criticize this idea as encouraging an 'I-Group relatedness'. This is described as an I-It relationship; the group itself functions as a substitute for the development of I-Thou relationships between responsible individuals. Thus, Wolf and Schwartz indicate that groups can further individual self-actualization if self is clearly differentiated from group and if the group is not viewed as a kind of self.

Slavson (1957) is also mistrustful of the attempts of individuals to respond to the group as if it were an entity. Although Wolf and Schwartz are relatively trusting of individuals' abilities to generate I-Thou relationships without the intervention of a group leader, Slavson (1953) views interpretation by the therapist as being essential to prevent group members' inevitable attempts to give up their egos, or portions of these, to the leader and the group. Slavson believes that bonds between group members, even if they appear cooperative or collaborative, have the effect of promoting regression and neurosis. Although there are many means for members to escape or resist the therapeutic process, group members can experience healing through relationship, catharsis, insight, ego strengthening, reality testing, and sublimation (Slavson, 1951). The group is a setting that allows for the therapist's analysis of individuals in a situation where their modes of relationship are apparent. For Slavson, self-actualization can only occur if members develop sufficient ego strength to avoid merging self with group.

## OBJECT RELATIONS AND THE HUMAN GROUP

More recent developments in psychoanalytic thought have come about through investigating dynamics (relations to human objects) that occur earlier in individual human development than the dynamics that were most important for Freud (see, for example, Mahler, 1968; Winnicott, 1958). These object-relations theories tend to show that healthy independence cannot occur without a developmental process that includes healthy dependence on healthy human objects (represented internally as 'good' objects, sources of security). Development toward self-esteem and autonomy is often impaired by experiences of anxiety associated with persecutory fears (represented internally as 'bad' objects). These theoretical constructs are used by group leaders to help members experience being cared about by others (reinforcing and developing 'good' internal representations); at the same time, feelings of anxiety and anger can be contained within the group, and members who experience these feelings can be gradually assisted to understand how defensive strategies related to internalized 'bad' objects are the basis for much fear and anger (Ganzarain, 1992).

Developments in object-relations theory support the concept that therapeutic benefit can arise from members receiving a kind of protective motherly warmth and acceptance from their therapist or group (Ganzarain, 1992). Object-relations theory indicates that early developmental difficulties with internalizing a strong and nurturing maternal presence underlie much psychopathology. Individuals may need to view the group as a strong and nurturant presence to internalize this image and thereby develop a more positive sense of self. Individuals who see the group as a 'bad mother' who cannot meet the participants' needs for recognition and sustenance may resist the group.

According to object-relations theory, much of what is useful for participants is the extent to which the group can satisfactorily meet previously unmet needs (for example, to feel cared about, to feel significant to others). These unmet needs are transferred into relationships in the group through unconscious fantasies (Bach, 1957). The primary benefit of groups for members, according to many neo-Freudian theorists, is not so much insight into one's past as it is the meeting of previously unmet needs. If needs are distorted by game-playing, group members are generally relied upon to sense when and how to confront games played by other members. These games typically involve attempts to meet unmet needs without consciously acknowledging their existence and nature. A healthy group will tend to develop intermember relationships that have increasingly less distortion, less defensive exploration of issues, and more accurate self-correction by group members (Bach, 1957).

Individual maturation can occur in a group if its power as a whole is used to support individuation. The individual's relationship with the group as an entity can be positive if this relationship allows the individual to internalize feelings of self-esteem. A person can be seen as having a need to experience belonging and acceptance within a cohesive group as a way to establish and maintain a personal sense of internal unity (Bach, 1957). Members may attempt to use the group as a whole to gratify unconscious fantasies that reflect unmet needs, but the desire to maintain group cohesion and acceptance from others will result in self-exploration, less defensiveness, and growth toward positive relationships. Bach (1957) views the individual as capable of using the group in ways that either negate or enhance the development of self-esteem. Object-relations theory has moved in a different direction than many of the earlier psychoanalytic group theories by associating the power of a group to exist as a cohesive entity with the development of members' perceptions of individuality. Interpretation by the therapist is less important for moving towards individuation than is the establishment of interactions that meet authentic needs.

In object-relations theory, group atmosphere becomes an important factor, perhaps an excessively emphasized one. It is possible to treat the group atmosphere as if it were a personality, a being in its own right, to which the members may look for nurturance. This kind of perception can lead to a kind of dependency that inhibits individuation unless members feel that it is safe to disagree with others in their group and to draw nurturance from sources other than their group. From the perspective of self-actualization, this theory emphasizes that human potentials can be actualized most effectively in an environment that provides supportive and caring communication.

## SELF PSYCHOLOGY

Self psychology, based on the psychoanalytic theorizing of Heinz Kohut (1971, 1977), places the development of a cohesive sense of self at the center of the therapeutic enterprise. Kohut (1971) indicates that the self develops through internalization of early experiences of merging with the mother (or other caregiver) and being mirrored by the mother. Merging provides experiences of security and well-being that gradually become internalized as a sense of self-esteem. Communications that mirror a child reflect the caregiver's awareness of the child as a valued being and thus contribute importantly to the child's sense of self and self-efficacy. Additionally, the child's sense of self is built upon the process of idealizing someone who is perceived as omnipotent and whose strength and ideals are gradually internalized by the child. Furthermore, a person who has deficits in self-esteem may move toward greater strength of self by developing a 'twinship' relationship with another—that is, a relationship in which the other is experienced as being very much like oneself (Kohut and Wolf, 1978). Thus, Kohut is more optimistic than Freud about people's ability to repair damage that they have suffered and to generate new 'self-structures' through relationships at various times in the life cycle.

Kohut's theory, among other theories derived from Freudian thought, probably comes closest to an overt conceptualization of a self-actualizing process that occurs through relationship. However, Kohut implies that the self can only be formed through passively transmuting and internalizing aspects of others. The ability of a person creatively to invent self through initiating new forms of relationship is minimized in this theory.

Object-relations theories and self psychology support the view that the group can provide a corrective emotional experience that can meet previously unmet needs for love and significance. Self psychology places less emphasis on fantasies about internalized representations of objects compared with object-relations theories. The felt experience of relationship, especially its empathic aspects, is stressed by Kohut (1977).

Applied to groups, the reactions participants have to feelings become important (Bacal, 1985). Relationships are experienced and felt by individuals, and these feelings and experiences determine who they become. Self psychology applied to group theory also attempts to explain how interpersonal dynamics can enhance or detract from the development of a positive sense of self (Berry, 1991). The person is not treated as a biological machine driven to discharge tension, but as someone who needs others to construct his or her perception of self. Applying Kohut's theory to group practice, it becomes plausible that a person could become stronger and healthier from experiencing him- or herself as a member of a cohesive and accepting group (Berry, 1991).

The use that members make of the therapeutic group has been understood, in object-relations theories and self psychology, as largely being activated by narcissistic motives (Bacal, 1985). The analysis of persons in a group focuses on how these individuals attempt to form relationships that will restore, maintain, and enhance the sense of self. Self psychology indicates that members want to establish a feeling of belonging in a group as well as a feeling of being special. They may seek mirroring responses, may attempt to merge with others or with the group as a whole, or may establish a twinship relationship with another. Since members have typically been hurt in the past, their resistance to forming intimate relationships is properly understood as their attempts to protect themselves from expected hurt or from the possibility of reopening old wounds.

Self psychology pictures psychological health as being derived from the establishment of a cohesive self, which is necessary for the recognition of a cohesive self in others, and an understanding of how to respect the self of others. Narcissism, or self-love, is viewed as playing an essential role in developmental maturation. The development of a cohesive self is achieved through transmutations of narcissism and is necessary for participation in mutually empathic relationships (Kohut, 1977).

## HUMANISTIC AND EXISTENTIAL THEMES IN GROUP THERAPY

Humanistic theories, such as those of Maslow and Rogers, value the realization of human potentials and use the theme of self-actualization to affirm human beings and their possibilities (Daniels, 1988). Humanism thus emphasizes trust in the human organism, based on a belief that innate potentials for physical, emotional, and spiritual well-being, as well as innate motivation toward prosocial interpersonal interactions, exist. Humanistic theories can be seen as a reaction against Freud's pessimism. At the opposite extreme from Freud, this philosophy declares that human beings are essentially motivated toward caring and prosocial relationships. However, like Freud, the humanistic school tends to validate its assertions about human nature by appealing to biologically rooted, pseudoscientific metaphors (Daniels, 1988). Human beings are considered to have an innate nature that unfolds in a predictable manner, that moves unerringly toward goals that are inherent to the nature of the human organism.

The existential movement in philosophy and psychology does not react so much against Freud's pessimism as against his determinism. The existential position generally places great importance on persons' abilities to make choices that influence who they become. The existential philosopher Sartre (1956) describes persons as creating themselves through their acts. Most existentially oriented thinkers would not view the person as essentially either destructive or prosocial (although people can make destructive or prosocial choices). One key difference between Buber, the existentialist, and Rogers, the humanist, is that Buber (in spite of his respect for Rogers' therapeutic work) philosophically rejects Rogers' belief in a universal core predisposition towards constructive directions (Friedman, 1986). Buber thinks that this belief in a positive core could inhibit therapists or other participants in relationships from engaging in certain kinds of growth-enhancing interpersonal dialogues. These dialogues would allow one participant, as an individual who has chosen values, to enter into another's struggle between constructive and destructive possibilities within that person's self. Buber uses the term *confirmation* to describe an effective interaction in which this kind of dialogue has occurred. Confirmation may result from a struggle between and within participants (Friedman, 1986).

One means to integrate existential and humanist views is to recognize that both are compatible with the assumption that the person is capable of constructing self and world creatively. Along with existentialism and humanism, the epistemologically oriented thinking of radical constructivists also emphasizes the human being as an active creator of reality (Watzlawick, 1990). Existential thinking tends to place more emphasis on individuals' confrontations with those factors that inevitably place limits on individuals than does constructivism, and existential theorists often see creativity as growing out of these confrontations (May, 1969, 1977, 1981; Perls, 1969). Relative to constructivism, the concerns of existentialism and humanism are generally more ontological (being-oriented) than epistemological (knowing-oriented). However, the view of the person as a creator of meanings, an organizer of perceptions, and a determiner of values seems to bridge the worlds of being and knowing. Within the process of being, knowing is integrated with action, and creation of meaning is inseparable from openness within perception. In the continuous activity of moment-to-moment existence, being is not separated from knowing, and emotion is not distinct from cognition.

A *central* assumption can be made in unstructured group therapy that integration occurs as being and knowing come together. This assumption will give a present-centered focus to therapy. Integration of being and knowing is evidenced by spontaneous actions and feelings as well as intuitive awareness of self and others. In self-actualization that is promoted by unstructured therapy, knowing and being are one immediate process. Members can be encouraged to think, to feel, and to know—and they can be encouraged to know their experience as they experience. Knowledge that is separated from being is less stimulating than knowledge that embraces being. From this perspective, experiential knowledge is preferable to attempts to formulate abstract 'truths' that are separate from ongoing experience and existence (Bugental, 1978).

## CONTRIBUTIONS OF ROGERS AND PERSON-CENTERED THERAPY

One major commonality of humanistic and existential theorists has been their recognition that the themes that evolve during therapeutic groups are most effectively and therapeutically treated if these themes are dealt with in the context of authentic present relationships (Rogers, 1970; Yalom, 1995). Carl Rogers' (1970) theory of individual and group therapy has had a significant impact on many leaders of therapy groups (Bozarth, Zimring and Tausch, 2002; Corey, 1990, 1991; O'Leary and Keane, 1997). One aspect of Rogers' influence is his emphasis on the importance of present-centered communication that is genuine and empathic. His emphasis on the importance of congruent perception and communication leads him to question whether psychiatrists and psychoanalysts have access to any special knowledge about human beings that make these professionals the sole proper authorities to conduct individual and group therapy.

Rogers' (1967b) theory proposes that the quality of communication is far more important to therapy than any special knowledge contained in the communication. Rogers (1967b) performed research that demonstrated that it is the quality of the personal encounter between a therapist and client that is most important in therapy; his research showed that therapists who show congruence, empathy, positive regard and unconditionality of regard in their relationships with clients are more likely to have successful therapeutic outcomes than those who do not exhibit these characteristics. Rogers was the first theorist to advocate that his own and others' sessions be taped and reviewed to discover what is therapeutic, rather than relying on what experts *say* is therapeutic (Bozarth, Zimring and Tausch, 2002; Garfield and Bergin, 1986). His analysis of the events that he observed to lead to experiences of healing and growth resulted in his departure from some of the premises of Freudian psychotherapy.

Rogers (1980) came to emphasize what is genuine and that which exists in the present, whereas psychodynamic therapy attempts to analyze and expose problems that are experienced in present relationships by focusing on the transference of early relationship patterns and needs. Rogers' method of working with clients focuses attention on the present dynamics between participants in therapeutic situations and builds on whatever authentic communication is occurring. The recognition of avoiding behaviors and strategies of communication is not considered necessary for therapeutic personality change (Rogers, 1967b). Avoidance can be assumed to diminish automatically as trust and openness become operating principles for communication. Analysis of past behaviors and situations is not required. Individuals move toward health and self-actualization as they learn that they can trust themselves, their perceptions of experience, and others (Rogers, 1977).

Interpretation is not a helpful therapeutic element in Rogers' theory. Rogers (1970) stresses that interpretation generally leads to a devaluation of the client's own judgment. The client is considered by Rogers to be the best expert on her or his own experience. The empathy of the therapist is considered far more helpful than the therapist's interpretive ability. Empathy is viewed as the means by which the therapist can understand the world of the client from that individual's perspective (Rogers, 1967b). This kind of understanding supports the client in his or her own self-exploration. Kohut (1971) also stresses the importance of empathy; however, he primarily sees it as a means to gain information that could assist effective interpretation.

A core belief in Rogers' (1987) understanding of human beings is that people are essentially constructive beings; they are prosocial and motivated toward health and growth. As individuals come in contact with their actualizing tendencies, each person can be expected to find vast inner resources to direct his or her behavior, relationships, and movement toward growth (Rogers, 1980). The group as a whole has the potential to become an expression of a universal movement toward self-actualization. Rogers indicates that if a group is functioning therapeutically, something universal begins to emerge. This process involves a loss of the experience of oneself as separate; the sense of 'me' and 'you' becomes less distinct (Rogers, 1980). Rogers (1980) reports that people in such groups have expressed highly positive feelings arising from their sensation that their consciousness is not separate from others in the group.

Wood (1982), a theorist of the Rogerian, or Person-Centered, school of thought, has stated that a therapy group tends to evolve as a distinct entity that influences its individual members. Bozarth (1981) has concluded that person-centered groups can work well with an unusually large number of people. As many as one hundred people have found they could function successfully and experience personal growth in a group according to Bozarth. Person-centered groups are conducted from the premise that individuals are the best authority for choosing situations that will assist their own growth. Therefore, group leaders would have little investment in trying to guide or direct members in any particular direction (Bozarth, 1986, 1998).

## CONTRIBUTIONS OF PERLS AND GESTALT THERAPY
Gestalt therapy has tended to view self-actualization as an activity that integrates polarities within the person. Integration is often seen in this theory as an individual rather than universal activity of awareness (Page and Chang, 1989). Perhaps for this reason, Gestalt therapists generally conceive of the group as a setting wherein members explore their experiences individually while others observe, rather than as a setting in which members cooperatively share explorations and develop a relationship with their group as a whole (Polster and Polster, 1973). Perls (1969) always used the 'hot-seat approach' when conducting therapy in groups (see also Polster and Polster, 1973). The hot-seat approach places one individual in the center of attention, and this individual works on his or her unfinished business—that is, unresolved personal issues. Other group members are placed in the position of learning vicariously from the experience between the therapist and the client. One can conclude that Perls (1969) relates to a group as a collection of individuals, and

his focus is on the resolution of individual issues rather than on the development of cohesive group process.

Polster and Polster (1973) have found that therapists can apply Gestalt theory to group work so that the leader surrenders more control to the group than Fritz Perls did. Polster and Polster (1973) advocate a 'floating hot seat' approach, a natural movement of members in and out of the center of their group's attention as they learn to attend to salient issues without the intervention of the therapist. Currently, Gestalt therapists vary greatly in the degree of control exercised by the group leader (Korb, Gorrell and Van De Riet, 1989; Strumpfel and Goldman, 2002). This variation in leader styles arises from the Gestalt emphasis on individual creativity, an emphasis that allows much freedom for the group leader to define his or her role in the therapy situation.

As we have seen, a consistent emphasis of Gestalt therapists who work in groups is that clients have individual needs and issues to resolve. The concept of a shared group spirit and the universal aspects of self-actualization tend to be emphasized less in Gestalt theory than in Person-Centered theory. Person-Centered therapy focuses on individuals but includes more emphasis on the social and universal aspects of self-actualization (see Rogers, 1980). Gestalt theory and Person-Centered theory can be integrated by noticing areas of agreement between the theories (for example, both intend to assist movement toward wholeness), valuing differences in emphasis (autonomy versus empathy), and reconciling these differences within a broader framework that creates a relationship between the theories (O'Hara, 1984).

## DIVERGENT VIEWS OF SELF-ACTUALIZATION

As participants use their group to affirm their individuality and universality, certain recurrent themes emerge. The theorists that we have investigated thus far in this chapter have noted the importance of similar themes but have arrived at different conclusions concerning how to treat them. We have noted differences concerning theorists' views on these key themes: (1) the need of group members for authoritative leadership, (2) perceptions of the group's existence as a coherent totality or as an entity, (3) the possibility of members being fully open to experience, (4) the possibility of attaining an authentic, present-centered focus in communications, and (5) the trustworthiness of human nature. We have noted that the varying assumptions and biases of leaders can affect group process and thus can influence what is observed in the process of therapy. Yet it is hard to believe that trained observers of human interaction could come to such divergent conclusions.

Divergent interpretations of human behavior in groups may have occurred because observers have focused on different facets of the process of estrangement and reintegration. Therapy groups take place to help members heal their interpersonal and intrapersonal estrangement and become more integrated through the process of relationship. If theorists focus on the activities that are evidence of estrangement, they may stress the apparent non-trustworthiness of human beings; their perversity, their interpersonal games, and their self-destructiveness. If theorists focus on events that demonstrate reintegration, they may emphasize the trustworthiness of persons, the emergence of the group as a coherent unity, and the potential for authenticity, self-direction and growth. It is therefore as incorrect to say that people are essentially untrustworthy as it is to say the reverse. People who feel estranged may behave in untrustworthy ways, but they can begin to move toward reintegration and trustworthiness when they can fully experience the dilemma of their estrangement.

Self-actualization has generally been associated with the assumption that there is a universal tendency to move toward growth and enhanced integration. Theorists such as Rogers (1977), Bozarth (1998) and Patterson (1985) have viewed self-actualization as evidence that there is a constructive core to all human beings. Patterson has postulated that self-actualization is an underlying motivation shared by all persons that can be evidenced by the continuous striving of all people to maintain and enhance themselves. This idea of self-actualization as a *core motivation* can be traced back to Kurt Goldstein's use of the term in the 1930s, when he observed how brain-damaged individuals strove to maintain their organismic viability (Korb, Gorrell and Van De Riet, 1989).

Maslow, Rogers, Bozarth and Patterson share the view that self-actualization is an innate, biologically inherited potential. Unlike Patterson, Maslow (1962) perceived only a small portion of the human population as being authentically involved in a self-actualizing process. Maslow's theory depended on a differentiation of 'deficiency' needs from 'beingness' needs (Goble, 1971). He therefore viewed self-actualization (a beingness need) as a potential that is latent within all persons but which requires the satisfaction of more fundamental needs before it can become a genuine motivation. Maslow thought that this potential for self-actualization could only emerge as a central concern if lower-order needs for safety and self-esteem had been met. Rogers and Patterson did not differentiate higher-order needs from lower-order needs and thus viewed self-actualization as a central and omnipresent organizing principle for human development.

On the one hand, Maslow's model of self-actualization is problematic because it is based on a predetermined hierarchy of needs contradicted by observations of unique patterns of individual growth and development. This theory also artificially dichotomizes the human race into 'actualizers' and 'nonactualizers' along lines that many view as arbitrary and reflective of personally and culturally bound value judgments (Geller, 1984; Lethbridge, 1986). The model proposed by Rogers and Patterson, on the other hand, is also problematic because it attributes human activities that foster growth to sources within organisms, and harmful activities to sources in the environment. Explaining hurtful behavior according to environmental influences alleviates guilt but avoids issues of responsibility. For example, a person can blame his or her parents for creating a hurtful environment, and these parents can blame their parents, ad infinitum. Basic questions remain unanswered concerning how individuals who are assumed to be essentially good can consistently and repeatedly make decisions to hurt others or themselves.

## TOWARDS A VIABLE CONSTRUCT OF SELF-ACTUALIZATION

Self-actualization needs to be understood, not as a rigid prescription or formula for growth, but as a concept that helps us to understand how people and communities establish patterns of relationship that lead to or away from growth. This concept should not be confused with self-conscious attempts to better life according to a predetermined plan for growth; similarly, self-actualization has nothing to do with egocentric gains for oneself at the expense of other people or at the expense of one's relations with others. Self-actualization should be understood as (1) a process of relationship; (2) the ability to affirm one's distinctness as a basis for caring about others, giving to others, and receiving from others; and (3) the affirmation and confirmation of one's own being, the being of others, and the source of being, which connects oneself with nature and with others.

Ultimately, self-actualization is the recognition that one's distinctness and one's universality are not opposed to each other. Distortions of self-actualization are therefore based on avoidance of either distinctness or universality. Individuals stifle their own growth if they are afraid to stand out and be noticed (Yalom, 1980), or if they are afraid to let go of themselves and experience a larger totality than their usual sense of self (Maslow, 1964; Wilson, 1988). Individual growth is moderated by a kind of contraction into distinctness as an individual and a kind of expansion into a more universal and infinite awareness (Schneider, 1990).

## DISTORTED FORMS OF SELF-ACTUALIZATION

*Self-actualization* can be viewed as a primary psychological process that establishes the integrity of human personhood. Self-actualization can never be totally blocked or denied because anyone who is alive will have some degree of integrity. However, as we have seen, self-actualizing processes can become distorted and misused.

Individuals can perpetuate distorted dynamics as they form new relationships. If the relationships that have contributed to who a person is have been hurtful or constrictive, people may have only a very vague sense of how to create constructive relationships. People may also have chosen modes of relationship that they believe help to protect them or insure their power. These choices can blind people to opportunities for constructive relationships of which they are indeed capable. Persons may need to acknowledge that they have committed their energy and awareness in a misguided or self-destructive direction before they are able to form new and more constructive patterns.

Commitment to a distorted form of self-actualization can be disguised by self-deceiving perceptions. People may perceive that negative interpersonal and intrapersonal dynamics 'have a life of their own', or just 'always seem to happen that way'. Individuals may feel that they are possessed by negative forces beyond their personal control. For example, patterns of drug abuse, fearfulness, or hurtfulness to self or others can become powerful compulsions against which individuals feel powerless, and by which they feel controlled. A person can 'know what is right' and yet can continue to perpetuate a pattern that leads to unhappiness, anxiety, and lack of fulfillment and success.

Nonetheless, the environment should often be considered as a factor in the perpetuation of negative patterns of relationship and behavior. Environments can support or hinder self-actualization. If individuals are taught to fear or ignore experiential possibilities, they are likely to mistrust their own awareness and creativity. Environmental support is helpful for the self-actualization of individuals, and some degree of support is essential. Still, individuals can choose a distorted form of self-actualization due to anxiety about emerging as a distinct individual or to avoid the responsibilities that emerge from awareness of universality. Self-actualization is therefore possible in adverse environmental conditions, and can be avoided even given a supportive environment. Apparently, adverse conditions can bring a person to a greater appreciation of the importance of relatedness, and supportive conditions can be misused to avoid self-confrontation that would enhance self-actualization.

Such factors as past conditioning, social prejudices, financial stressors, and lack of emotional support in a community can make it difficult for individuals to thrive. Therapy generally focuses, however, on what an individual can do to create change—in areas such as attitudes, relationship patterns, and experiences. This focus should not blind us to the very real effects of environments and should allow us to enhance the ability of persons to recognize whatever personal power and responsibility are possible within given circumstances and situations. Therapy can help members to reframe and redirect energies that have been misapplied. Reframing involves the recognition that 'this is me' rather than 'this is outside me' and redirection involves making connections where there were previously disconnections, interpersonally and intrapersonally (for example, see Perls 1969, 1973).

As can be seen, groups can either move toward healing or away from healing and can either create an environment that encourages or discourages self-actualization. This movement within groups is largely associated with members' perceptions of the possibility and desirability of realizing their ability to communicate relatedness within the psychological environment provided by the group. The actualization of these potentials may involve risk-taking; there are likely to be risks involved in becoming distinct—for example, criticism or rejection. Members tend to heal and grow if they perceive their environment as one that is encouraging and trustworthy. Yet their self-actualization reflects personal decisions and choices that are influenced, but not controlled by the environment. Members' collective choices and decisions within relationship help create what their environment is and what their environment becomes. A group that becomes an optimal environment for self-actualization thus provides sufficient support for trust to develop and sufficient challenge to assist members in questioning their complacency and static systems of belief.

## SELF-ACTUALIZATION AND GUILT

The choice to realize the potential to experience and communicate relatedness can disturb the psychological status quo of the person who communicates, the person who receives the communication, or the group in which it takes place. Secure roles that have been established to regulate transactions may be called into question. However, the decision to maintain an avoidance-based status quo at the expense of self-actualization is also a risk. The hazard is that estrangement from the process of being will become an entrenched way of life and that it compulsively will govern responses within ongoing encounters. Because the universal process of being is essentially whole, this unified process exerts a 'pull' on aspects of individual processes that are disunited or split.

The movement towards reunification can be denied, but the price that is paid is anxiety about avoiding growth, that is *ontological guilt*. Ontological guilt is not tied to feelings of shame due to introjected values. Ontological guilt is the anxiety that attends disconnection from being. This kind of disconnection arises from refusal to be distinct and refusal to be aware of universal values that connect people to each other and to nature. Disconnection from being leads individuals to experience estrangement and attendant guilt. Yalom (1980) referred to this kind of guilt as 'existential', a guilt that 'is a positive constructive force, a guide calling oneself back to oneself' (p. 280).

Differentiation of ontological guilt from introjected guilt that is created by the imposition (and subsequent introjection) of others' values and others' expectations for conformity assists effective therapy. Perls, Hefferline and Goodman say that 'an introject consists of material—a way of acting, feeling, evaluating—which you have taken into your system of behavior, but which you have not assimilated ... you take it on as a forced acceptance ... as if it were something precious. It is actually a foreign body' (1980: 23). The experience of ontological guilt is a potentially corrective experience that can be worked through unless a person becomes inflexible and reacts in a defensive manner and seeks to defend the behavior he or she is guilty about. Ontological guilt has the potential to permit an enhanced process of self-actualization to be realized.

On a cultural level, ontological guilt can bring about changes in patterns of relationship within a culture. Such changes do not occur to meet expectations or legal sanctions imposed from outside sources (which leads to introjected guilt), but take place because the culture has learned to question its own assumptions and biases. Since culture is an abstraction that expresses a collective dynamic formed by individuals, it cannot question its assumptions unless individuals within the culture are questioning theirs. Therapeutic groups are minicultures that can be models for how a group atmosphere can encourage self-questioning by members of assumptions and biases. Therapeutic self-questioning is encouraged, not when members attempt to instill guilt, but when they help each other to recognize potentially constructive aspects of ontological guilt that have arisen within the life experience.

## DYNAMICS INVOLVED IN DISTORTION

As we have indicated in Chapter 2, the lack of empathy, caring, and respect within primary relations in childhood can play a central part in the establishment of the patterns that lead to estrangement from the process of being. However, persons can also develop problems that lead to distorted forms of self-actualization if they become estranged later in life and in spite of a rewarding childhood. Whatever the causes of estrangement, on a deep, often unconscious level, the estranged person senses that he or she cannot be truly alive until he or she reunites with the process of being, and regains a sense of power within self and fulfillment in relationship.

One of the authors had a client who illustrates how people can resist the pull of being, or the messages provided by ontological guilt, in their efforts to maintain a semblance of being in control of their own lives. 'Robert' was a member of a therapy group led by one of the writers that was conducted in a hospital setting. When Robert was young, he was a member of a gang in a large metropolitan area. As he described himself later, he felt completely crazy in the ways that he acted. He was continually fighting with the members of other gangs and was regularly breaking the law to obtain money to support a life in the fast lane. Gradually, Robert became extremely unhappy with himself as he lived an increasingly antisocial and violent lifestyle. Eventually Robert decided that life was not worth living, and he ended up trying to commit suicide by shooting himself in the head while looking in a mirror and laughing at himself.

Though Robert did not kill himself, he did sever his optic nerve and became totally blind. He spent some time in the psychiatric ward of a hospital. Yet, as Robert himself later said, becoming blind completely changed his life for the better. When Robert made this statement, he did not appear to this writer to be in denial of being blind; instead he seemed to mean what he was saying. One way of explaining why Robert was glad to be blind is to show how ontological guilt contributed to the general lack of meaning he felt when he was living the life of a hustler.

Robert gradually became more and more unhappy with himself because of his basic estrangement from the process of being until he reached the point where he attempted suicide. Once he was blind, as Robert indicated to this writer, his life slowed down, and he was forced to develop new and more satisfying interests and relationships. One of Robert's activities once he became blind was to become actively involved with associations for the blind. His therapy group assisted Robert to reconnect with others in ways that enabled him to feel that he was contributing to the welfare of others. This allowed Robert to develop a radically new perception of himself; he no longer saw himself as being disinterested in or even hostile to others' welfare but instead came to think of himself as being socially engaged with others in a constructive manner.

Robert was able to develop a new sense of being worthwhile, creative, and socially engaged. A person capable of authentic creativity and aware of power within self responds positively to evidence of creativity and power within others. A person whose awareness of power is distorted strives to control others' power and to dominate others' creativity. A twisted awareness of power never truly senses power within self; power is only experienced when something outside oneself is controlled. Thus a person one does not control becomes a threat. The threatened individual may try to control the other through intimidation or punishment or through manipulations and rewards for compliance. Distorted power can lead a person to invalidate spontaneous expressions of feelings or creative approaches to situations.

Distorted forms of self-actualization run the risk of becoming self-perpetuating vicious circles. Defensive maneuvers and resistance against ontological guilt may lead a person to avoid communicating relatedness, a failure that engenders more ontological guilt, which then must be defended against, and so on. Awareness must be fragmented and aspects of experience split off in order to maintain this vicious cycle. In extreme forms of distortion, often termed 'psychotic', awareness can become tortuously twisted. For example, persons can deeply hate themselves for attempting to exist, can annihilate their own attempts to organize experience, or can attempt to refuse any communication of relatedness. Seriously distorted forms of self-actualization are evidenced by repetitive and compulsive patterns of behavior that often seem beyond individual control. The individual's attempts to suppress the experience of ontological guilt play a part in these self-created vicious cycles. Attempts to be in control lead to experiences of being out of control.

Before they can end a vicious cycle, persons may need to reach a point where they perceive that control has been lost at least to the extent that self-control is impossible. The person can then let go. This letting-go experience has been reported in Zen Buddhist descriptions of satori, or enlightenment (Watts, 1961; Wilber, 1980), in Gestalt-oriented therapies (Perls, Hefferline and Goodman, 1951/1980) and Person-Centered descriptions of movement toward health (Rogers, 1980) and in descriptions of the path by which members of Alcoholics Anonymous generally have to 'hit bottom' before they can change destructive patterns of behavior and relationship (George, 1990; Lewis, Dana and Blevins, 1988). Descriptions of letting-go processes that lead toward health and wholeness are so pervasive that an ontological basis for these experiences seems likely. Therefore, therapy groups assist members' movements towards self-actualization if these groups become settings wherein members feel safe to release some of their self-control and wherein members can reveal their impasses or the ways in which they have experienced hitting bottom.

## HISTORICAL MANIFESTATIONS
## OF DISTORTED SELF-ACTUALIZATION

Distorted forms of self-actualization have been evident throughout human history. Politically, these have often revolved around political parties and group leaders who espouse slogans that verbalize the importance of unity, power, and growth at the same time that forms of relationship are instituted that eliminate individual freedoms and responsibilities. Language that encourages identification with the party or group is used simultaneously with dynamics that undermine abilities to resist the party or group. The followers of such leaders often wish to identify with a powerful figure; they may want someone to control them, and they are willing to surrender their own distinctness to become part of a collective mass movement that promises identification with a group (Fromm, 1964). These dynamics are a distortion of the dynamics of authentic self-actualization. Letting go to control by a leader is substituted for letting go to experience within awareness. Power achieved through identification and subjugation is substituted for personal power that arises from responsibility. The necessity of maintaining law, order, and control of deviants is generally a central theme in these movements.

The same dynamics that work in social and political situations can operate in therapy groups (Leszcz, 1992). A group leader can act in ways that are similar to political leaders who encourage dependence by undermining opportunities for responsibility. Group members may also look for authoritative leadership if they experience too much anxiety or perceive the beginnings of chaos as conflict emerges. A leader can present him- or herself as a powerful figure, assist members in avoiding becoming distinct individuals, and encourage participants' willingness to believe that they need someone to be in authority to help keep them in control of themselves.

In extreme forms, this negative dynamic produces cult-like interpersonal patterns of relationship. Leaders and organizations may attack members' self-integrity by recruiting members using social influence to create double-binds that are resolved through conversion, and by inducing altered states of consciousness which are used as 'proof' that a new person has emerged through a miraculous process (Cushman, 1989). Thus, the ability of the self to form directions and make sense of the world is undermined in a manner that encourages allegiance to the organization's program and a willingness to adopt a new more 'positive' ideology.

An example of the process of distorted self-actualization occurred with the Synanon movement in drug rehabilitation. Charles Dederick, Synanon's leader, gradually assumed a hierarchical position of near-total control in this therapeutic community. Therapeutic process became subordinated to a structure that encouraged certain members to control other members who were viewed as morally inferior (Yablonsky, 1965).

In less extreme forms, a distorted form of self-actualization encourages conforming and role-oriented relationships as well as judgmental attitudes about members' contributions. These milder forms of distorted actualization occur in those groups that McClure (1990) calls regressive (or immature) as opposed to generative (or mature). According to McClure (1990), the members of a regressive group abdicate responsibility, become numb to feelings, use hatred of enemies and out-groups to generate cohesion, rely on allegiance to a myth of intragroup harmony and lack of conflict, and react negatively during stressful situations. Generative groups are characterized by curiosity, openness, respect, love, and trust. Participants feel safe and are free to express themselves. They sometimes feel a sense of surrender to a greater whole that differs from the loss of autonomy that occurs in regressive groups. Individuals do not lose their identities, but 'integrate the "I" with the "We"'. Group members become spontaneous, rather than autonomous, and are engaged and carried along, not in spite of themselves, but beyond themselves' (p. 167).

## ENHANCEMENT OF SELF-ACTUALIZATION IN A GROUP SETTING

When people join an unstructured therapy group, they are likely to introduce the distortions and anxieties they have previously experienced in past relationships into their current relationships with other members and the leader. People tend to repeat what they know rather than move into an unknown form of relationship. A therapeutic group is therefore an opportunity for members to work through avoidant relationship patterns. Robert, the client who was discussed earlier in this chapter, illustrates how group members can take interpersonal risks to develop new forms of relationships. During the unstructured therapy group that Robert joined, he consistently showed the ability to develop helpful relationships. He also served as a model by trying to change his life outside of the group. Robert was ultimately successful in turning his life around by becoming creatively involved with others and by obtaining a job he liked.

A group becomes a setting that encourages the self-actualization of its members if they can begin to move away from predictable patterns of being with others. Someone who knows a person only casually may have difficulty recognizing whether that person is choosing or avoiding the actualization of potentials for creativity and integration. However, these choices are often apparent to others in a group because self-actualization involves relationships and can be seen in changes in the quality of these. Changes are likely to include movement toward authenticity, enhanced awareness of self and others, trust in self and others, and acceptance of mutual responsibility to form directions.

Rogers (1970), a careful observer of group process, noted that certain themes emerge in groups that promote self-actualization of members. The following themes are in general agreement with Rogers' (1970) observations about constructive groups and are likely to characterize interactions as the group encourages growth: (1) the members do not seek authoritarian leadership from any one participant but become flexible in taking leadership roles themselves; (2) the members often make comments that reflect their perception of other members as individuals; (3) participants express willingness to be open to experiences in their group; (4) members value an authentic, present-centered focus in communication; and (5) members move towards a view that they and others in their group are trustworthy.

The development of such basic themes as authenticity, the nature of the group as an environment that can support individuality, and members' awareness of each other's strengths and trustworthiness reflects the degree of support for self-actualization. It is impossible to predict how or if self-actualization will occur for members; they themselves often do not know beforehand. Self-actualization is an integrative movement that brings individuals into contact with others in ways uniquely meaningful for those involved, and that must develop from mutual perceptions rather than from preconceived labels, roles, predictions, or explanations.

## SELF-ACTUALIZATION AND PRESENTNESS IN ORIENTATION

We have indicated that an individual's process of self-actualization is encouraged by a focus on the present in communication and relationship. This focus may be a different temporal orientation than is promoted in many settings outside the therapy situation. Many cultural institutions in the West emphasize a future-oriented perspective based on what one can expect to become if one works hard or sacrifices for a cause. Because members of therapeutic groups are also members of society, it is important that their group allows them to freely explore their future concerns as well as permits them to focus on the present. Much of the growth that members experience, however, occurs because they are able to look at both the types relationships they form in the here-and-now of the group and their current personal concerns.

There is a rationale—one with implications for self-actualization—for focusing on present experience in group therapy. Although past patterns influence the present, people can spend endless hours gaining understanding of the past while remaining stuck in the present. Change in the present tends to come when a person breaks, at least to a degree, with the past. Dwelling on the past extensively can make it more difficult to risk change; people can become habituated to ruminating over past events in a manner that detracts from recognition of present opportunities.

Individuals can also use a focus on what will happen in the future to avoid awareness, action, and change that can occur in the present. A person can avoid changing by focusing on all the possible disasters that could occur. People can also discuss wishes or hopes for the future while their present behavior remains inconsistent with these ideals. Additionally, goals can become impositions associated with introjects if these objectives are not congruent with present experience and awareness.

Resistance to present-oriented awareness can be evidenced by excessive storytelling that lacks emotional involvement and experiential reality, by theatrical dramatics that are used in ways that prevent the establishment of relatedness, by abstract intellectualization that masks noninvolvement, or by an insistence on focusing on general events outside the group. Resistant members may find ways to distract others from current interactions. They are likely to characterize a focus on here-and-now encounters as an undesirable use of time in the group and as inappropriate or falsely intimate.

This kind of resistance is understandable; if norms that would regulate most social situations involving strangers are applied to the therapeutic group, present-centered interactions might be deemed risky or inappropriate. Resistance in a group to present interaction needs to be allowed to occur. If group members begin to recognize their own avoidance as an obstacle to what they would like to gain, they can confront resistance constructively. Typically, group members become bored with avoidant forms of relationship and begin to confront tired interactions. A group leader can support members who risk a here-and-now focus (while not necessarily discouraging other forms of communication), and can encourage discussions in which members are willing to reveal their perceptions of the quality of interactions in their group.

## PART-WHOLE RELATIONS IN GROUPS

Groups can be settings that recognize and value individuals' paths of self-actualization. As members experience increased permeability of interpersonal barriers, they may sense that their own existence is a process of mutual definition that includes others and nature. In this event, they are likely to accept experiences that others present as demonstrating aspects of themselves as well as others (Agazarian, 1992). An unusually intense perception of part-whole relatedness joins the individual and collective aspects of group functioning so that individuals experience a sense of surrender to the flow of interaction in their group (McClure, 1990). We have noticed that this unusual kind of openness occurs if the group's atmosphere is experienced as safe, trustworthy, and free.

Group members are affected by the atmosphere in their group, which they in turn create through the process of their interactions. This experience does not necessarily lead to a perception of the group as an entity, but it does support a perception of universality, of a collectively shared reality. As we have already seen, awareness of differences between members' individual worlds does not interfere with their sense of a shared world if the group atmosphere supports individuality and universality. Adler, (1969), Buber (1970), Jung (1958), Maslow (1962), Tillich (1954), and Yalom (1995) are among those who have found purpose, meaning, and well-being to be associated with perceptions of universality within human experience. The theme that existential aloneness is an essential aspect of the experiential encounter of individuals with the ground of being can be found in the writings of Bugental (1978), Jung (1916), and Rank (1945) and in the psychologically oriented philosophies of Buber (1970), and Tillich (1952). All of these authors share the recognition that congruence within the process of being is simultaneously an awareness of relatedness and an acceptance of aloneness.

Although members of therapeutic groups may experience aloneness as they come to terms with their own questions about themselves and the process of being with others, this aloneness should not be taken as evidence that people exist as separated beings. Members often wrestle with feelings of aloneness as they come to terms with their awareness that they are not as separate as they had believed. In recognizing that one's existence is not separate from others, an individual becomes more vulnerable. This vulnerability can bring feelings of aloneness. Members can experience themselves as part of a shared process with others; yet within this unitary process, I am nonetheless I and you remain you. Although I do not exist as an enclosed entity that is separate from you, my 'I-ness' is distinct from your 'you-ness'. This distinctness is the basis of our uniqueness, of our ability to learn to share empathically (Friedman, 1986).

Members struggle with the relationship of their limitations with their ability to grow, of their distinctness with their universality, and of their self with their group. Sometimes, individuals work through the feelings related to perceptions of themselves as a part within a whole and come to experience a kind of self-transcendence (Maslow, 1964; McClure, 1990). Self-transcendence is appropriately considered as an aspect of the development of self-actualization (Daniels, 1988; Vaughan, 1991). Experiences of self-transcendence can occur if a person reaches a new awareness of relationship between self and a larger totality. *Transcendence* of the self is a paradoxical and somewhat confusing term. Who other than the self can even talk about such an experience? How can the self have been transcended if it remains to talk about its own experience of transcending?

Transcendence has been discussed by Frankl (1966) and Yalom (1980) as a movement of attentional focus and involvement towards others and away from oneself. Maslow's (1964) research into peak experiences and Jung's (1933) research on the collective unconscious led them to believe that integration was possible in which the usual feeling of self was transformed. Both of these theorists viewed such experiences as being essential to growth towards full humanness. Transpersonal psychologists have generally followed Maslow's lead and have discussed self-transcendence in terms that indicate the desirability and importance of this kind of encounter with the ground of being (Vaughan, 1991; Wilber, 1980).

In both interpersonal and transpersonal terms, transcendence is a construct that portrays individuals as capable of gaining new perspectives, more comprehensive forms of awareness—a new center for experiencing life and others. Transcendence, going beyond one's limits, implies that an individual has reoriented and formed a new perspective, a new gestalt within awareness. Transcendence in this sense is neither self-negation nor a means for making a person more 'special' than others (Vaughan, 1991). Rather, the centering of ongoing experience around an enclosed and separated self is transformed so that more attention can be given to experiencing others and the world. It is thus possible to assert that members of therapeutic groups can experience degrees of self-transcendence as part of their self-actualization within group process.

Participation in a group has the potential to provide learning about part-whole relations. In an effective therapeutic group, the whole (group) exists because of its parts (members), and the parts communicate within the context of the whole. Because the whole provides a context that would not be possible without others, the whole is more than the sum of parts. The individual's sense of self can be enhanced and recreated through participatory acts that involve others and the group atmosphere can become enriched because of individuals' participatory acts.

CHAPTER 4

# AWARENESS, FREEDOM, AND RESPONSIBILITY

Awareness, freedom, and responsibility act as a gestalt within human experience that affects human perception and action in the world. Awareness, freedom, and responsibility all imply one another within human experience. For example, unless people are aware and act responsibly in human relationships, they will undermine their co-participatory freedom. Therefore awareness, freedom, and responsibility are interacting aspects of a gestalt that is basic to unstructured group therapy.

## AWARENESS

*Awareness* can be viewed as the activity of registering, maintaining, and connecting aspects of experience. This activity leads to the formation of perceptions, cognitions, affects, and actions. Recognition of a human ability to experience certainly implies awareness of experience (Egan, 1970).

To a considerable extent, experience is 'given' by biological and physiological processes that predetermine forms for sensation and perception. Awareness constructs experience, relates and links experiences to one another, defines experiences, creates boundaries and may form rigid boundaries or splits within experience. Therapy taps into the ability of awareness to reintegrate what was previously split, thus opening areas of experience that were previously compartmentalized.

### RELATIONSHIP OF SELF-ACTUALIZATION TO AWARENESS

Actualization is an inherently ontological concern of human beings, or as Rogers (1980) put it, 'a way of being' that thrives on congruent awareness of experience, and empathic communication with others. A way of being is a way of being aware. Awareness is necessary for being as a person because awareness allows us to recognize our potentials and enables us to find ways to actualize them.

Experientially, self-actualization involves healing through reunification of the self with all aspects of present experience. Persons integrate themselves within present experience as they become open to their own potential to be fully aware. The activity of awareness becomes evident as people perceive meaningful wholes, or gestalts, within experience. The activity of awareness is also evident in human perceptions of groundedness within the process of being. Awareness can be seen in persons' abilities to be empathic with others and to recognize the world of experience communicated by another person. Awareness can potentially integrate the self with the other while preserving and enhancing the distinctness of persons.

From both Person-Centered (Bozarth, 1998; Rogers, 1961) and Gestalt (O'Leary, 1992; O'Leary and O'Connor, 1997; Perls, 1971) perspectives, growth is related to being open to present experience. Both of these theories imply that abilities to be interpersonally open and related are associated with abilities to experience life fully. When persons become open to their experience, they use fewer strategies and techniques designed to avoid, split, or compartmentalize experience. If group members accept the challenge to embrace awareness in their group, they will decrease their reliance on defensive strategies that restrict aspects of the experience of being with others.

To grow in awareness, people need to have a faith that there is more to be gained by acknowledging experience than by denying it. The person who is not ready for integration will find ways to reinstate the same patterns of distortion and blocking of perception that worked in the past. Attempts to coerce a group member into greater awareness are generally counterproductive, if not literally impossible. Although one can invite a person to explore experience, it is ultimately a matter of personal responsibility and subjective choice.

## THE GESTALT OF AWARENESS, FREEDOM, AND RESPONSIBILITY

Awareness, freedom, and responsibility can be imagined as three points that form a triangle. The triangle can only emerge as a stable form when all three elements are present. When awareness, freedom, and responsibility operate in an integrated manner within human consciousness, the self-actualization of an individual is enhanced. On the other hand, it is difficult to imagine that people can be free or self-actualize if they are not aware of themselves or what is going on around them. Persons who act irresponsibly in their relationships with others, even if they are aware and make choices, generally are unhappy because they feel disconnected from other individuals and humanity as a whole. Thus, the stability and happiness of individuals require the integrated functioning of all three elements.

A therapy group is simultaneously a social organization and a gathering of distinct individuals who have different concerns. The gestalt of awareness, freedom, and responsibility has implications for the functioning of the unstructured group as a group, as well as for the individual functioning of members. Structures and directions that define interactions are not supposed to be imposed by the leader or the institution that is sponsoring such a group. Therefore, an assumption is being made that the unstructured group setting can potentially allow awareness to function without the imposition of restrictions.

Frankl (1965), the creator of logotherapy, gives the creation and discovery of meaning a central position in his therapeutic framework. Frankl found that survivors of concentration camps in World War II, of whom he was one, were able to maintain their sense of personal integration if they were able to focus on events that were perceived as meaningful. By contrast, those victims of the concentration camps who encountered their experience as completely without meaning became hopeless, lost their former sense of identity, and sometimes gave up struggling or might turn on others. The ultimate human choice is not the determination of what one will encounter but what meaning will be given or discovered within that experience (Frankl, 1963).

If regarded as equivalent to the formation of perceptual wholes and associations within experience, meaning can be viewed as simultaneously discovered and created by awareness. The idea of awareness, freedom, and responsibility as a gestalt assists us in connecting individualized forms of meaning-making with collective processes that form meanings. The individual gestalt interacts and resonates with the collective gestalt.

Human awareness is never truly separate from nature, although people may experience a split between themselves and nature. Nature can be considered as a gestalt within which individuals and communities form subsystems of meaning. Group members generally have a sense of sharing a collective gestalt, a sense that is allied with awareness of sharing a common nature. Those who are unable or unwilling to acknowledge this gestalt will sometimes create difficulties or conflicts within group process. If members are to deal constructively with these difficulties, they need to draw on their awareness of their group as a whole, and its place within a larger whole that includes humanity.

The authors were in a group together that illustrated to them how the members can have a sense of sharing a collective gestalt where the whole is larger than its constituent parts. We were both members of a person-centered group or workshop that included more than fifty members. We experienced much of this group as fractious and involving a lot of game-playing where the members tried to avoid discussing personal issues or how they regarded one another. The group was not particularly meaningful to either of us until a turning point occurred after about four hours of talking.

At this moment, everyone in the group suddenly decided to be quiet. The group came together during this silence and developed a bond that is difficult to explain. One aspect of the 'coming together' was that by mutually deciding to become silent, members tacitly acknowledged that trivial chatter and melodramatic expressions of opinions had outlived their usefulness. The two co-authors felt as if they were a part of a collective gestalt that was experienced as being personally meaningful. One of the members who had previously been dominating the group finally broke the silence because, as he later indicated, he was feeling uneasy. According to subsequent disclosures, most of the participants had similar experiences to ours when this silence occurred. We felt more connected with the group as a whole after this experience.

As we have seen, awareness can be considered an activity that is simultaneously individual and universal in its functioning. Because awareness is the basis for choices, particularly choices in the formation of gestalts of meaning, awareness has an individual aspect. At the same time, awareness arises from within nature, and is based on an intrinsic organization given by nature, reflecting a universal aspect. Yalom (1995), a group theorist who recognized universality, interpersonal learning, and interpersonal cohesiveness as important therapeutic factors, has also noted the importance of more individually centered activities (for example, catharsis, self-understanding, and personal responsibility and control).

### AWARENESS AS AN INTEGRATIVE ACTIVITY

The creation of meaning is often conceptualized as occurring at different levels of awareness. For example, Freud (1940/1964) and Jung (1916, 1936/1968, 1956) refer to conscious and unconscious aspects of human psychology. Human beings can be seen as forming different levels of meaning at both conscious and unconscious levels. The conscious mind can be viewed as a system of meanings that can be held, reviewed, and changed intentionally. Unconscious meanings are outside the conscious system or have been blocked from interacting with the conscious meanings. Unconscious meanings affect experience but cannot be intentionally reviewed and changed. Awareness of intentionality defines the boundary between conscious and unconscious processes. Changes in perceptions of intentionality (i.e., shifts in awareness of responsibility) can alter the boundary between conscious and unconscious levels of meaning.

The unconscious represents those aspects of functioning that a person has been unable to 'own'. Unconscious thoughts or feelings are things for which a person does not experience himself or herself as being responsible. The work of therapy groups is to assist members to allow more of their experience into the sphere of self-disclosure and self-reflection, and to recognize themselves as more fully responsible for their perceptions and actions. Thus, we could conceptualize therapeutic work as changing the boundary between conscious and unconscious aspects of self. This idea seems limited because we can never be precisely clear about what exactly is being defined by the terms conscious and unconscious. More adequately, we can conceptualize therapeutic group work as activity that helps members to move toward integrated awareness. Members can learn to be aware of aspects of their process of being that they had ignored, or of which they were unaware.

Awareness is always working to form distinctions, gestalts, and relationships within experience. If this work occurs within self-imposed barriers, awareness is blunted and tends to create tensions related to self-contradictions. Awareness constructs wholes from the level of sensation to the level of abstract thought. Self-created barriers exclude aspects of awareness, interfering with self-organization and also affect the formation of relationships between people. Thus, awareness can be said to exist simultaneously at a social level and a personal level. Members extend their personal awareness of one another to include one another, and thus create a social aspect of awareness through their interactions.

## POLARITIES AND SPLITS

A primary polarity that many members deal with in therapeutic groups is the split caused by their beliefs as to which feelings and thoughts are 'good' or 'bad'. If experiences are evaluated as bad, they are often rejected, and awareness will not be able to complete its work of integration. 'Bad' experiences may be maintained within gestalts of unfinished business that have an impact on ongoing patterns of relationship and perception (Perls, Hefferline and Goodman, 1951/1980).

For example, one of the writers had a client who was a member of an unstructured group that was conducted in a women's prison for two years. The story of one member of that group illustrates how hurtful experiences of rejection can contribute to having unfinished business and to the maintenance of splits that keep a person psychologically trapped. 'Nancy' was a heroin addict who was ignored by her alcoholic parents as a child. She started dating a man who was a heroin addict when she was thirteen years of age and quickly became addicted to heroin after she married this person. Nancy engaged in a lot of personal exploration during her group experience. When the group was finished, the members filled out evaluations of their group experience. She wrote out a statement that was quite simple: 'the group helped me to accept reality'.

What this statement meant to Nancy (based on what she had discussed in the group) was that she was finally able to accept the fact that her parents had treated her horribly when she was a child. Nancy finally had developed the courage to give up her illusions about her parents; she then became free to quit trying to hurt her father and mother by hurting herself because they did not live up to her expectations about what good parents are supposed to be like. Before experiencing this insight in this group, Nancy was caught between the conflicting perceptions that her parents had to be either good or bad parents. She was finally able to accept the reality that her parents were neither good nor bad but instead had their own problems that prevented them from responding effectively to her needs when she was a child. She was able to accept some of her life experiences that she had previously denied. Nancy became less conflicted in her attitudes towards her parents and herself because of this group experience.

Individuals can attempt to escape negative experiences that haunt them by denying their existence or by projecting the badness outside themselves and onto others. These tactics require people to minimize the costs of failing to integrate these experiences. The work of therapy groups may lead members to feel uncomfortable if feedback from others brings awareness to the costs of denial and projection. Such feedback is most likely to be helpful if the group has an atmosphere that promotes confidence among members to self-disclose and that allows participants to feel accepted when they do so.

Many theorists have recognized that therapy encourages participants to recognize and integrate polarities. One of the central polarities that has been addressed in existential therapy is clients' split motivation between authenticity versus conformism (Maddi, 1985). Perls (1971) focused on those aspects of a person's internalized dialogue that involved the 'top-dog' (representing internalized 'shoulds') versus the 'underdog' (representing resistance to 'shoulds'). Freud (1923/1962) emphasized the polarity created between the instincts of the id versus the rationality of the ego. Jungian therapy works with polarities such as the persona (or social self) and the shadow (rejected aspects of self), as well as the ego (personal center) and the self (transpersonal center) (Jung, 1964).

The reason that so many prominent therapists have focused on this area is that the tension created by a polarity exists as potential energy that can be tapped and released through therapy. As tension is released, it can be used to formulate a new gestalt, a new organization of experience. The means to tap this energy is to increase awareness of the polarity and to work toward acceptance of both sides of it. The work of therapy is not to make the polarity disappear but to explore it in a manner that enhances self-acceptance and the growth of awareness, and that allows access to emotional and physical energy.

During a therapy group for college students conducted by one of the authors, a female member indicated that she had been abused by her parents who used to continually expose themselves to her when she was young. These experiences were traumatic for her, and she developed many phobias that revolved around her attitudes towards sex and seeing the human body. 'Mary' began to think of her own body and sex as being something alien to her and as being essentially bad. Much of Mary's energy was spent in trying to avoid thinking about anything sexual or that involved the human body. By participating in an unstructured therapy group, Mary was able to make progress toward openly discussing issues related to dating and sex and her past erotic experiences with her parents without feeling uncomfortable. Mary began to accept her own sexual feelings as not being ugly and bad by discussing these in the group.

Awareness becomes rigidly self-limiting when it accepts internal splits as being necessary for self-maintenance. Integration is facilitated by the acknowledgment and acceptance of a split. Acceptance becomes integration as the person gains experiential understanding that both sides of a split have been affecting the person's interactions and sense of self.

Because experiential understanding plays a major role in the process of integration, members can benefit by directly acknowledging feelings, perceptions, and memories that play a part in the split. A member can be encouraged directly to verbalize these thoughts and feelings. Perls (1969, 1973) advocated the use of techniques that encouraged individuals to make hidden splits overt and that used individually oriented psychodrama to create a present-centered focus for the energy involved within a split. Other therapists have used psychodrama techniques as advocated by J. L. Moreno (1964) and Z. T. Moreno (1965) to involve more than one member in an 'acting out' process to explore internalized conflicts or splits. Although psychodrama role-playing that involves two or more members (as well as individual acting out of internalized dialogue) can be helpful techniques to facilitate exploration, these techniques may not always be comfortable or perceived as appropriate by members of a group.

Members may generate present-centered dialogue that assists explorations of splits in awareness without recourse to specific techniques. At times, a great deal of emotional energy can be released simply because a person talks about an event to others who are relating to that person in a concerned manner. When a person feels that others really care and are attempting to understand, a situation evolves that can be highly conducive to releasing emotional energy and physical blocks of tension. It is the experience of oneself being accepted by others that seems to be the essential dynamic involved in the process of healing. An individual can then move toward experiential understanding and integration of a polarity within awareness.

For instance, in a group of college students dealing with eating disorders, a woman named 'Rhonda' was divided between the image she tried to maintain with others and her inward feelings of loneliness and unworthiness. This split between inward and outward selves was rectified through a group process conducted by one of the authors. Rhonda had always feared she would 'go crazy' if she began to express her negative feelings about herself. When she took the risk to acknowledge and express feelings of sadness and anxiety about loneliness, she found that strong feelings do not equate with being crazy. She found that she could be accepted by others and could accept herself as a whole person. This improvement of a split in awareness formed the groundwork for Rhonda's subsequent work to change compulsive patterns in relating to people and food.

## THE INTERPERSONAL FIELD OF AWARENESS

The dynamics of unstructured groups lend themselves particularly well to an ongoing assessment of the question, 'What is happening between us?' Individuals' connections and splits affect a group's atmosphere. The unfinished business that members carry 'within' is inevitably experienced 'without' in the interpersonal realm of awareness. If members are able openly to confront their experience of being with others, they will be able to work on themselves by working on what is occurring *between* themselves and others. As members address the question, 'What is happening between us?' they increase their awareness of relational context. Awareness of relational context, the *between* aspect of being, is essential to the process of the therapeutic work in a group setting.

Awareness of a relational context is often manifested by explorations of the questions, 'How are "you" affecting "me" and "us"?', and 'How are "we" affecting "you"?' Underlying these questions is the awareness that 'you' are an aspect of 'us'. The dynamic relationship between the 'self' and the 'we' is necessary to create group process.

Questions about how an individual is affected by being in a group can be addressed in a general context when members discuss how they perceive their group experience. Exploration of specific incidents in which members have affected one another can also provide important learning about the process of 'self' being with others.

Participants are likely to manifest their internal splits and polarities within the dialogues that emerge as relationships develop between members. Internal splits tend to make it difficult for individuals to move out of themselves and into the 'between'. Thus, individual splits in awareness mirror those that occur in the relations between members. Addressing differences of opinions or attitudes and learning about discrepant perspectives can become the means to help individuals to move toward personal integration. Members can provide feedback to help each other learn about dynamics that either assist or interfere with constructing the relationships that individuals are attempting to form. Such feedback is generally most helpful if it reflects ongoing observations and reactions on a personal level rather than an abstract or philosophical level. Personal reactions enhance awareness of relatedness. There are times when abstract or philosophical feedback can be useful, but only when such feedback does not assist intellectualization and distancing from awareness of present experience.

## THE GOAL OF AWARENESS

Perls states that 'in Gestalt therapy, *the goal is always awareness and only awareness*' (1969: 55, italics in original). This statement sets up the intriguingly paradoxical possibility that awareness is its own goal. However, this paradox disappears if we assume that barriers to awareness have been formed by the activities of awareness.

Other theorists (for example, Adler, 1969; Berne, 1961; Moreno, 1947; Yalom, 1980) believe that awareness must be joined with a particular kind of insight that is based on cognitive understanding. To these theorists, simply being aware is not enough; one must learn something from the contents of awareness. These theorists imply that participants in therapy must increase their awareness in order to grow, but they must also learn certain principles at the same time. Members can then apply these principles to events and relationships outside their group and their present field of awareness. Naturally, various theorists and schools of therapy recommend focusing on different types of insights or cognitive formulations.

A basic issue underlying differences between schools of therapy, as well as between individual therapists, concerns definitions of the goals of awareness. There are also differences concerning how to define directions that assist clients to greater awareness, and how to describe what should be done with this awareness (if anything) once it is achieved. An integrated therapeutic approach can be developed by learning from various perspectives about the importance of enhancement of awareness as a central movement of effective therapy. Recognition that there is no one 'correct' goal or approach is likely to lead practitioners to develop a flexible attitude toward these objectives. Perhaps there is no predetermined correct direction for awareness. In this case, situational, cultural, and historical contexts, personal issues and concerns of participants and ongoing modes of relationship must all be taken into account as directions are formed. Because these variables shift and change as group processes evolve, predetermined goals for awareness are of limited value.

Observation of therapeutic group work is likely to lead an observer to conclude that each member seems to have a different perspective about what is important in a given situation. An observer of almost any unstructured group is likely to find that individuals vary in how (and if) they want to use their group to improve their awareness, how and where they wish to focus awareness during a particular event, and in what direction they seem to want to develop that awareness.

As we know, members often struggle with their ability to enhance their own awareness. They may have trouble believing that their own feelings are important, or may not experience their own perceptions of events as valid. If one participant dictates to others how to manage their problems, they may not learn that they can trust their own ability to form meanings and directions. Rather than supporting the group's need for a manager, norms can be developed that support the person as a creative, potentially self-directing being. The person can be assisted to find his or her own ability to form directions that make sense and that feel right. When members assist each other to form directions, they tend to exchange leadership roles in different situations. Members begin to use their interactions to generate an atmosphere of freedom. They can use this freedom to learn about their mutual influence on one another in the process of exploring awareness.

If members develop a sense of having a shared field of awareness, group interactions begin to form gestalts of meaning that may develop into ongoing themes. One person alone does not determine the flow of energy and awareness in a group. As freedom develops, all members perceive themselves as able to influence directions at any given time. Areas of focus form according to members' mutual perceptions of their own needs and wishes and those of others. The question of whether awareness within the present is itself a sufficient goal or whether some type of additional cognitive insight is important becomes relatively unimportant. Members learn that they are capable of attending to their own awareness of events, can use this awareness to assess each other's emergent needs, and can contribute to one another accordingly. Through finding out about each other, members learn if a member needs to explore a new cognitive perspective, needs to express feelings, or needs to experiment with new behaviors.

## FREEDOM

The perception of freedom within the field of experience facilitates opportunities for developing new learning (Cain, 1989; Rogers, 1983). *Freedom* can be experienced 'inwardly' as the unrestricted openness to and acknowledgment of thoughts and feelings and as the formulation of perceptions according to one's own integrity.

Freedom can be experienced 'outwardly' as openness in communication of thoughts and feelings (without interference from imposed values), and as interpersonal encouragement for investigation of experience. Ideally, a group atmosphere can support a merging of both fields. The personal and interpersonal fields of perception can then interact to create and develop gestalts of meaning. Freedom then becomes a shared and inclusive experience, and members can support and encourage each other's freedom.

The perception of freedom is a useful foundation for the recognition that the individual is responsible for forming her or his meanings and directions (Polster and Polster, 1973). In the absence of freedom, a person would not be able to view self as responsible. If a member does not perceive freedom to exist within the group, the member might have to fight the group to assert the reality of freedom and to self-actualize.

History has not yet provided us with an example of a large society that has been able to surmount the limitations created when one group uses force to gain and manipulate resources at the expense of others. Therapeutic groups struggle to achieve on a microcosmic scale what has not yet been achieved in the social macrocosm of the world. Because members may have adapted to social systems based on exploitative norms, they may carry these patterns into relationships with others in their group. When individuals have adapted to exploitation as a reality, they may have difficulty experiencing freedom as a reality. Individual participants may struggle to understand whether freedom can be real in their group, and if so, what they would want to do with that freedom.

There are certain resources available in a group for which members may compete. These resources include attention, respect, sympathy, admiration, and control of themes and norms. Members' distorted patterns of self-actualization may become evident as attempts to manipulate or dominate discussions in a group, or to influence group norms to fit personal values. Much of the therapeutic work done in an unstructured group has to do with recognizing freedom and learning to use it constructively. As members learn to use freedom for each other's mutual benefit, they generally move toward more cooperative and less competitive modes of interaction.

No group will achieve complete freedom based on total awareness of mutual responsibility. People, being imperfect, will create misunderstandings, will share power unequally, and will have disproportionate effects on the development of group themes and the use of group time. Growth does not often come by a sudden leap into a totally new way of being with others. Growth more often comes by learning how to compromise, cooperate, affirm oneself and others, and create win-win situations in interactions rather than win-lose situations. Competition becomes balanced by cooperation, and self-assertion becomes balanced by respect for others.

A member's expression of self sometimes represents an imposition on or a misunderstanding of another, or it may be intended to establish control through imposition (Gans, 1989). Group members can move towards freedom by dealing with how an imposition or misunderstanding is experienced by others in the group. If members are unnecessarily polite and avoid disagreement, they will not experience real freedom (Burnand, 1990). The more of themselves that members feel must remain hidden, the less free is the atmosphere in a group, regardless of the norms that are consciously espoused. Group participants may not consciously perceive that they must hide aspects of themselves, but may simply experience a reluctance to disclose feelings or a lack of any thoughts or observations to share.

Three related assumptions that underlie the formation of an unstructured therapy group are (1) that individuals are capable of choosing to be aware, (2) that an atmosphere of freedom maximizes opportunities to choose to be aware, and (3) that individuals will value freedom, and relationships and new learning that result. An atmosphere of freedom reflects acceptance of diversity, openness to novelty, and a willingness to live without the certainty of prearranged outcomes. This atmosphere of freedom will not come into existence simply because a group leader has determined that an unstructured format will be used. Members must experience themselves as free, and must be willing to use their freedom to make choices to move toward awareness.

## LIMITS OF FREEDOM

Although predetermined roles are not provided, members generally take on roles within their unstructured therapy group. Members will also typically institute a subtle system of rewards and punishments (using attention and feedback), and create ritual forms of interaction with predetermined outcomes (using politeness or another set of norms). Members tend to institute roles and norms that have prevailed in other social groups in which they have participated. Roles and norms form limits that regulate free expression. These limits are necessary insofar as interpersonal relationships require a degree of predictability concerning how others will respond and how one will respond to others.

Group process provides opportunities for members to observe how they create roles, rules, and rituals. They may learn that they have created these roles and rules through their own choices. If members can acknowledge choices that they are making, they become aware of their abilities to influence events in the group. An unstructured format, because it does not provide predetermined norms, allows members to learn about themselves as they observe themselves structuring their own interactions. If they learn about the patterns that they create by adopting certain roles and rules, members may then assume more responsibility within their interactions. They can learn that they do not have to repeat roles and rules that they used previously, but can choose new ways of interacting that are more authentic, that meet needs, and that allow for creative expression of self.

People tend to institute those roles with which they are most comfortable when they are in an unpredictable situation with unfamiliar people (Leszcz, 1992). Some participants will use politeness and being agreeable to attempt to win the goodwill of others, to reassure themselves that they can belong in their group and that others will support them. Some may use wit or charm to gain the attention of others. Other participants may demonstrate a no-nonsense practicality, attempt to define group tasks, and generally assert leadership. These participants may find that others contest their attempts to guide their group, and some members may compete by trying to show evidence of their own intelligence or knowledge. There may be members who ask others for something or who identify themselves as people who need help. Still other members may find a place in their group by showing that they can be empathic, supportive, or caring. Sometimes participants withdraw from their group or evidence anxiety and uncertainty. Any or all of these means for creating one's presence in a group may be part of the interplay of dynamics by which members establish a role. As roles are defined, they help set the foundation for the establishment of norms that will guide interactions.

In creating roles for themselves, members learn about one another. Their roles are not created in a vacuum but in relation to one another's presentation of self. Most, if not all, individuals are capable of presenting themselves in different ways or according to the perceptions they have of various situations. These perceptions of the group environment will guide their decisions in creating a part for themselves. The more members establish roles with each other, the more easily they can predict one another's responses. A degree of security and certainty is created and can be the basis for establishing trust. However, if trust depends on maintenance of roles, members will hide aspects of themselves from each other. They can hide those aspects of self that would conflict with a role or those aspects that might create conflict with others in their group.

To deepen the atmosphere of interpersonal trust, members must be willing to reveal aspects of self that do not fit into group norms or into roles and expectations that have been established. If members value their group's potential to create an atmosphere that joins trust with freedom, they will experiment with interactions that are 'out of role'.

Freedom, the basis for choices and decisions, is a fundamental quality of awareness. Individuals can choose to limit their awareness, to expand it, to focus it on certain events and situations, or to avoid attending to these events. Although there are many factors that determine our lives, we are also free to form perceptions and to explore awareness in ways that diverge from past patterns. At the same time, we are not free to do whatever we wish. For example, we will not be able to walk through a wall simply because we decide we can, and we can never control our environments totally, although some people might wish to do so. A common misconception about freedom is that freedom represents the ability to do whatever one wishes or to become whatever one wants to become.

A realistic awareness of freedom does not disregard limits and does not ignore factors that determine peoples' lives (May, 1981). The experience of freedom is the experience of one's own creativity within interactions. While acknowledging the impact of environments, physiology, and their own history, members find that they can create new perceptions of who they are and who they can be with others.

Environments can condition the perceptions of people in many different ways. Sometimes, the members of groups may question the kind of conditioning that is promoted by environments they have experienced. Women and members of various minority groups have attempted to form their own perceptions of valid roles and have had to struggle against the ways that societies in many countries around the world have framed their behavior and attitudes. As women and minority groups have struggled in different societies, they have helped focus the attention of others on the power of messages that are conveyed in families, through the mass media, and through the dynamics of power in social systems.

Unstructured therapy groups can become environments wherein it is acceptable to question whatever stereotypes have limited individuals' perceptions of freedom. Rather than using stereotyped roles, group members may feel free to step out of these roles or to experiment with new roles. However, in the process, members are likely to find that their own stereotypes and unfinished business affect the roles that they create. If trust has been established in a group, members can grow by sharing their own prejudices and preconceptions. Members can then learn to recognize each other's individuality, and can validate each other's unique ways of using freedom in their group to explore awareness and experience. They can acknowledge the psychological limitations, as well as the physical and environmental limitations, that have affected their life experiences. Members can help each other to see if they are responding to one another habitually, in ways that have been conditioned by environments in which they had to survive.

Sometimes struggling with issues of increased psychological freedom can be menacing to group members. For example, Rhonda (who was mentioned earlier in this chapter) struggled with feelings of being overwhelmed when she expressed sadness and anger about how lonely and self-despising she had been. She gained in freedom, and this provided her with motivation to continue her therapeutic path. However, as she opened to the freedom of revealing feelings openly, she became concerned about the uncertainty of where she was going. New ways of expressing herself led to unknown areas of awareness and relationship that were genuinely scary for her. She ran the risk of being rejected as the person she really believed herself to be, a possibility far more frightening than that of being rejected for playing a role poorly.

Sartre (1956) wrote of freedom as something to which people are condemned, and Fromm (1964) wrote of freedom as something from which people long to escape. People can be viewed as condemned to freedom because they cannot escape the responsibility of choice and as longing to escape freedom because it demands awareness of anxiety-provoking aspects of reality. May and Yalom (1984) indicate that intense anxiety can arise from perceptions of freedom. This anxiety is due to feelings of groundlessness related to lack of certainty and external authority and to a fear of dying (May and Yalom, 1984).

Group members may try to escape from freedom by making the leader an authority or guru. This kind of escape may be instigated by the leader or by group members but cannot be accomplished unless there is collusion from all involved. Group members can also institute rigid norms to regulate behavior, and thus escape the anxiety that comes with awareness of choices. Freedom seems to create anxiety because it reveals life to be a process that does not have absolute or final rules and regulations.

### PERSONAL AND INTERPERSONAL FREEDOM

People are free to the extent that they can change their lives by changing their perceptions of self and others, by creating new forms for communicating with others, and by generating new goals. This kind of change represents personal freedom. Participants in relationships explore interpersonal freedom as they learn how they can use interactions to explore ideas and feelings. If members accept the challenge of freedom, they often find that along with anxiety, they can experience excitement and fulfillment. Rogers has emphasized the positive aspects of freedom. He points out that as people learn to trust their own perceptions and their own ability to function autonomously, they can use freedom in ways that enhance growth and create fulfillment (Rogers, 1980, 1983). Though freedom may be associated with the anxiety of insecurity, it can also be used to release the anxiety that develops from adhering to unnecessary limitations. Freedom is a basis for the affirmation of creativity and for movement towards personal fulfillment in relationships.

As members explore possibilities for freedom in their group, they also learn about limits to this freedom. A person may have the freedom to explore authentic communication, but this situation does not guarantee that everyone in the group will accept and admire this person's use of honesty. People's freedom does not allow them to control the responses of others. Individuals may also find that if they strive to obtain affection from others, they have sacrificed the freedom to express those aspects of self that others don't like. Freedom involves choices, and these mean that certain alternatives are sacrificed as others are actualized.

If members decide that they do not have the right to control others, they begin to move toward an ethic that can support the freedom of others as well as the freedom of self. This movement is associated with the movement from I-It relations to I-Thou relations. As we have seen, freedom in I-It relations is that which comes when the responses of the other can be controlled and predicted. Freedom in I-Thou relations is that which comes when participants can validate and affirm each other's creativity, self-direction, and spontaneity.

It is possible for a person to act spontaneously in ways that others perceive as hurtful. Examples include choices to leave a lover or spouse, decisions to reveal negative perceptions of others, and various communications and behaviors that do not meet the wishes of others. I-Thou relations involve mutual affirmation of spontaneity, something that is usually diminished if one person perceives that another is acting in ways that seem unnecessarily hurtful. As members move toward I-Thou relatedness, their spontaneity becomes tempered by their empathy. Self-created limitations on the use of open communication can assist the development of effectively therapeutic transactions (Kaplan, 1985). These kinds of boundaries to self-disclosure are most useful if they are motivated by a consideration for others that grows out of empathic resonance, rather than from attempts to conform to imposed norms. Group norms of consideration may not be an imposition if members genuinely respect and care about each other's feelings.

Empathy is itself an expression of freedom because people choose to enter the perceptual worlds of others. If spontaneity can be integrated with empathy, members can experience freedom as a mutually supported condition in their group. Empathy is not a magical device to protect people from being hurt. There are times when hurting another person can be unavoidable—for example when people have conflicting needs or wishes. Empathy helps members to use freedom responsibly, so that unnecessary hurt is not inflicted on participants.

## EXPERIENCING FREEDOM IN THE GROUP SETTING

Members' experience of freedom in a group setting involves the perceptions of several individuals as they affect one another. If someone takes risks that enhance perceptions of freedom in the group, others may feel relieved and may also begin to take more risks. A participant may experience the reality of freedom, but others may dislike the way this participant uses it to relate to others. Conflict will most likely arise at this point. Such a conflict represents an opportunity to enhance perceptions of freedom in a group. Group members will need to discuss their perceptions of events and will need to learn about each other's views of these events. If they can learn enough about each other to discover how they are affecting one another, the development of a therapeutic group atmosphere can continue.

Freedom makes demands on people by involving them in interpersonal contact that is open to change and which does not have clearly defined rules that predetermine outcomes. When members perceive the reality of their freedom, they sometimes recognize the illusory nature of those conventions and proscriptions that are supposed to make interactions predictable. They may have learned from listening to others that everyone has had experiences that did not follow the rules. They may have learned by observing their group that interactions have often diverged from whatever norms had been established. Members who have invested themselves in a fixed set of beliefs often find these challenged by the diversity of life experiences and personal attitudes that are revealed in their group. Perceptions of freedom may challenge individuals' needs for security but may also help them to become more flexible within evolving relationships, more accepting of diversity, and less dogmatic in their conceptualizations of themselves and others.

As a group develops a therapeutic atmosphere, and as members begin to value each other's freedom, a person who negates or invalidates others may be seen as hurtful to that atmosphere. A group can be challenged to extend acceptance to those who are deviant (according to group norms) and to help these members to learn about how their actions affect the group (Gans, 1989). Extending acceptance to a deviant member allows him or her the opportunity to choose a new approach. Without acceptance, such a member simply receives reinforcement for those stereotypes that allow him or her to picture others as members of a different species. Although group members may honestly disagree with the values of a certain participant, they need to validate that participant's value as a human being who is capable of growth. If they are unable to validate the potential for growth, they have in effect given up on that person. Giving up on someone is an expression of a group's sense of their own inability to heal and to care. This awareness of an inability to accept will be a limitation that negatively affects the group atmosphere.

All groups have a limit to their ability to heal, of course. No therapist and no group can be all things to all people. In very unusual cases, the members or the leader may suggest that a member should leave a group because this person has repeatedly and frequently interfered with the work that others wish to do. Other group members are more likely than the leader to question whether a disruptive member should continue to participate in a group. If such a suggestion is made, this suggestion should be discussed with the member, preferably in the group. It is hoped that this individual can learn how the group perceives his or her behavior. Then, the individual can make a choice about whether to accept the responsibilities involved with group membership.

Asking a member to leave should only be a last resort in extreme situations. Even if a consensus exists in a group to expel a member, the group leader will often intervene to assist members to explore the issue further. A participant should not be asked to leave as a 'punishment' for misbehavior or to allow other participants to feel powerful or self-righteous. Some members may become demoralized after a participant leaves their group, either for voluntary or involuntary reasons. These members may perceive themselves as having been unable to include and care about all who were present. The future ability of a group to generate an atmosphere of freedom will be affected if someone has been asked to leave. Members will know that if one person can be told to leave, anyone may have the same experience.

Given an atmosphere of freedom, members will usually work out for themselves the question of whether to participate and how to participate. Members are usually capable of understanding the needs of others in their group. They may decide to leave for a while and to return later when they are ready for group interaction. As we know, meeting others in a group setting can be a stressful experience. If they realize that their freedom includes the freedom to choose not to attend the group, they may feel less stress. Attending an unstructured therapy group should be a voluntary commitment, should not represent an obligation or duty, and should not represent an imposition of values. The value of freedom underlies attendance and participation in these groups.

# Awareness, Freedom, and Responsibility

## FREEDOM AND RESPONSIBILITY

Because awareness not only registers but also creates experience, freedom is not merely passively perceived; it too is actively created. Freedom, an aspect of nature, also is a potential of the self that it brings into being within its interactions and through its choices. This implies that freedom is not bestowed by an outside force or entity. Freedom is not so dependent on environmental conditions that it is impossible for a person to realize freedom unless he or she exists in a free environment. At the same time, freedom is not so independent of environmental conditions that these are unimportant. People need to discover freedom within their own experience of life and self to create freedom in their environment. Freedom originates from awareness and becomes real within awareness.

As individuals recognize their potential for freedom, they also realize their creativity. If individuals can create, they also can destroy (Perls, Hefferline and Goodman, 1951/1980). They can affirm their own possibilities, and those of others, or they can choose to negate their own and others' potentials. Freedom implies that we are responsible for nurturing and affirming our own capabilities, and for creating an atmosphere that can nurture and affirm others' capabilities. Individuals cannot be responsible for the choices others make regarding the development of potentials within their lives, relationships, and environmental interactions. Individuals are responsible for respecting others' capacities to choose, and for contributing to a supportive environment.

If people avoid the responsibility associated with freedom, they inevitably distort their own processes of self-actualization. The operation of awareness, freedom, and responsibility as a gestalt becomes unbalanced and this affects the self-actualization process of the individual. This distortion leads to estrangement from others and nature. The movement through estrangement into reintegration always involves an acceptance and affirmation of one's own capacity for freedom. Freedom is the necessary foundation for the ability to make creative choices that can change one's perceptions, one's relationships, and one's life. Thus awareness of freedom implies responsibility, because this awareness implies that one can make choices that improve the quality of one's relationships and hence the overall quality of one's life.

## RESPONSIBILITY

The individual's ability to be responsible is reflected to some extent by the willingness to make clear choices and not to disown feelings. Yet, most definitively, *responsibility* is the acceptance and willingness to be distinctly who one is. Realizing the individual aspects of responsibility leads a person to become more aware of the potentials of others. A person then recognizes and acts on an awareness of responsibility to self and others.

RESPONSIBILITY AND THE GROUND OF BEING

Responsibility allows a person to recognize a common ground that connects self, others, and nature. Thus, responsibility can be conceptualized as the activity by which a person establishes groundedness within the process of being and within the process of relationship. The experience of gaining a sense of groundedness is often described as a sense of *centering* within the flux of experience. To center is to balance and harmonize diverse sensations, thoughts, feelings, and perceptions. Through centering, the person creates an integrated wholeness within the multiplicity of feelings and perceptions that are formed from experience. Awareness increases its intensity and extensity as the person centers.

Centering is not the creation of a static structure or position for the organization of experience. Centering can best be understood as an integrative movement, as the forming of meaningful connections between and within experiences and persons. The development of empathetic resonance between members therefore becomes possible when individuals become centered. Members become centered in a group as they are increasingly able to trust the perceptions they have of themselves and others and to express what they feel. Centering becomes a basis for interpersonal grounding of the self as members are able to use interpersonal interactions to move into the *between* or a shared field of awareness and freedom.

The person establishes and expresses responsibility within the context of a matrix of ongoing relations with others and in the context of relatedness to the ground of being. (Paul Tillich (1954) has used the term *ground of being* to describe the underlying essence or source of all that exists and the interconnectedness and relatedness of self, others and nature.) Ultimately, it is groundedness within being that is the basis for responsibility. Responsibility within the ground of being takes precedence over responsibility to a given relationship or to a system of relationships. A responsible person may decide to break connectedness with a community, with a family, or with a particular person, because of his or her perception of groundedness in being (Fromm, 1964; Tillich, 1954). For example, a grounded person may resist the pattern of community relations in a society that is becoming totalitarian, may break ties to a group of others who have become destructively oriented toward nature, may leave a family whose norms require hurtful interpersonal interactions, or may leave a personal relationship that is thwarting centering. Groundedness in being provides the basis for awareness that one's own being participates in the being of humanity and in nature, and that one is responsible for one's own and others' freedom.

A member of a human group expresses responsibility by recognizing the humanity of others in the group (Buber, 1970). Membership in a group involves responsibilities that arise out of recognizing one's relatedness to others. Each individual is formed within a complex web of human relations that begin at the moment of birth and which are developed and elaborated throughout a lifetime.

The ground of being is not separate from the process of being. People make contact with the ground of being in the present by becoming aware of a shared field of relationship. Group members may move toward groundedness within being by exploring the nature of present relationships or by looking at unfinished business involving relations with those who are not present. As members discuss their past and their hopes for the future, they may gain an understanding of themselves as beings within relationship. Through exploring their involvement in beginning, moving into, and ending various forms of relationship, members become aware that their distinctness has evolved through an ongoing process of reciprocal connectedness. Throughout this process, they have related to others, and others have related to them. As members learn from the process of being with others, they become encouraged to experience contact with the ground of being.

## LEARNING ABOUT RESPONSIBILITY

By experiencing various aspects of relatedness with others who are present, members develop an awareness of the connectedness and mutuality through which interactions gain meaning. As members experience meaningful connections with others, they also tend to learn experientially about the importance of responsibility within relationship. This learning occurs because connections form opportunities for sharing and closeness and present opportunities for responding with awareness to what is learned about others. Norms, rules, and prescriptions that define responsible behavior have limited value in helping members to learn experientially about responsibility. If norms and rules are used to substitute for experiential learning, they are likely to form barriers to the development of authentic responsibility.

There can be no prescription that dictates how a person should establish himself or herself as a responsible being. To enhance responsibility, each person has to begin where he or she is, become aware of life experiences and important relationships, and make connections between feelings and perceptions. Responsibility grows as a person becomes clearly aware of present situations and relationships, of unfinished business, of the being of others, and of the larger context within which individual lives unfold. Responsibility involves awareness of one's own needs and feelings and of the context in which these are expressed.

Members of therapeutic groups often do not discover how to interact responsibly until they are ready to face very simple truths about themselves and their relationships. These are often perceived when members allow themselves to be open to emotional aspects of being with others, to feelings that are powerful without being complex. These feelings must be integrated into awareness to contribute to the development of responsibility, and this integration involves forming direct connections within experience more than it involves abstract cognitive processing of information. An excessive degree of cognitive processing usually interferes with work on integrating simple experiential truths.

91

## RESPONSIBILITY AND 'LETTING GO'

Awareness of a ground of being prevents responsibility from being equated with control over events or other people. As we saw in Chapter 3, someone too intent on controlling others or him- or herself will maintain a split that prevents experiential awareness of freedom. A responsible person is aware of when controlling a situation or a feeling is appropriate and when letting go of control is appropriate.

Awareness establishes the basis for understanding when and how a person can function most appropriately within a situation by releasing control of people, events, or the individual's own feelings. For example, sometimes it is necessary to let go of control over children so that children can recognize themselves as responsible. At other times, a parent needs to exert control over situations in which a child is unable to foresee consequences or is looking for guidance. The release of the tension caused by a false sense of responsibility based on control of self and others can lead to greater personal balance and less distortion.

Rhonda, the woman who has been described as struggling with an eating disorder, experienced a strong sense of letting go when she chose to express chaotic feelings of anger, hurt, and sadness to other group members. She gave up her distorted sense of responsibility that entailed controlling the image she presented to others. She gained a sense of balance that allowed her to think more clearly about herself and others and to express what she was feeling and observing more honestly. Ultimately, the experience of letting go of a distorted sense of responsibility formed the foundation for a more grounded and useful sense of responsibility.

As Rhonda's case shows, attempts to control our feelings can result in our feelings controlling us. When people try to contain, deny, and exert too much control over their feelings, the result is tension. Tensions created by denied feelings often exert a perpetual influence on the quality of a person's relationships and process of being. Letting go of resistance to feelings can help a person to move toward a more relaxed and integrated process of being. Letting go of feelings, responsibly, as opposed to destructively, requires awareness. If individuals are in a situation where they can receive support for letting go (for example a therapy group), they can use the resulting experience to enhance their learning about who they are. If individuals let go of feelings in an inappropriate context, they may lose a job, may escalate an explosive situation, or may precipitate a destructive interaction with a person who is unprepared to deal with strong feelings.

## RESPONSIBILITY AS CO-CREATION

Black-and-white thinking leads to the conclusion that either people are viewed as responsible for what happens in their lives or as victims of events beyond their control. Beyond black-and-white categorizations is the view that individuals co-create their lives through transactions with others and the world. As co-creators, people can be seen as being affected and even formed by external circumstances and events. However, no matter how random these events, a person's creativity is still involved in how these are perceived and interpreted. Individuals' perceptions of events create their meaning. From these meanings, people generate their sense of self and their life goals. Their sense of self influences the relationships that individuals develop and the fulfillment experienced in their lives.

Contact with the ground of being often emerges as an experiential reality when individuals are willing to let go of control. This contact is necessary for co-creation to be an experiential reality. As a person recognizes those events that are beyond control, and as a person is willing to let go of attempts to control feelings, thoughts, and other people, she or he becomes more open to experiencing life in an open manner. This openness is essentially creative, capable of forming novel configurations in awareness as well as stability and balance (Perls, Hefferline and Goodman, 1951/1980).

If individuals become open to the ground of being, they recognize their potential for communion with others on a basis of equality. This type of experiential learning provides a basis for greater control within relationships. When others perceive a person as able to interact on a basis of equality, these others are much more likely to give to that person. If a group's atmosphere is supportive of members who allow themselves to let go, the movement towards groundedness for these individuals is facilitated. The creativity of group members' responses allows awareness of co-creativity to become part of the group's atmosphere.

All the aspects of existence that are perceived as outside individual control are interconnected within the ground of being. Additionally, the ground of being is not separate from the interpersonal world of culture and community. In a group context, contact with the ground of being often emerges through those experiences that help a participant to learn that there are limits to the power that any individual can exert upon a group. Members then become freer to co-create their group because they recognize that no one person will direct this creation.

CENTERING WITHIN EXPERIENCE

As members release illusions of control and permanence based on self-images, they become more open to experience as flux and change. They become more open to freedom as a reality because they are seeking less to control others and experience and more to learn from others and experience. As authentic self-actualization is perceived to be possible, members ground themselves in what they experience rather than what they wish they were experiencing. A present-centered focus emerges within awareness and communication. Members learn that responsibility is based on centering within experience rather than on an image of self. If participants can view themselves as responsible without requiring themselves to control everything that happens, they can enjoy freedom (and even find it exhilarating) rather than perceiving it as threatening.

Freedom assists self-actualization as a person centers within the experience of freedom. If freedom is continually perceived as anxiety provoking and groundless, a person will have no basis for making life choices that enhance self-actualization.

Members of unstructured therapy groups or personal growth groups may feel

93

deeply meaningful connectedness if they begin to center awareness within the flow of group interactions. At times, members may report feelings of communion or unity with others, and become aware of deeper levels of their own experiencing (McClure, 1990; O'Hara and Wood, 1983; Rogers, 1980). These events are evidence of the potential that unstructured groups have, at least for some individuals, to enhance awareness of groundedness in a shared field of awareness.

## CONNECTING SELF WITH OTHERS

A natural movement of connection between self and others may be evidence of a universal center that becomes accessible through dialogue (Arnett, 1989; Friedman, 1986). Within the unique and individual aspects of experience, members find ways to universalize their perceptions and connect with others. For example, as one person acknowledges a need to mourn a loss, others will find corresponding aspects of their own experiences. As members communicate these experiences and center within them, they simultaneously connect with one another in a manner that evidences the universality of loss and grief. Members may then find that freedom can enhance rather than threaten their sense of meaning in life.

The concept of centering is related to an understanding of meaning as a creation within experience rather than an imposition upon experience. The center is a point of contact between the individual and the universal, between the uniquely personal and the shared ground of being. This point of contact allows experience to organize meaningfully and permits individual experience to find relationship with the life events of others. As they share their experiences, members affect one another's lives on an ongoing basis.

If members accept the challenge of centering themselves within experience, they tend to create four types of changes within ongoing encounters: (1) Members become willing to 'own' aspects of experience that they have previously denied or projected. (2) They discover new meanings in situations and interactions, meanings of which they were previously unaware. More comprehensive awareness of experience forms the foundation from which members can create new perceptions of meaning. (3) Members recognize decisions and choices that influence present situations. They recognize interactions as co-creative processes. (4) Group participants are willing to initiate changes that alter levels of exploration and communication. These changes tend to move from lesser to greater openness and contact and to win-win forms of contact based on mutual acceptance, rather than me-against-you kinds of contact based on adversarial relating.

Win-win situations allow members to feel greater personal power (Rogers, 1977). Centering within experience provides a foundation for movement towards a balanced and creatively integrated expression of love, power, and justice in relationships.

# CHAPTER 5

# THE DYNAMICS OF LOVE, POWER, AND JUSTICE

Human awareness can be understood to consistently operate within a relational context. Therefore, we can make the assumption that the individual creates and integrates splits in awareness within a field of relationship and that relationships affect the formation and healing of splits. Integration is simultaneously an intrapersonal event and an interpersonal event. Members' sense of self moves from enclosed or rigidly bounded to one that functions in the 'between'. What happens within persons influences what happens between them, and what happens in the between influences what happens within.

If group members are to integrate awareness and extend awareness to include others, they open themselves to relations that are based on mutual caring and responsibility. This extension of self to include others can be viewed as the operation of love between persons. An atmosphere of freedom in a group can support mutual care between the persons involved. If group members are willing to use their freedom in their group to be aware of what another experiences and to respond with openness and acceptance, then they move toward love. If they sense the potential of a group's atmosphere to support loving interactions, members may feel encouraged to choose the openness that allows the self to include others.

## UNIVERSAL DYNAMICS OF THE INTERPERSONAL FIELD

One way to explain this tendency of the self to move toward inclusion of others is to postulate universal dynamics in the 'between' that can bring people into integrated forms of relationship. Simultaneously, these universal dynamics encourage and support the integration of individuals.

An individual who experiences contact with the ground of being comes into relation with universal aspects of being. This contact with the ground of being opens the individual to the potential for love, to the possibility of including others in the person's process of being. Individuals define and influence their relationships; yet at the same time, those relationships reveal the nature of self to individuals. A person learns about his or her potential for integration from participating in integrated relationship dynamics. These dynamics allow for the expression of love.

Therefore, actualizing the potential for love within relationship can provide a basis for the grounding of individual participant's awareness, just as the grounding of the individual in awareness can lead to actualization of potentials for love.

Because awareness and relationship imply one another, it is possible to conceptualize universal dynamics for healing, growth and development. Universal dynamics for healing and growth exist as a potential within human relationships because all people need relationship to express awareness and all human relationships can enhance awareness. Those dynamics that integrate awareness within relationship provide a universal basis for growth and development— that is, for self-actualization.

The elements of love, power, and justice can be understood as aspects of the process of being. Tillich (1954) views love, power, and justice as central and universal elements that emerge within an *ontological* analysis, an examination of what it means to be. For Tillich (1954), ontology was 'the elaboration of the *logos* of the *on* ... the "rational word" that grasps being as such ... being-insofar-as-it-is-being' (p.18). Tillich's attempt to grasp 'being as such' leads him to conceptualize the functioning of individuals as an expression of universal dynamics. He indicates that universal dynamics are evident when individuals establish relatedness to each other, to nature, to their cultures, and to their world. According to Tillich, awareness of universal dynamics in no way minimizes the importance of individuality or diminishes the importance of the individual's encounter with meaninglessness and non-being. Rather, the operation of universal dynamics helps to explain commonalities that emerge among different individuals and cultures as people attempt to live meaningful lives.

*Love, power, and justice* are terms Tillich says possess 'ontological dignity' (1954: 21). They are terms adequate for a discussion about universal aspects of relationship because these terms reflect core ideas that have shown themselves to be relevant in diverse cultures as well as in contemporary Western culture. Love, power, and justice have played a role in various political systems, philosophical systems, religions, and mythologies that have been created as expressions of human attempts to comprehend a universal reality. Thus, these core elements reflect an ongoing dynamic that is essentially universal within the field of interpersonal interaction. Although it is universal, this dynamic develops through different formulations that arise within various situations, group settings, and cultures.

## ANALYSIS OF INTERPERSONAL DYNAMICS

Cultures that do not encourage their members to see the universal dynamics of being human may believe that people who live in other cultures are strange or exist as objects to be exploited or removed. Like individuals, cultures can refuse to learn from, can interfere with, and can disrespect one another. One motive that frequently leads cultures, groups, or individuals to create interpersonal barriers is the need for power based on control of resources. People may seek this kind of power to protect themselves, to feel secure, or to dominate others. As we shall see, the integration of self with others is blocked or distorted whenever power operates separately from love—that is, when the need for power functions without care for the well-being of others. Similarly, love that operates separately from power can distort relationships by refusing to acknowledge differences or boundaries. However, if love and power can be integrated, an interpersonal ethic of justice can become the basis for interpersonal and between-culture interactions.

In an unstructured therapy group, an ethic of justice operating within an atmosphere of freedom supports members' co-creation of shared experience and enables participants to actualize potentials for integrated love and power. People who are aware of and care about each other can create dynamics of justice that function with flexibility. Justice that is flexible can meet the demands of changing situations and changing needs of individuals within those situations. The universal healing dynamics that promote the growth and development of group members are those that function as an integrated gestalt of love, power, and justice.

Members could learn to analyze the dynamics of relationships in a therapy group in a similar manner to analysis of a chemical reaction. One could isolate the components of a relationship, figure out how these components are interacting, and formulate a strategy to combine these elements in a new way. For example, a person could be helped to comprehend how certain needs for security are interfering with meeting other needs for affection. The person could be assisted to understand how to express love more clearly and to act more assertively to meet his or her needs.

However, this kind of analysis will not necessarily help a person to learn how to reassess situations on an ongoing basis. Real change occurs in the present; there is an alteration of a pattern of ongoing interaction. Therefore, a more constructive way of learning about relationship dynamics occurs when a person experiences the self as a dynamic process that creates changes and adapts to changes within various contexts. This kind of learning is more likely to involve human emotional resonance and intuitive forms of awareness than is the kind of learning related to analyzing chemical reactions. An important aspect of this kind of intuitive learning involves how one expresses love in all of its forms.

## LOVE

The longing for love is a recurrent theme in individual and group therapy. Obviously, many people have been hurt because they did not receive love that they wanted or needed. Many people are in pain because they see themselves as essentially unlovable. Some people are afraid to love, or to be loved by others. People sometimes know that they wish to have the feeling of love, but they are uncertain what it involves. People can have stereotypical ideas about or highly idiosyncratic definitions of love. Very different actions can cause people to feel loved or not loved by another. In spite of these different perceptions and divergent ways of expressing love, there is something universal about the longing for love. This universality is evident in the key role that love has in the problems and in the fulfillment that people experience.

Tillich (1954) defines love as the 'reunification of the separated'. He writes, 'Reunion presupposes separation of that which belongs essentially together ... separation presupposes an original unity' (p. 25). Tillich views love as a kind of force that reaffirms unity after it has been broken. In this view, a person could never feel love unless the person had felt separation. Tillich (1954) presents this observation, as he does his other ontological analyses of the human condition, as assertions validated by what can be determined experientially. Love, in this view, is essentially not quantifiable. Love cannot be reduced to the operation of other elements, such as instincts or desires to gain rewards. Its effects can be observed, but love itself must be felt to be understood, as opposed to being observed from outside. The healing effect of love comes through its experience.

## LOVE AS A DYNAMIC ELEMENT IN UNSTRUCTURED GROUP THERAPY

Love plays an important role in the dynamics of healing and growth that occur in therapy groups. Individuals' desires to experience love are often present from the beginning of an unstructured group since it is not uncommon for members to join with the hope of finding acceptance, openness, and caring. Members may have experienced separation from others with whom they were once unified. If they experience reunification with others in their group, some of their wounds may be healed. Group members can also often provide useful feedback about other members' longing for reunification with significant others in their lives. Such feedback can help members to learn how to ask for love or how to deal with situations when love is not being offered.

As their problems are frequently associated with their difficulties in giving and receiving love, members may be concerned about issues such as self-esteem, feelings of inadequacy, and difficulties achieving certain life goals. These issues are often closely related to the self-image created by relationships in which there were difficulties in expressing love. With the acceptance and understanding of their group, members' self-esteem can improve. Positive self-esteem decreases feelings of inadequacy and makes it more likely that individuals can set and achieve life goals. Love alone is not the only element involved in successful therapy. However, experiences of love can play a significant role in many therapeutic encounters. For example, members can be affected by perceptions that others care about them or understand them, and may gain self-esteem when they express their own caring toward others. The presence of the experience of love—if love is considered broadly— is a fundamental element in therapy.

Another theorist who may be viewed as having presented an ontological analysis of love is Carl Rogers. Rogers (1967a) delineated congruence, unconditional positive regard, and empathy as three necessary and sufficient conditions that promote therapeutic personality change. These three core conditions are central in Rogers' lifetime work (see Rogers, 1980). The conditions of congruence, unconditional positive regard, and empathy can readily be understood as aspects of love. When love is expressed from one person to another, this expression must be authentic (i.e., congruent with experience), if therapy is to heal rather than manipulate. Unconditional positive regard, the second core condition, represents the expression of love as respect, caring, and involvement. Empathy, the third of Rogers' conditions, can also be understood as an important aspect of love; empathy is necessary to understand how the other person feels. An individual must be able to assess how the other feels if love is to be communicated and demonstrated in a manner that the other can appreciate. The absence of any of these conditions weakens the ability to love and to express it.

Referring to empathic understanding, respect, genuineness, and specificity, Patterson (1985) writes, 'the essence of these conditions is love, in the sense of the Greek *agape* … love is the most effective agent for change that we know' (p. 8). Defining conditions that are conducive for therapeutic change, according to Patterson, is equivalent to analyzing the components of a loving relationship. If Patterson's premise is valid, then therapy heals through the experience of love. However, love cannot simply be provided by one person (the therapist) to another person (the client). Love implies a dialogue, and persons who participate in dialogue can experience a loving relationship only if they create one together (Arnett, 1989; O'Hara, 1984).

The therapist and group members may work together to create a climate wherein members can congruently express thoughts and feelings, respect and value each other without placing conditions on their mutual acceptance, and can form empathic relations with one another. Participants may also choose to work against the creation of a loving group climate (McClure, 1990). One frequently cited barrier to such a climate is the maintenance of fear and resentment as a reaction to participants who express negative feelings towards other members (Gans, 1989). Another barrier can arise if members communicate their lack of respect or valuing of certain other members (Unger, 1990). A third barrier can be the difficulties that members experience if attempts to communicate lead to misunderstandings or mis-interpretations (Leszcz, 1992).

The creation of a loving group atmosphere can only occur if members are willing to acknowledge the barriers to mutual caring that exist and are willing to experience these barriers and work on them (McClure, 1990). A loving atmosphere in a group is not created simply by believing that it would be a nice thing to have. The group needs to struggle with doubts, self-esteem problems, the need to maintain roles, and various other impediments. The creation of a loving atmosphere requires awareness and commitment as well as good intentions.

ASPECTS OF LOVE

Awareness and love are linked because one must be openly aware of who one is, and who the other is, for love to function as authentic acceptance and care. Participants in unstructured therapy groups are very likely to be consciously or unconsciously wishing for exposure to unifying love in the group. Members would like to be accepted by others and would like to extend acceptance to others.

Although members wish for the experience of love, they may find ways to undermine love through mistrust, aggression, or self-protection (Agazarian, 1992; Gans, 1989; Yalom, 1995). Mary, the client who was described in Chapter 4, demonstrated with one of the writers this tendency of seeking love and acceptance while undermining her own efforts. Mary let the therapist who was conducting the unstructured group know that she wanted his affection and respect; at the same time she attempted to become dependent on her facilitator. She had a previous history of trying to develop close relationships with other counselors or psychologists and then becoming overly dependent in these relationships. Once Mary became involved in therapy, she never wanted it to end. Mary was able to avoid assuming responsibility for her own actions in this manner. This facilitator encouraged the other members to provide Mary with feedback in the group when they observed her being too dependent on others, including the facilitator, and gradually she was able to develop more self-confidence and an enhanced ability to function independently.

Love can be characterized as having four basic aspects: *agape* (or universality), *epithymia* (or desire), *eros* (or life-enhancing values), and *philia* (or friendship) (Tillich, 1954). Tillich (1954) thought that although love has been treated traditionally as a fragmented process by various religious and secular institutions, love actually operates without fragmentation if it is accepted as a whole or totality. If, as Tillich (1954) suggests, the different aspects of love are all expressions of integration in human relations, it would therefore be incorrect to regard the expression of one aspect of love as being more valuable or worthy than another.

Patterson (1985) has noted the connection between *agape* and therapy. Agape is selfless concern for others and represents a willingness to give to others. A person who expresses *agape* is not concerned about whether others reciprocate love or give in return. Because it does not favor one person over another, *agape* is considered to be the universal form of love. Yet, it would be a mistake to equate the growth of group members in therapy only with the experience of *agape*. Agape arises from the awareness of a shared context for all beings. Perhaps the experience of *agape* is always present to some extent whenever members feel that they are part of a caring group atmosphere. However, members also move toward mutual acceptance by finding ways to enjoy one another's presence in the group and by experiencing a bond that is established when intimate aspects of oneself are shared with others. Members extend their centers to include others not only because they sense a universality that is shared with others but also because they enjoy talking to specific others and because they have confided in specific others.

100

# Dynamics of Love, Power, and Justice

Thus, love also has an individual aspect—one that joins specific people for particular interpersonal aims. In unstructured therapy groups, members generally move to accept and include specific others in the group. The individual center of one member can be extended to include another member because of shared values, because of attraction or desire, or because of the potential for friendship. The more that two members are willing to include each other, the closer their personal relationship comes to the I-Thou form of encounter. Although the joining together of individuals can sometimes create discomfort for other members who feel left out, it can also be a positive experience for the group. The joining of two members who experience a bond can be helpful if other participants feel gratified to observe that two members have connected on a meaningful level. Jealousy or feelings of rejection may surface as barriers that must be acknowledged and experienced before the group can move to acceptance of this bond.

As we saw earlier, Tillich (1954) believed that different forms of love were expressions of one force in human affairs. The apparently selfless *agape* aspect of love is not, in reality, separated from the *epithymia* aspect of love, which is expressed as the seeking of pleasure and self-fulfillment (Tillich, 1954). Groups become more cohesive (that is, members experience more mutual acceptance) if members can accept the various expressions of love that can be important to individuals. If a male member strives for selfless love and denies his selfish side, he may not connect as fully with others. If a female member denies her more selfless or universal feelings because she thinks others will take advantage of her, she may also limit her fulfillment in the group and in life. Any one-sided approach may be limiting.

Some people, including Freud (1930/1961), have viewed the foundation of all love as a drive for pleasure. At the other extreme are people who believe that love is a spiritual reality that sometimes may contradict the self-centered tendencies of sensuality and desire (Maslow, 1964; Vaughan, 1986). *Epithymia*, or desire, has traditionally been treated by many religions as the lowest form of love. Yet *epithymia* is present in all desires whose fulfillment brings pleasure, including eating, movement, sexuality, or participation in a group. These activities provide pleasure as they unite the person with the environment and the person with others. Pleasure is the by-product of integration with the world, with individuals, and with the human community.

If pleasure is sought as an end in itself, the integration of the person with the world becomes limited. In therapy groups, members who have tried to live only for the experience of pleasure often express a confrontation with meaninglessness in life and in relationships. Groups can provide environments where members learn that integration within relationships includes pleasure but that fulfillment through relationship may be limited if pleasure is seen as the only goal.

Tillich (1954) relates the movement of human energy toward life-affirming values to *eros*, the form of love that is expressed as an enhanced experience of life, nature, and culture. He related the movement of human energy towards friendship and personal involvement with the form of love that the Greeks called *philia*. These two aspects of love form a polar relationship, with *eros* representing a transpersonal aspect of love and *philia* representing a deeply personal aspect of love. *Philia* and *eros* can be conceptualized as existing in interdependent relationship, and neither aspect would be possible without the existence of the other (Tillich, 1954). People cannot fully appreciate the meaning of nature and beauty if they are unable to personalize feelings in the context of specific encounters and relations. The dynamic relationship between *philia* and *eros* can be seen in the context of group therapy. As individuals' personal interactions and relationships develop in the group, their values are often affected. As a result of group interactions, members may develop more positive views of society, relationships, certain ethnic or minority groups, males, females, or the potential for beauty and love in life.

At the same time, *eros*—according to Tillich (1954)—is founded on *epithymia*. *Eros* can use desire to transform persons who are estranged from the positive possibilities of life. *Eros* is the attraction that people may feel towards reunification with values that disclose beauty in nature and the potential for meaning and truth in culture. Therapy groups can be considered to begin to work successfully as members become attracted to the group and to each other. This attraction, along with mutual interpersonal acceptance, is a necessary part of the development of cohesion in the group (Yalom, 1995). Members are much more likely to experience a positive transformation of values if they first experience attraction to others in their group and to their group as a whole.

The *eros* aspect of love may affect members throughout their group experience, whenever they experience the possibility of life-affirming values. *Eros* can lead members to prize their group experience as a whole for the values that it represents— for example, openness, honesty, and equality.

The *philia* aspect of love is most evident when members disclose and respond to specific others in the group with the understanding that there is a fundamental equality between the individuals. Perceptions of fundamental equality are likely to be more readily available if members see others in their group as coming from shared environments or life experiences. Equality can also be recognized between those from different backgrounds, usually if members come to experience empathy and respect for one another.

The *philia* and *agape* aspects of love can intertwine in experiences of empathy. Through *philia*, a member can experience a unique kind of bond with another who has shared an empathic encounter. Through *agape*, a member can experience the potential universality of empathy, the possibility of joining with any other who is willing to be joined. Empathy represents an attitude of openness and a willingness to learn from the experiences of others. Empathy, like awareness and love, cannot be forced. Empathy can be viewed as awareness and love working together. By relating empathically, a person is able to become aware of the world of another, and to care enough about that world to be affected by nuances of the other's perception that are highly personal and subjective.

Therapy groups have the potential to help members learn how to unite aspects of love that may be fragmented in the experience of individuals (for example, *epithymia* and *agape*). A group can help members to learn that they can care about the group as a whole and can integrate this caring with a special feeling of attraction for one or more members. Members can get feedback from others that helps them to validate all of who they are—their spiritual longings as well as their desires for 'earthly' pleasures.

The person who has adapted to an environment where it is emotionally unsafe to express or seek love is likely to repress longings for love. Theorists have had different explanations for difficulties that people have in engaging in loving relationships. Kohut (1971) emphasizes that a person's lack of empathic relations with a significant nurturing figure leads to lack of self-esteem and an emotional emptiness that makes mature love difficult or impossible. Maslow states that people adapt to emotionally deprived environments by learning a form of love that he termed 'deficiency-love' (Goble, 1971). This is a kind of love that attempts to fill a void. A person who experiences self as deficient attempts to take from others to feel better about self. Perls (1971) might say that this kind of person wants to fill self-created holes in the personality by taking from others. Kohut (1971) would probably say that the person only created these kinds of holes because of experiences of deprivation or rejection.

Most likely, experiences of a loving nature can help heal the kinds of wounds preserved as negative self-perceptions, whereas experiences of a rejecting nature will maintain or exacerbate these wounds to the sense of self (Bacal, 1985; Kohut, 1971). Although loving relations in therapy can promote healing, therapists are constrained by their roles from engaging in a fully equal and loving relationship in which partners express and meet needs and wishes of the other (Yalom, 1980). Therefore, an advantage of group therapy is that members can learn about love on an equal basis from each other. Members may experience greater benefits from the relations that they form with others whom they perceive as equals than with a group's therapist (Yalom, 1995).

Therapeutic groups provide opportunities to meet the kinds of needs that help build self-esteem—the needs with which theorists such as Kohut (1977), Combs and Snygg (1959), and Maslow (1962) have been concerned. A person can find others who are willing to give, but just as important, a person is likely to find others who are willing to receive. A person's belief that she or he has sufficient resources to contribute meaningfully to others and can experience joy within the act of giving is a central aspect of the love that Maslow (1962) termed *being-love* and Patterson (1985) termed *agape*.

DISTORTIONS OF LOVE IN THERAPEUTIC RELATIONSHIPS

The gestalt of love, power, and justice within present relationships becomes skewed when participants in relationships deal with unresolved emotional issues from the past in ways that are unjust within the context of the present relationship. Whether this distortion is evaluated in terms of transference dynamics (see Greenson, 1967) or the maintenance of unfinished business (see Polster and Polster, 1973), therapists often attempt to aide their clients to give up old, ineffective relationship patterns and to form more effective ways of relating in the present. Therapists who work in terms of transference tend to focus on learning about a client's past, whereas work on unfinished business tends to focus more on here-and-now effects of communications. In unstructured therapy groups, participants may be invited to assess how past relationships affect current interactions (Wolf and Schwartz, 1962; Foulkes, 1975) or may gain potent experiential learning by being invited to communicate within the context of present dynamics in ways that challenge distorted patterns of relationship (Leszcz, 1992).

A person who has experienced rejection from a significant other in the past often rejects the possibility of empathic encounters in the present. Such a member can be assisted to reconstruct important past events and to be open to experiential aspects of these events that were shut out. Additionally, this individual can be encouraged to be open in the present to empathy offered by another member. A member will usually provide cues whether an exploration of past or present events is central in his or her awareness.

A client named 'James', a member of an unstructured therapy group conducted in a residential drug treatment center, shows how people can benefit from both examining their past and learning about how to relate effectively in the present. James was a black, multidrug user who had intimidated many of the staff and other residents in his program. He had the reputation among the residents as being dangerous and crazy enough to do about anything. He was also a former Vietnam veteran. James tended to undermine his relationships with other residents by projecting a violent image of himself. During one group session, he described having seen his best friend killed by a policeman for what he thought was no good reason. The policeman was white, and since that time James had developed some highly unfavorable opinions about white people—especially white authority figures.

After a fairly extended interaction with the leader wherein James described his friend's death and his own feelings about the incident, James became more open and honest with the facilitator and the other participants. The leader and James ended up the group by indicating that they liked each other. James was able to describe a tragic incident in his group that had affected his attitudes toward white people unfavorably, and he also learned that he could relate in some rewarding ways to an individual whom he considered to be a white authority figure.

If therapists are unaware of their own uncompleted or unacknowledged longing for love, they may create skewed relationships with clients. Such patterns can become evident if a therapist plays the authority role and encourages client dependency, if a therapist demands or manipulates caring from the client, or if the therapist attempts to play an exclusively intellectual role. In a group situation, such a therapist tends to be either under- or over-involved in controlling the group process. By being over-involved, the therapist tries to win affection and the perception of his or her importance from clients. By being under-involved, the therapist portrays an image of self-sufficiency and emotional distance.

## CENTERING THERAPEUTIC RELATIONSHIPS IN THE PRESENT

As we saw in Chapter 3, present-oriented concerns can be assumed to be valid therapeutic issues without necessarily or automatically relating them to past patterns (Perls, Hefferline and Goodman, 1951/1980). Although awareness of unfinished business can be helpful, the present relationship should not be reduced to a vehicle for understanding the impact of past events. Instead, the past can be considered significant insofar as it forms part of the meaning of the present. The unknown aspect of the present, its becoming, can never be sufficiently translated in terms of the past, which is known. Therefore, powerful therapeutic work can be done within the context of the present to assist people in becoming more open to unknown aspects of their own processes of being-becoming.

An ontological perspective of therapy leads us to view being as centered in the present. From this perspective, unfinished business is a kind of resonance of events that is reconstructed within each current moment. If the person is viewed as a creative, present-centered being, then unfinished business is the person's own construction based on perceived similarities of the past with the present. Unfinished business is a means to learn about how the person is constructing self within the present. Viewing unfinished business in this manner requires a unique view of transference and countertransference issues.

Unfinished business can be considered as constructions within the present that reflect a person's commitments, beliefs about self, and goals for relationships. As we have already seen, these can distort current relationship dynamics and limit the atmosphere of love that can be created between participants. Unless members can learn to express their needs to give and receive love effectively in the present, it is doubtful that they will be satisfied with the results of their therapy. Love is not an intellectual idea that can be grasped solely from the analysis of past interactions—although sometimes this may help. Members who work to own feelings within the present and to confront dynamics based on blame and shame will challenge their reconstruction of unfinished business and may be able to take the risk in their group to express their needs to love and to receive love.

## POWER AND LOVING SELF AND OTHERS

The integration of power and love has been seen by many theorists to involve the ability to care for and love one's self in a manner that can include loving others (for example, see Fromm, 1956; Kohut, 1971, 1977; Bozarth, 1998; Rogers, 1977). The ability to make decisions based on one's own experiential process and perceptions of relationships, including awareness of worthiness of self and other, is evidence of an awareness of power (Bugental, 1978; Rogers, 1977). Thus, power is necessary to love, just as love is necessary to power. Power without love degenerates into exploitation and eventually degenerates further into self-destructive and other-destructive behaviors. In unstructured therapy groups, members can explore options for integrating love and power in an interpersonal context.

The person who has ambivalent feelings about self is likely to develop fragmented relations with others. Fragmented relationships are evidenced by the inability of participants to connect as fully as they would like or to express themselves completely. The price can be a loss of personal integrity, a disassociation of love from power. Love may be withheld in such relationships. If group members risk expressing themselves openly and fully with others in their group, they will experience congruence between the image that they present and their own experience. This congruence ends fragmentation in relationship.

Constructive self-love is not narcissistic self-love, that is, it includes and is aware of the other, rather than excluding and investing in remaining nonaware. Self-love includes others, because one cannot have a self without others. The atmosphere in an effectively therapeutic group allows members to feel that it is safe to allow one's self to include the others in the group.

Clients involved in therapy often complain of low self-esteem or a poor self-image. These clients can be taught new ways to think about themselves, but if they lack the experience of constructive self-love that includes others, their new thinking is unlikely to have much of an impact. A therapeutic group can provide opportunities to experience interactions with others that provide a basis for the experience of authentic self-love.

## POWER

*Power*, as a basic element of anything that exists, is the identity and coherence of that thing (see Tillich, 1954). In human life, power is demonstrated by a coherent awareness of self, and by the ability to use that sense of self as a basis for formulating directions and influencing events.

### ASPECTS OF POWER

If love is the inherent movement of reunification that connects a thing with everything else, power is the inherent movement towards distinction that differentiates a thing from everything else. Power is an assertion of distinctness associated with knowing what one wants and needs, expressing these wishes or needs, and acting to move toward what is desired. Thus, personal power is evidenced by a person's willingness to function as an active agent (see May, 1972; Yalom, 1980). If power is integrated with love, a person is able to express wants and needs in a manner that is considerate of the feelings of others and that respects their integrity. If power is expressed in a manner that is disconnected from love, others are likely to feel imposed upon, coerced, or manipulated in a dishonest manner. Therefore, integrating power with love usually helps people to meet needs in interpersonal situations more effectively. Power and love are intrinsically unified, and their separation in interpersonal dynamics diminishes the ability of either of these elements to function fully and effectively.

Power must be aligned with awareness in order for individuals' influence over events to be congruent with individuals' actual needs, feelings, and values. For power to be used responsibly, the freedom of others must be recognized and respected. Thus, the element of power interacts with the gestalt of awareness, freedom, and responsibility. Awareness assists the integration of power with love; through awareness a person can recognize the needs of others, and can also understand the destructive consequences of power that acts without love.

## POWER AND COURAGE IN GROUP THERAPY

The initiation of interaction in a therapy group may involve risk for the initiator, particularly if this action upsets the status quo. Yet a person can also take a risk by not initiating an action that others expect or require. Personal power may be expressed by not moving or not reacting to a stimulus as well as by initiating an action. For example, a group leader who does not provide an answer to a question may assist others to construct their own answers. A participant who listens or asks a simple question about what is occurring in the group may be showing personal power in a situation where others are excessively concerned with asserting the significance of their opinions. A group member who does not respond to name-calling from another member may also be showing personal power. Thus, personal power is expressed as the ability to choose how and when to engage others within ongoing interactions. Power allows a person to maintain a centered presence with others and to choose how to react to situations.

One theorist who noted the prevalence of the theme of power in human relationships is Alfred Adler. Adler has observed that a central motivation for the achievement of power is the individual's perception of insignificance (Mosak, 1984). Adler also believed that people become healthier as they learn that they make choices that alter events. They can then learn to be creative in their approach to life, and can gain significance without hurting themselves or others. People may often wound themselves and others by attempts to overcompensate for feelings of insecurity, by trying to demonstrate their superiority to others, and by trying to control situations and people (Adler, 1972).

Tillich takes a broad view of the theme of power. He postulates that individuals are motivated towards power in an attempt to attain victory over nonbeing (Tillich,

1954). The *threat of nonbeing* encompasses feelings of guilt, perceptions of one's own inadequacy and insignificance, experience of life as meaningless, and insecurity due to awareness of death. People sometimes assert their power over perceived threats through behavior that is self-destructive. Fromm (1964) and Perls, Hefferline and Goodman (1951/1980) have asserted that the threats that people perceive may be projections of disowned aspects of their own experience. If this assertion is true, people are trying to overcome an externalized aspect of their own experience when they act against these threats. No amount of external victory will be able to alleviate their disowning of themselves.

According to Tillich (1952), courage is an essential characteristic of people who are able to act in spite of perceptions of the threat of nonbeing. It is this willingness to risk that can lead to greater fulfillment and self-respect. Group members often help each other to take risks that require courage. A participant can sometimes be comfortable initiating actions that others see as risky and dangerous but will be afraid to acknowledge feelings of vulnerability. Feedback from group members can assist participants to clarify perceptions about those areas of life—including feelings of vulnerability— that are personally challenging and that require courage. Courage is always an individual matter because actions that require bravery for one person may be habitual for another person, and vice versa. By helping each other to take risks in what is owned and what is expressed, members help each other to experience themselves as having more choices within interpersonal interactions.

## DEVELOPING AN EMPOWERING GROUP ATMOSPHERE

Power is generally perceived as a coherent sense of self that includes trust in one's perceptions, a belief in adequate resources to meet needs, a sense of one's adequacy to deal with challenges, awareness of the capability to affirm self and others, and the ability to initiate changes in situations. Members can assist each other's empowerment if they are able to give each other feedback about perceived strengths. Yet, more importantly, members grow through new experiences of asserting power integrated with love in actual group relations. This sense of power is likely to include the courage to acknowledge perceived weakness and 'negative' feelings. By being open with each other about who they are and who they are becoming, members experience power in a new way.

If members avoid disclosure of perceived threats and experiences of nonbeing, work toward empowerment and self-actualization will be inhibited. Members may need to develop a strong sense that their group is trustworthy before they acknowledge perceived threats of nonbeing. Aspects of being that are not usually part of social discussions (sexuality, aggression, history of physical or sexual abuse) may emerge as participants confront perceived threats. As a group becomes a safe place to work on issues of personal power, members tend to confront each other about interactions that they perceive as manipulative or dishonest. A central way that a group can empower members is by helping members to become aware of covert activities designed to influence others and by creating norms that validate directly asking others for what is desired or needed (Leszcz, 1992).

## NORMS AND ROLES IN POWER RELATIONS

In therapy groups, the group process evolves as members (1) form perceptions of their own power in their group, (2) form perceptions of the power of other members, (3) find ways to relate their own sense of power with the power of others, (4) gain an understanding of the power of the group's leader and their relationship to the leader, and (5) gain insight into the power of the group as a whole and their power within the group. These five aspects of members' perceptions of power can change throughout a group, depending on the course of interactions.

Members gain or lose status in their group depending on a general, often subtly formed consensus based on members' understanding of norms, and of each other's personal power in relation to these (Napier and Gershenfeld, 1987). Determining which people have power requires careful assessment, because members who are not overtly controlling can sometimes have a great deal of power in determining values or directions for the group as a whole.

Those who have more power generally command more attention from others when they speak (Napier and Gershenfeld, 1987). They may be allowed to take more of the group's time without being interrupted. One value to developing an awareness of how a group shares power is to determine if all members have access to attention from the group as a whole. A group leader may wish to draw attention to the dynamics of power in a group to assist members in taking responsibility for the way they are choosing to spend time and energy. However, if a leader is too assertive about the importance of his or her observations or comments, that person may assume a dominant position in group process that interferes with the opportunities for others to feel that their observations count.

Power struggles can become overt at certain times in a group's process. These struggles may express one or more members' rebellion against dynamics that have been experienced as unfair. A power struggle can also represent an attempt to control the direction of a group or to determine the values and beliefs that will guide decisions that influence directions (Gans, 1989). At the same time, struggles for power often are engaged in covertly. A member may direct comments only towards certain other members. If one subgroup dominates by directing comments and eye contact toward one another, other members not included in the subgroup may feel excluded (Agazarian, 1992).

Relationships can be based on a pattern that prohibits the sharing of power— that sets and maintains unequal power between participants. These relationships by definition are those wherein the purposes of power are separated from the purposes of love. Love is oriented toward inclusion of the other; if power is used in ways that exclude or diminish the other, then it operates in a manner divorced from love. Power becomes divorced from love when the power of the other is perceived as a threat.

Participants may generate conflicts in which other members tend to take sides, or may seek to establish exclusive relationships with the leader or others. Group members may seek to establish a role in the group that allows them to gratify needs for attention because they are anxious about a situation wherein roles have not been defined beforehand. Members may, for example, define for themselves such roles as caretaker, complainer, challenger, mediator, victim, commentator, comedian, and so on (Vander Kolk, 1985). If they can explore feelings of anxiety and uncertainty, members may then learn how they use roles as a way to diminish uncomfortable feelings such as uncertainty, insignificance, or powerlessness (Vander Kolk, 1985).

## CHANGING ESTABLISHED ROLES

Strategies that lessen opportunities for fulfillment through interaction may be attempts to maintain power while avoiding the discomfort of enhanced awareness. Enhanced awareness can bring a realization of imperfections in oneself and others that might increase perceptions of vulnerability and decrease illusions of security or superiority. Enhanced awareness can reawaken experiences of anxiety that have been sealed off by stereotypical structures for perception and relationship. Unstructured therapy groups can support participants who are willing to experience anxiety as they confront self-limiting patterns or previously denied perceptions.

Members' experiences of anxiety can be viewed as opportunities for growth, learning, and actualization of possibilities. If members become more open toward the experience of anxiety, they are more likely to be able to do the work on the self-confrontation involved in changing patterns that have separated the goals of power from those of love (see McClure, 1990; Yalom, 1995). When power is aligned with love, people allow themselves more vulnerability with each other. Power can be expressed in a context of love by learning how to give and receive and by becoming more open to the uncertainty of an evolving relationship.

As we have seen, people separate power from love because they would like to believe that they can be strong by eliminating uncertainty and vulnerability, by controlling as much of life as possible, and by controlling their forms of self-expression and relationship. Conversely, people who perceive themselves as inadequate to gain this kind of control but who also want to eliminate uncertainty and anxiety may have fantasies of being controlled. Change is a journey into unknown aspects of self and relationship. Members can learn that there is a kind of power that comes from entering and sharing experiences of anxiety and intimacy with others, power that is not based on maintaining a protective self-image (Gemmill and Wynkoop, 1991).

## BOUNDARIES AND INTERPERSONAL JUSTICE

As group participants let go of attempts to defend a self-image, they release their defensive interpersonal strategies (Leszcz, 1992). Although members become open to being influenced by others, they may also become more definite about setting

# Dynamics of Love, Power, and Justice

limits for their own participation and communication. Self-definition within a relational context can be described as a formation of boundaries (for example, see Agazarian, 1992; Perls, Hefferline and Goodman, 1951/1980).

The ways that individual boundaries are formed in overlapping patterns with others' boundaries result in bounded subsystems for interactions within the overall group system (Agazarian, 1992). *Boundaries* define where one's perception of 'self' ends and perceptions of 'other' begins and how different from self another is perceived to be. These perceptions of inclusion and exclusion influence how close a person is willing to become to specific others and to the group as a whole. Boundaries, along with norms, help define how much time and attention is given to individuals. Nonverbal expression of boundaries can be exhibited by physical distancing, seating arrangements, and attentional cues (see Applbaum, Bodaken, Sereno and Anatol, 1974). Perception is the basis of boundary formation. Persons may perceive certain others as included (or partially included within the self at one time in a relationship) and may exclude those same people at another time. Thus, boundaries of selves and subsystems of selves shift throughout the life of a group.

As power aligns with love, boundaries can become firm yet permeable. Members will then neither seek contact compulsively, nor compulsively refuse contact. In a group that functions therapeutically, members tend to learn from and with each other how to move toward flexibility in interpersonal boundaries (Agazarian, 1992). They will feel able to choose vulnerability if they don't fear rejection or misunderstanding, and will recognize that they can grow through allowing themselves to be affected by the experiences of others.

For example, a young graduate student named 'Paul' attended an unstructured therapy group for college students. Many of Paul's difficulties had surfaced in sexual relationships in which he would back off quickly before emotional intimacy could develop. Paul was able to talk openly about his difficulties in relationships and felt free to explore the impact of childhood sexual abuse that involved his mother. However, Paul always carefully maintained a barrier to others' feedback by maintaining a 'storytelling' presence in which he commented about himself as if he were an objective observer, thus limiting how much of his vulnerability he exposed.

Later in the life of the group, Paul began to feel confident of his ability to maintain boundaries. He could then relax and let others into more of his experience. He was then able to respond to feedback more immediately and emotionally. At this time, he also began to respond with emotion to others' revelations of problems and difficulties in their lives. Members began to express appreciation of Paul's perceptiveness and ability to demonstrate understanding of others. Paul's attempts to carry these newfound patterns of communication into his relationships outside of the group proved to be difficult when romantic feelings were involved; yet he made slow but steady changes in his willingness to let the woman he was dating into his emotional life.

111

Shared risk-taking occurs as interpersonal connections and trust develops. The atmosphere of love in a group can support and assist members' empowerment as they risk new ways of experiencing and interacting. These risks can further intimacy, facilitate centering within ongoing experience, and encourage an individual to initiate changes in relational patterns. Thus, the processes of growth and healing in a group form interpersonal patterns that unite the purposes of love with the purposes of power.

## JUSTICE

The patterns of an individual's interpersonal relationships, as well as interpersonal patterns in groups and societies, can be considered as embodiments of forms of justice (Tillich, 1954). *Forms of justice* mediate the integration of love and power by determining how needs, demands, expectations, and wishes are expressed and met in interactions.

### CHANGES IN FORMS OF JUSTICE

As members experience increased permeability of boundaries, they change the form of interpersonal justice that mediates their transactions and interactions. Members can move toward a more dynamic and creative form of justice if they (1) support an open atmosphere in which everyone can freely express their individual modes of caring and personal power, (2) develop awareness of others through actively listening to that which is expressed and revealed, (3) develop sufficient caring for others to value their work on personal and interpersonal problems, and (4) view others' self-revelations as potentially important contributions to interpersonal learning. Thus, justice includes the dynamics of awareness, freedom, and responsibility, as well as connections between power and love in interpersonal interactions.

If members perceive that each participant has opportunities to contribute and receive, members will perceive that their group is just. Justice supports new learning because members become willing to express more completely whom they experience themselves being with others, and others being with them. Creative justice allows members to respond spontaneously and openly to novel challenges to group interactions. Group norms, the quality of communication between members, and structures of power and authority that members create reflect forms of justice. The form of justice of a group determines who gets heard if there are competing needs for group attention. Justice is also involved in how members are heard and responded to and how judgmental or nonjudgmental group members are. Each member has needs for love and power that the group can potentially meet. Members' individual perceptions of their abilities to satisfy their needs for love and power form the basis for their sense of personal boundary in the group.

# Dynamics of Love, Power, and Justice

## THE CHALLENGE OF CREATIVE JUSTICE IN GROUP THERAPY

Forms of justice are created by people through an interactive process and provide the structures through which people make sense of their feelings, needs, and desires. Any ongoing interaction evolves a form of justice because participants constantly make choices about what to offer and what to withhold, how much to care about the experience of the other, what to request or demand from the other, how to assert self in relation to the other, and how to respond to assertions made by the other. Forms of justice exist along a continuum. At one extreme of the continuum are rigid forms of justice that attempt to predict and regulate exactly what will transpire during the course and outcome of interactions. At the other extreme are forms of justice that attempt to be totally adaptable and flexible to constantly changing interpersonal dynamics.

In practice, interpersonal justice lies somewhere between these two hypothetical extremes. Even the most rigid forms of human justice need to allow for some accommodation to unpredictability because of interactions that break with predetermination and predictions. Nevertheless, even the most fluid forms of justice must maintain some structure that regulates behavior because a degree of continuity and predictability is necessary as a basis for human communication and relationship.

*Creative justice* arises as participants ask something of each other, hear each other, become aware of each other, and respond spontaneously without preconceptions about who the other is capable of being and becoming. The unstructured therapy group is an environment that can challenge members to develop forms of creative justice within ongoing encounters. The unstructured group is never without form but makes demands on all the participants involved to form structures within interactions that meet everyone's changing needs.

In the unstructured group mentioned earlier in this chapter, for example, Paul's willingness to reveal aspects of his emotional and sexual life formed a challenge for other members who had not broached such intimate material. His tendency to back away as others got closer led to some confusion among members about how they could best help Paul as well as learn from interacting with him. Members had to create a structure of justice that was new for their group. This allowed Paul flexibility in asking for help or retreating from exposure and also permitted members to express their reactions about Paul's maneuvers honestly. The basis of this new mode of justice was a willingness to give and receive at a new level of intimacy, along with respect for individuals' abilities to regulate their own exposure of thoughts and feelings to others.

The determination of forms of justice for relationships and communities is a creative activity. Justice has a creative element that emerges as individuals perceive themselves as adequate authorities for determining the forms for their relationships. Justice lacks creativity if participants simply accept a predetermined form of justice from an authority figure or social institution. If people are willing to repeat

113

unquestioningly the forms of interaction that have become habitual and comfortable, they are avoiding the anxiety of a creative encounter with life and other people.

Self-actualization requires a creative form of justice that is adequate to the demands of changes in situations and environmental realities and to shifts in personal and interpersonal needs and wishes. If members are able to question their stereotyped responses and their predetermined ways of relating to others, they can engage in a process that moves them toward a mutual creation of a more creative form of justice. If the challenge of constructing a creative form of justice is avoided, then members may continue to experience themselves as isolated units, and their potential to become a group may not be realized.

Members will not function fully as a group until they can recognize a mutual purpose that can align individual desires for love with those for power. This unifying purpose is the recognition that each person is responsible within each interaction to participate in a manner that is creatively just. Of course, this kind of responsibility is seldom addressed specifically and cognitively. To address it overtly may defeat the very process that moves towards this form of justice. If members become self-conscious about the mode of justice that they are forming, they are likely to develop an excessively cognitive approach to being together and may miss learning opportunities that arise spontaneously.

## CREATIVE JUSTICE AS MUTUAL AWARENESS OF SIGNIFICANCE

Members reflect a concern for justice when they interact with the unspoken recognition that participants each have the right to ask something from their group. In Tillich's (1954) view, each member has an equally valid claim for justice from a group. Participants move toward creative justice if they begin to understand each person's claim on the group from the perspective of that person. If a member makes a claim that is perceived to be unfair or illegitimate, the others should be willing to investigate and understand that person's point of view. They will assert their own reactions in terms that acknowledge the humanity of the other, even if the other's claims seem unfair. Thus, their response will not be designed to humiliate, stereotype, or reject. A creatively just group will help members to understand how others are seeing them, and why certain demands seem unrealistic or unfair.

Unjust claims made on others in a group are often based on unfinished business (for example, see Johnson, 1963). A person may demand something from others based on unmet needs in other relationships or may think of and relate to others based on previous relationship patterns (Johnson, 1963; Wolf and Schwartz, 1962). A group can become a setting where members can confront each others' unjust claims, can learn about each others' unfinished business, and can give and receive honest feedback concerning how members are establishing relationships with others.

Of course, participants often feel uncomfortable making *just* claims on their group. Effective group therapy generally focuses on assisting members to recognize the value of their authentic claims for justice. Members are not assisted to feel self-righteous, or to expect that life can be expected to be fair to everyone. Instead, they are taught to experience and value their own need for justice, one that may have been disowned due to powerful and unjust relationship patterns with others.

Just as life is imperfect, no group can create an environment that meets all members' needs, or even all of any one member's needs. A creative mode of justice encourages members to listen, to ask, and to respond. Although creative justice does not guarantee that all needs will be met, it does optimize potentials for a group or community to meet the needs of as many members as possible.

A person can act in a creatively just manner towards herself or himself or towards others. The person who is creatively just towards self will not impose 'shoulds' that require maintenance of a façade. Rigid forms of justice result in self-imposed perfectionism for a person who strives always to be reasonable and always to account for every action. Members in a group encourage each other's self-actualization by creating an atmosphere wherein members can be heard and can receive open and honest responses. Creative justice thrives on mutual caring, commitment, and honesty rather than on perfectionism, legalism, and self-consciousness.

Because it is always based on the dynamic flux of present experience and interpersonal encounters of power with power, forms of creative justice cannot be determined *a priori*, or from a formula of what is loving or just (Tillich, 1954). Creative justice can, however, be recognized by certain qualities that appear in members' interactions as they move toward it. These qualities are listening, giving, and acceptance (see Tillich, 1954).

## CREATIVE JUSTICE AS NEW ORGANIZATION

Members who have split off and disowned feelings and experiences have been influenced by experiences and patterns in relationship that were perceived by the person as being unjust. The split is evidence of a mode of justice that is punitive and rejecting toward the self. To create order (justice) within a disorderly (unjust) life experience, people disown aspects of self that they associate with negative or unjust experiences. In the example given earlier, Paul was dealing with a past mode of justice within his family that allowed his boundaries to be disregarded. As he discovered his feelings about times when his mother had acted seductively toward him, Paul recognized that he had cut off his feelings to allow himself to maintain a relationship with his mother. He began to acknowledge feelings of hurt and self-negation, and this acknowledgment preceded his willingness to allow himself to be more affected by others in the group.

An interpersonal dynamic is involved in the process by which a person disowns experience. This dynamic is based on being rejected by important others (for example, parents) for having thoughts, feelings, or behaviors that are deemed to be unacceptable. Rejection is used to punish the person for having these feelings, thoughts, or actions. People who feel rejected in this way have usually learned self-rejection. In an effort to create an illusion of perfection, a person can become more rejecting toward him- or herself than others have been (Perls, Hefferline and Goodman, 1951/1980). People who are approving of others can also be unduly harsh and rejecting toward aspects of themselves. They expect themselves to achieve a moral superiority that they do not demand from others. If members are generally accepting and provide feedback about a participant's self-rejecting behavior, they may assist that person to re-evaluate rigid forms of justice used toward self.

As we stated in Chapter 4, reclaiming disowned aspects of self can establish a new self-organization (Mahoney, 1990). A new self-organization is a form of justice within awareness of relationship; it allows a person to accept what was previously rejected. Because denial and projection are no longer useful, this form of justice encourages acceptance and contact. Likewise, if members create forms of relationship that negate denial and projection, they can assist each other to internalize new interpersonal forms of justice as self-acceptance.

The operation of creative justice in a group generally moves the leader from a position of special authority or power to an equal footing with other members. This form of justice can be recognized when members are willing to maintain different values from each other and the leader and are comfortable and appreciative of these differences. Creatively just norms allow members to learn how their needs and perceptions differ. They may then attempt to give what they perceive that each needs, and what they feel can be legitimately given. One person may need attention, another may need to be comforted, another may need space, and yet another may need to receive feedback. If members intend to balance and meet each others' needs, they must develop a sensitive and comprehensive awareness of one another.

## THE GESTALT OF LOVE, POWER, AND JUSTICE

The unified functioning of love, power, and justice as a gestalt within relationship is similar to the Chinese Taoist's thinking of the unified movement of Tao, the way of life. The Tao was said to move without resistance or fragmentation, to nurture strength when strength is appropriate and to be able to yield when flexibility is appropriate (see Fung, 1948; Lao Tzu, 600 BC/1963). If love, power, and justice are experienced as integrated, group participants are able to respond assertively or receptively according to the dynamics of a specific encounter. They are open to the possibilities of becoming, and are receptive to their own and others' experiencing within an ongoing encounter. They also are able to experience a unification of thinking, feeling, intuition, and acting. The degree to which love, power, and justice are integrated or balanced at different times provides an indication of whether or not a group is functioning therapeutically at these periods.

Taoists say that the Tao is essentially beyond definition (Fung, 1948; Lao Tzu, 600 BC/1963). Similarly, the dynamic functioning of love, power, and justice evades full description. The purpose of delineating these elements of relationship is not to propose a complete definition of love, power, and justice. Rather, we seek to understand how the operation of love, power, and justice provides a field or context for the interactions of people in group therapy (or in any other group or relationship). We additionally endeavor to understand how the denial or distortion of one element leads to imbalanced expression of the other elements. In the same way, we find that an overemphasis of one element leads to neglect of at least one of the others. Integrated relationship is therefore understood as balance within an ever-changing dynamic. Of course, love, power, and justice never operate in a completely integrated or balanced manner in any human relationship; this gestalt also never operates in a completely imbalanced way although sometimes it can seem as if it does. It might be helpful to view the operation of love, power, and justice as a continuum that can range between being highly integrated or balanced to being highly imbalanced or hurtful.

Because the integration of love, power, and justice is centered in the present, this gestalt cannot be used as a formula for predicting how a person should grow or how the developmental stages of relationships and groups should be formed. Thus the functioning of this gestalt cannot be used to forecast the course of events that will lead a person to a balanced life. The essential unity of this gestalt allows participants in relationships to construct their being together in ways that promote their own healing and growth according to their own experience.

The reunification of love, power, and justice for a group member often occurs through a spontaneous experience that allows her or him to express and trust perceptions, to be open to feelings, and to trust in the process of sharing with others. Members can also learn from the experience of not trusting the interpersonal process of a group that has unbalanced dynamics. They may learn that relying on their own perceptions involves refraining from sharing with people not viewed as receptive or trustworthy. Essentially, however, members grow by learning that they have an awareness of timing that allows them to sense when to share with others and when not to contribute. This awareness of timing is an awareness of relatedness.

Integration of love, power, and justice cannot be defined as any type of final goal because the dynamics of relationships always require reintegration as contexts and forms of interactions change. The integration of this gestalt should therefore be viewed in terms of process and dynamics, as a movement that deepens awareness and experience and which helps direct choices and decisions. Movement toward an integrated dynamic of love, power, and justice can help group members to develop an increased motivation to initiate changes in relationships and can encourage them to develop more confidence to give voice to new expressions of self. Finding and creating a balance within the gestalt of love, power, and justice can empower a person to regard self as an initiator of change.

As members develop relationships in their group, they learn that relationship has continuous and discontinuous aspects. Some aspects of relationship are developed continuously over time, as members share, disclose, react, and elaborate themes.

Through this kind of interaction over time, members can develop increasingly rich and complex perceptions of who others are and are capable of being. The discontinuous aspect of relationship occurs through the immediacy of encounter. People are who they were not, and are not who they were. Each moment offers a fresh opportunity for discovery. Often people learn through spontaneous self-expression that they are not limited to being who they have been.

The gestalt of love, power, and justice functions, not as a machine functions, but as an organism functions. This gestalt is given form by human awareness and human spirit. Through dynamics created by the feelings and perceptions of participants in moment-to-moment encounters, this gestalt functions to give form to human relationships.

CHAPTER 6

# THE DEVELOPMENT OF THERAPEUTIC PROCESS

An integrated dynamic of love, power, and justice allows participants to express individuality and to experience communality and universality. Therefore, an optimally therapeutic group encourages the development of cohesion between individuals while also supporting members increasingly to experience themselves as free to reveal (and even celebrate) differences from others. In an effective therapeutic group, an ensemble of individuals moves from an initial awareness of separation to an increasing awareness of being connected. As connections form, members can learn about their distinctness in relation to others as well as discovering their universality.

## GROUP DEVELOPMENT AND INDIVIDUAL DEVELOPMENT

An unstructured therapy group can offer members opportunities to examine the motives, beliefs, and expectations they bring to encounters when they meet others who may become 'we'. Members can learn through experience about their tendencies to surrender their individuality in a group, to become an observer or follower, or to become an engaged and individuated participant. Members have opportunities to encounter basic human emotions and choices that are involved in the creation and use of collective realities.

Tillich (1954) has observed that people frequently relate to the groups they create as if these groups were organisms or beings. Tillich (1954) also points out that members of a group are free to come and go, whereas constituent parts of an organism are not. This freedom of movement represents a significant difference between organisms and groups. If individuals reject their own freedom of movement because they feel responsible to a group that is an entity, they deny the value of their own individuality. A more useful motive for remaining within a group is the recognition by an individual that caring and responsibility mutually involve him or her and others.

Foulkes (1957) has written that groups exist as matrices for interpersonal communication. This matrix is seen as the necessary basis for communication between individuals, a view implying that a person cannot truly become who he or she is capable of being without the existence of groups. If groups are matrices for communication, individuals can become different people in different groups, depending on how each group influences modes of communication, interaction, and experiencing. Each group has a different atmosphere based on the unique dynamic gestalt of interpersonal process. The meanings of individual interactions occur within this relational context. Interaction between participants in a group simultaneously influences, and is affected by the group matrix.

Although group dynamics affect who the individual becomes within a relational process, individuals affect how this relational process is created, maintained, and acknowledged. As members interact, they help create, maintain, and enhance the group gestalt that, if creative in its integration of love and power as justice, affects members by challenging them to grow in and through relating. This gestalt can assist them to work constructively with perceptions of self and relationships as members create a context wherein they connect meaningfully with others and communicate authentically and openly.

## INDIVIDUAL AND COLLECTIVE TRANSACTIONS

Awareness and acknowledgment of individual and collective responsibility for growth are basic for the construction of an effective therapeutic group process. One way to imagine this responsibility is to view growth as a movement that evolves through specific actions and events. If we can find specific ways in which individuals can contribute, we can then understand how growth as a principle of group development operates.

A group cannot force an individual to choose actions that foster healing and growth, although the group can provide a context that encourages caring and authentic modes of participation. Transactions can be considered as interactions that affect participants across boundaries, not merely at boundaries. If an interaction is an effect of one entity upon another, a self-actualizing transaction can be understood as an effect between entities in which they function synergistically. Through these transactions, each participant allows self to change by accepting the other into self.

Much of the impact of transactions appears to occur outside individuals' conscious focus of awareness. Group therapy can help members to recognize how these transactions alter a person's sense of self. Members can learn how specific encounters can influence them and how mutuality between members can alter the group gestalt. Individuals may perceive themselves being affected by transactions, and, at times they may experience that their group as a whole has been affected.

## THE NATURE OF GROUP PROCESS

Theorists such as Bonney (1974), Corey and Corey (1987), Page (1983b, 1984), Rogers (1970), Vander Kolk (1985), and Yalom (1995) have used a model of stages to describe the sequential progression of therapy group members' interrelatedness. Though these theorists' definitions vary, all serve as a basis to discuss perceptions that change occurs predictably within group process, that temporal as well as interpersonal effects exist, and that alterations take place in meaningful patterns between individuals who relate over time. Each stage develops from what went before and in some cases is described in relationship to what is expected to come after. Stages consistently represent a sequential ordering of interactions related to changes in gestalts of meaning for individuals and the group as a whole. The stages represent a syntax that gives overall meaning to the specific and individual interactions of participants.

### THE EVOLUTION OF GROUP PROCESS

All groups deal with achieving the degree of cohesion that the members perceive as necessary to gain what they need or want from their participation in a group. For cohesion to develop, members must create structures in the form of norms and themes that affect communication between participants. Certain norms (for example, nonviolence) and themes (for example, interpersonal healing and growth) are inherent in the situation and influence process from the initiation of a therapy group. Additionally, all groups deal with the temporal structure that forms during the beginning, middle, and ending of relationships. These three basic stages tend to evoke basic human feelings associated with beginning an association with others, working together with others, and ending one's association with others.

As has been stated, a stage-oriented model of group therapy presupposes that there is an evolutionary aspect to the development of a group. Cohen and Smith (1976) view 'evolution in the group' as an 'unfolding' and a 'development' that occurs in a process of 'gradual, orderly change from one stage to the next'. Evolution implies the existence of 'progressive states' that are expected to lead to 'improvement in group and individual effectiveness' (pp. 160–1). The idea of evolution, according to Cohen and Smith, has a Darwinian connotation that implies that effective behaviors are born and survive, whereas ineffective behaviors are extinguished. Members may learn through experience that trust, self-disclosure, and cooperation help them to use the group effectively, whereas mistrust, denial, and competition limit their ability to receive what they need and want from others.

However, the metaphor of evolution may be extended too far if we forget that individuals and groups can benefit from relaxation and free play, from temporarily abandoning concerns with survival and progress. As members move toward acceptance and freedom, they become less defensive, less concerned with how to survive in their group, and less vigilant about which behaviors should be extinguished.

Therefore, if we discuss the evolution of group process, we need to examine the playful development of themes and relationships, as well as the serious work on problems that members do. We believe that defining group process in terms of phases rather than stages allows us to stress the unpredictable features of group process as well as its more predictable aspects.

## STAGES OR PHASES IN GROUP PROCESS?

One potential limitation of defining sequential group stages is that a leader can impose his or her idea of stages on the process. A leader who wants to 'progress' to the next group stage may begin to steer the group in that direction. Sometimes leaders can unconsciously expect the stages of groups they are currently conducting to unfold in predictable ways because this has happened in past groups they have led. The group members might sense, however, that they would benefit from working at their present level of exploration. Thus, a leader who insists on moving on can create unnecessary resistance and impede the therapeutic movement of the group. If a group leader recognizes that the conceptualization of stages simply provides a convenient framework for the theoretical analysis of process, he or she will allow each group to find unique paths that fit individual members' movements towards integration of love, power, and justice within relationships.

Although unstructured group therapy is based on the assumption that structure does not need to be imposed, this theory acknowledges inherent form in the development of any group. The theory also recognizes that structures are created as leaders and members respond to their perceptions of their own and others' needs and wants. Thus, groups can be considered in terms of imposed, inherent, and created structures. Unstructured group therapy attempts to minimize imposed structures. Phases in unstructured therapy groups reflect members' coming to terms with a lack of imposed structure, their growing awareness of inherent structure, and their growing assumption of responsibility for creation of structure.

Love, power, and justice are inherent forces that interact to form structures within each group phase. Awareness, freedom, and responsibility are factors that also influence the development of modes of communication and interaction. As we have seen, these forces have a degree of predictability in their impact on the evolution of human groups because there is a universal aspect to how people interact. At the same time, there is a degree of unpredictability to the interaction of these forces within group process because each group is unique and is formed through the specific interactions of the distinct individuals who comprise the group. If we look at groups' phases rather than stages, we can infer that there is some predictability in the themes that arise when unstructured therapy groups are conducted but that the sequential ordering of these themes is relative rather than absolute, and reversible rather than irreversible.

Specific interactions are the result of the unique individuals who engage in interactions, and their results could not be meaningfully predicted without a deep personal understanding of those individuals. Even with a personal understanding of participants, prediction would be difficult, except in a general manner. Each person represents a unique and constantly changing gestalt constructed from present perspective and experience, personal history, physiology, goals, desires, and so on. Not only do complex factors influence interactions, some of these factors may change unpredictably within the present. The course and outcome for a group as a whole, or for an individual in a group, can never be considered as predetermined at the beginning of the group. Our purpose in discussing group phases should be considered less important for comprehensively predicting group behavior, and more important for understanding ongoing behavior, appreciating how the forces in a group can lead to its constructive evolution, and for setting goals within a present moment of interaction.

Identifiable themes can sometimes have an effect on the dynamics of a therapy group. A theme may develop throughout the life of a group or may appear at a particular phase. A theme may be general (for example, the importance of trust in relationships) or specific (for example, what Mary and Mark can learn from each other). Themes serve as focal points for members' awareness and conversation. Maintaining a focus on an individual's, a dyad's, or a group's theme promotes the theme's evolution. Examples of group themes that tend to develop are the group's purpose, reactions to leadership and authority, questions about personal responsibility, issues of control and security, intimacy issues, and feelings about termination. These themes are not always addressed directly; members' communications about themes can be metaphorical, can be presented in the form of humor, or can be expressed through actions and tones rather than words (McClure, 1987, 1990; Roller, 1989; Rossel, 1981).

Themes change as members develop more trust and openness for each other and in the process of the group as a whole. For example, members often need to develop much interpersonal trust before they are willing to expose and explore their intimacy issues. Cohen and Smith (1976), as well as Rogers (1970) and Yalom (1995), have examined how groups typically evolve from relatively lower levels of interpersonal trust and understanding. These authors agree on their finding that a shift of power and responsibility moves from the leader to group members as the group evolves, a finding that is consistent with the observations of psychoanalytic group therapists such as Foulkes (1975) and Wolf and Schwartz (1962).

As members' perceptions of personal power and responsibility change, the themes that they discuss usually alter. Members become more willing to confront and discuss each other's needs for control and power in interpersonal relationships. As members become more comfortable in asserting themselves, they often discuss interpersonal issues related to themes of justice. Members assert themselves in ways that reveal their perceived closeness to others. Group phases evolve through movements between and within central themes (for example, between separation and relatedness, or within increasing recognition of the reality of termination).

Group phases thus develop in a manner that might be imagined as a spiral rather than as a line. Members may leave a theme, become involved in a new meaning-orientation, and then return to the first theme. When members return to a theme, they often address it with different attitudes or feelings than they previously had. For example, group members may shift from an apparently consistent atmosphere of mutuality to repeat an earlier phase of mistrust or conflict. However, their new discussion about mistrust may demonstrate enhanced knowledge of each other's issues. Group phases can also be altered unpredictably by specific events. An unexpected conflict between two members who had previously agreed can alter the themes and dynamics about which members are concerned. If a new member enters a group or a member decides to leave, the process will be influenced (Yalom, 1995). In spite of various unpredictable occurrences, certain trends tend to be consistent within the group. Members tend to deal with issues of trust at the beginning of a group, themes related to disclosure and intimacy toward the middle phase, and feelings about ending relationships toward the termination phase of a group (for example, see Bonney, 1974; Vander Kolk, 1985).

## DEFINING GROUP PHASES

Using the Hill Interaction Matrix (HIM-G) as a measure of types and levels of interaction, we have analyzed the phases of a 16-hour-long group conducted with illicit drug users (Page, Davis, Berkow and O'Leary, 1989). The results of this analysis showed that various levels and types of interaction occurred in any given phase of the group. Whereas many types and qualities of interaction occurred during any phase, the types and qualities of interaction considered most therapeutic by the HIM-G occurred most frequently during the middle two segments of the group, rather than during the initial or ending phases. This research supports the findings of previous research conducted with unstructured 16-hour-long groups composed of illicit drug users (Page, 1982; Page and Bridges, 1983; Page, Weiss and Lietaer, 2002; Page and Wills, 1983).

The collective results of these studies indicate that the unstructured groups that were studied did not have distinct stages (on the Hill Interaction Matrix– Form B) characterized by the predominance of any one level or type of interaction. They did, however, exhibit an overall tendency to work toward the establishment of trust, then intimacy, and then towards mutual disengagement. These studies confirmed our experiential learning from participation in personal growth groups and from facilitation of various groups with physically disabled individuals, psychiatric clients of various ages and differing levels of impairment, secondary school students, and college students in Ireland (Page and O'Leary, 1992) and the United States.

We have defined five group phases that serve as a framework to explore the dynamics that form members' movements toward and through trust, intimacy, and disengagement. The five phases that we will describe are based on frequently occurring themes in groups we have led, in which we have participated, or which we have observed. We have drawn no firm lines that discretely separate portions of group members' ongoing interpersonal experiences; phases are merely convenient constructs useful for discussing the development of a relational process. Practitioners of therapy should be able to orient themselves toward group phases as a way to enhance awareness of certain key themes and messages.

## PHASES OF UNSTRUCTURED THERAPY GROUPS

The following phases are relevant to either single-session marathon groups or to ongoing unstructured therapy groups or personal growth groups that last more than ten sessions: (1) Preliminary Socialization, (2) Ambivalence Towards Authority, (3) Exploration and Self-Revelation, (4) Mutuality, and (5) Ending. These phases can be viewed as constructs around which themes and potential knowledge gained from the group can be organized. Themes may build on each other sequentially, or may appear and reappear throughout the life of a group.

### PRELIMINARY SOCIALIZATION
When participants first enter a group, they tend to feel anxious and apprehensive about what is about to happen. They often feel unsure of the degree to which they can trust the leader and the other members. Although some participants may be ready to trust in others, most members build toward it. Many members find that they need to interact with others before they have a basis for trusting them. These members may feel anxious because they hope to establish meaningful relationships with others but are uncertain about how safe it will be to do so. Such people may wonder whether if they ask for something from the group, they will become vulnerable and may be hurt or manipulated by others.

The anxieties that members initially experience are frequently based on past experiences with the process of gaining membership in a group of people. On the basis of previous experiences in social groups, members may believe that they need to find out with whom they are interacting and what consequences will follow from membership before they commit themselves to an interactive process. Some members may ostensibly express themselves openly and freely. However, they may not trust others fully and may be interacting in a pattern that is (for them) stereotypical. Most members experience initial anxiety and interact during this phase in personally safe ways.

Group participants may try to find common ground with others by talking about themselves as they would at a cocktail party. They may discuss sporting events, the political situation in the world, or may seek out information about others' occupations and domestic situations. Discussing safe topics affords participants protection while they investigate whether others in the group are approachable or are worth approaching. As members learn more about each other, they can process the ways in which they are different and similar. As their awareness of each other's lives increases, they learn which experiences are shared and which may not be.

Themes related to trust are frequently emphasized during the initial phase although these themes are frequently hidden because members generally feel each other out by interacting in stereotypical ways. Later in the life of a group, the importance of interpersonal trust is often addressed more directly and openly than in the initial group phase.

The leader of a group may need to exert special effort in remaining attentive to these apparently meaningless and superficial discussions. Yet hidden within these apparently superficial exchanges are clues about who each person is and who they may become. If the group leader disregards early exchanges as meaningless chatter, he or she will lose the opportunity to begin forming an understanding of these individuals.

It is a useful therapeutic approach for the leader to view all communication in a group as meaningful and significant. The themes upon which individuals choose to focus for a discussion of current events may later emerge in a different form as an immediate personal concern. For example, a member who discusses protest marches early in the life of a group may later express rebellion toward group norms or may question the authority of the leader or other members. If members project a great deal of emotion or animation about an apparently innocuous theme or humorous exchange, they can be communicating around a metaphorical message or theme (Rossel, 1981). Humor may represent an attempt to gain acceptance, may be used to indirectly reveal aspects of who a person is, or may be a form of resistance.

Many participants are careful when they first enter a group because they have learned from past teachings and experiences that otherness can be a dangerous aspect of interpersonal encounter. Otherness may be associated with possible threats from strangers who are perceived as possibly harboring negative intentions towards oneself or whose goals and desires are thought to be incompatible with one's own goals. When members learn about otherness, they may begin to question their own stereotypic perceptions of reality and how their unfinished business has affected the ways they have defined themselves in relationship to others. These members may need to discover how their perceptions of otherness (for example, differences in perceptions, attitudes, past experiences, desires, opinions, goals, economic status, appearance, culture, and so forth) have influenced their communication and relationship patterns in the group before they can begin to develop increased trust and empathy for certain participants.

The initial phase of the group is therefore exploratory in nature. Members may first seek to discover where and how they are similar to one another before they can feel safe to explore the extent and degree of their mutual estrangement. It is unlikely that members will begin to experience their estrangement until they feel and acknowledge that they want or need something from one another. Some members may take risks that help them to establish whether they can give something worthwhile to another, such as honest feedback or open revelations of self.

Members who initiate personal contact and self-disclosure early in the life of the group may find themselves accepted and cared about. They may initiate a change in the group atmosphere that leads to more disclosure and to work on personal issues. However, if their timing is off, such members may be rebuffed. This experience can hurt a member's sense of confidence in relating to others in the group. Members whose timing is off when they decide to reveal themselves to others may also sometimes be confirming their own negative expectations that others are untrustworthy and not accepting. Although it can be painful when members are rejected, these rebuffs can also lead to learning about being with others and can be viewed as part of the process by which members learn how to establish appropriate interpersonal boundaries. Members can benefit from learning that they can survive rebuffs from others without suffering catastrophic consequences.

There are often cases where the preliminary socialization phase of a group is very brief. Members may have an interest in interacting directly and openly, and if one member risks disclosure, that may lead to another member reciprocating. It would be a mistake to believe that all groups involve prolonged social chat or a continuing phase where members experience ongoing reluctance to share openly.

The atmosphere early in the life of a group may move quickly towards increased openness or may be constricted simply because members are uncomfortable and uncertain in the group therapy setting. Some members may additionally want to make a point of expressing their independence from group norms or indifference to demands for sharing. As a group evolves towards creative justice, such members may become more comfortable in their interactions. If they have successfully established comfortable boundaries, they may subsequently relax and decrease defensiveness. The healing group does not force members to make certain choices through peer pressure or the imposition of norms by the leader; rather it provides the opportunity for people to experience freedom to choose how to interact with one another.

In unstructured group therapy, members may test their freedom by expressing their resistance to the goals that they believe that the leader seems to have. They may express negative feelings about their leader if that person has presented herself or himself authoritatively or in an aloof manner. Members may show mistrust toward specific others or the group as a whole. If participants feel free to resist possible impositions from the leader or to express doubts or anxieties about group process, their openness can usefully lay a foundation for later perceptions of mutual responsibility. If members do not feel able to express doubts or resistance, they may never perceive themselves as being responsible for determining group norms and as being free to reveal negative feelings and attitudes.

### AMBIVALENCE TOWARDS AUTHORITY

This phase of the group generally evolves from the previous phase in which members tend covertly or unconsciously to form impressions of the leader's persona and character. Members develop a sense of the degree to which they can trust their leader and by extension the group that the leader has organized. On the one hand, members may feel frustrated if their leader is too distant, aloof, or analytical about group events (Leszcz, 1992). A leader who is experienced as consistently maintaining an emotionally distant position is likely to seem uncaring, self-protective, or unapproachable. On the other hand, a leader who establishes a powerful presence that demands attention from members may be perceived as imposing, intimidating, or superior. Such leaders tend to elicit overly dependent responses from group members in therapy settings (McClure, 1990).

One reason that the group participants might be anxious about the leader is because they are aware that this person often has the power to hurt them in various ways. For instance, the leader may work in a hospital setting where he or she can make recommendations that alter the course of treatment or the rewarding of privileges. The leader in a mental health clinic may be required to report to judges if members are receiving treatment as the result of legal proceedings or have been mandated to receive treatment by the court. In prisons or in other treatment settings, there may be concern that the leader cannot be trusted to maintain confidentiality. These kinds of role conflicts may make it difficult for the leader to gain the trust of members.

Members may additionally be influenced by the images and wishes that they project onto the leader because of their past experiences with authority figures. Psychoanalytic theorists such as Wolf and Schwartz (1962) have emphasized this transference aspect of members' patterns of relating to group leaders. Transference is likely to show itself through ambivalence related to feelings of attraction and anxiety that are expressed toward authority.

According to Yalom (1980), transference can contribute to members perceiving a therapist as an omnipotent rescuer. Such members may then experience love and hate for a leader who is longed for as a rescuer and resentment as a withholder of rescue. In particular, members who were affected by abusive relationships with significant others in childhood may continue to hold deep feelings of mistrust and anxiety towards authority figures, coupled with a desire to receive love from a powerful other. As they learn that the leader cannot rescue them from themselves or make them feel significant, the members will hopefully begin to take increased personal responsibility for themselves in the group.

Although members may rebel against or refuse to cooperate with suggestions from their leader, they may also at the same time expect their leader to provide directions or to clarify issues. Thus, if a group's leader is attacked by one member, another member may defend the leader or may launch a counterattack against the first member. A member who confronts the leader may back down if he or she perceives the leader as vulnerable. Members may not only question the leader but may begin to ask her or him for help on personal issues. A member's ambivalence may then continue to be expressed in the form of difficulty accepting help that has been requested, responses that demonstrate a lack of listening, or dissatisfaction that the problem is not adequately 'solved' by the leader and the group.

Because the leader is viewed as the organizer of their group, members who criticize or express frustration with the group may be indirectly expressing frustration with the leader. Members may express frustration and resentment toward another member while at the same time blaming the leader for much of their anger. For example, if a member is attacked for talking too much, members may also resent their leader for failing to restrain this person's actions or failing to provide direction and structure. As their group is increasingly experienced as safe, these members may become willing to express feelings directly toward their leader. The leader can then help them to understand how members can become responsible for generating their own directions and structures.

Members may express anger or ambivalence toward the therapist as a kind of test. This test may help members to discover whether there are unspoken limits that regulate authentic expressions of self. Although participants may feel hostility toward the leader, they also tend unconsciously to wish for the leader to withstand their anger and to help them move toward a balanced and mutually responsible dynamic. Members usually want opportunities to move toward creative justice, and will spontaneously create these opportunities if given the chance.

The group benefits if the leader can intuit the function that a particular expression of anger serves for a group. If a leader prematurely acts to confront what seems to be a member's inappropriate hostility, this action will have implications for the role that other members will come to expect the leader to play. The leader may be seen as expressing his or her perception that other members need to be taken care of or protected; a leader who protects members will influence the formation of group norms concerning responsibility. Creative justice can also be impaired if a group leader is perceived as someone who takes sides or who is highly evaluative.

A leader can react effectively in challenging situations by remaining aware that attacks from group members may have a constructive purpose on the group's dynamics. If the leader responds to expressions of anger as if she or he had been rejected as a person, this reaction will have effects on the group's perception of the leader's power and perhaps on how involved the members are willing to become in the group. If ambivalence and overt or covert expressions of anger can be treated by the therapist as meaningful communications of emotion rather than as a threat to his or her control of the group, interpersonal dynamics in the group are more likely to move towards listening, giving, and acceptance.

If members are accepting of a complacent atmosphere where risks of self-disclosure are avoided, a group leader may wish to challenge others by expressing her or his awareness of superficiality of the communication or by discussing specific aspects of this that she or he perceives as not being genuine. This kind of challenge can stimulate members to respond by expressing their dissatisfaction with the leader or by taking risks to reveal self to others.

Members of groups conducted in specific settings may have similar backgrounds that create common assumptions about authority figures. Illicit drug abusers, for instance, frequently exhibit overt or covert discomfort or hostility when they approach authority figures in a therapy situation. Unstructured therapy with illicit drug users often brings anger to the surface, anger that often seems disproportionate to the present situation (Page, 1979). Members may attack the personality or capability of their group leader. They may pointedly discuss the unfairness of authorities or society, and they may focus on incidents in which they received unfair treatment from past authority figures. If a leader clearly makes an effort to listen and to understand, the participants may begin to re-evaluate how they perceive authority in this particular situation.

Members may allow or encourage one member to express anger because they can allow this person to be their spokesperson and thus can avoid responsibility. Participants can avoid responsibility by directing anger toward a safe target (for example, 'the system') or by encouraging one person to act out the angry feelings shared by others (Gans, 1989; Unger, 1990). If members covertly act out their anger, this manipulative behavior can lead to passive-aggressive interactions. Passive-aggressive strategies allow members to withhold feelings and can have a detrimental impact on the group norms concerning honesty and openness. On the other hand, as members establish a free and caring atmosphere, passive-aggressive strategies become increasingly unnecessary and are perceived as counterproductive by members.

Members who are addicted to rage may feel very comfortable expressing anger although they may have blocked awareness of what it is about (unfinished business). A therapy group can provide such persons with a setting where they learn that it can be safe to explore submerged feelings of hurt and vulnerability that are intertwined with compulsive expressions of anger. Once anger or frustration has been expressed, members can receive help with the issue of how they can effectively act on these feelings in a socially constructive manner.

Many people in our culture have problems acting on their anger in a positive way (Rubin, 1969; Travis, 1982). For example, people may ignore or stifle angry feelings, may displace anger onto inappropriate targets, or may communicate anger in hostile ways instead of ones that invite communication. Participants may have learned in their families or peer groups to avoid anger or other strong feelings or to use anger to control others. Moreover, men and women often learn different rules for dealing with certain emotions. Men may feel that anger is acceptable but sadness or vulnerability is not. Women, on the other hand, may have learned that expressions of vulnerability are appropriate but anger is not. As members begin to express anger or other strong feelings, they can experience their group as a place where they do not have to limit themselves to stereotypical reactions and interactions.

# Development of Therapeutic Process

Some groups may not involve a phase in which angry or ambivalent feelings are openly expressed. Some groups may not present opportunities for the members to work on angry or ambivalent feelings they have; other groups may contain members who do not have many issues related to anger or ambivalence towards authority. Effective group work can sometimes be conducted without giving overt attention to issues related to anger. However, anger is often considered to be a socially dangerous emotion, and the members themselves are not likely to propose that their group atmosphere shift so that individuals have increased opportunities to work on anger. This is likely to be true even for participants who have many angry feelings.

Once the members are able to express anger or ambivalence towards the leader, they often learn that it is safe to express anger in the group about family issues or other situations they face. Members can then receive feedback from other participants about how they are handling the situations that make them angry in addition to being able to express repressed angry feelings. If members feel free to express feelings of anger, their awareness of personal responsibility is likely to be enhanced. This can occur because once anger is expressed, the members can make choices about how they deal in the future with the situations that have caused their anger. A group setting can be a useful environment for participants to deal with past and present situations in which they have felt abused or frustrated. Other members can help a participant to look at options, to recognize strengths, and to process the experience and meaning of feelings.

As members discuss negative feelings, they become more consciously aware of choices they are making and of the personal and interpersonal consequences of various feelings that they are experiencing. They may learn that negative feelings represent opportunities to learn about justice (by learning about perceived injustice), power (as members make themselves known to others), and love (as members give and receive acceptance and caring about the pain of others). Therefore, dealing with ambivalent reactions to authority and to group process is an important foundation for moving toward integrated interpersonal dynamics in a group situation.

Members' basic ambivalence frequently is based on a desire to be included in their group coupled with anxiety about being dominated or smothered by it. This anxiety may be expressed by demonstrations that one cannot be cajoled into becoming involved with what is going on in the group. In the phase of ambivalence, members are often unsure of their motives. They may express anger although they also feel a desire to join or may attempt to join in ways that also demonstrate a need for control.

The phase of ambivalence toward authority is thus one of membership versus self-exclusion. Members learn from their interpersonal process as they work together to determine a direction for their group in spite of equivocal feelings about belonging. They learn how and when each participant seeks inclusion or self-exclusion. Some participants may want to belong and be accepted, but they may not want to be constrained by the expectations and demands that a group can make on them.

If members can begin to work through their ambivalent feelings about being in an unstructured therapy group, they can facilitate an open atmosphere for the discussion and expression of feelings. Confrontation and questioning that moves members towards greater responsibility can grow from challenges to the leader, challenges between members, or self-confrontation that members disclose to others. As members decide to work through their ambivalent or negative feelings, they may develop trust through a process of shared experiencing and are likely increasingly to facilitate each other's self-revelation.

## EXPLORATION AND SELF-REVELATION

The assessment that members make about the trustworthiness of their group may be cognitive and may reflect judgments about how accepting group members have overtly shown themselves to be. Additionally, members' sense of the trustworthiness of the group is influenced by unspoken norms that regulate self-disclosure, and by intuitive awareness of emotional safety (Napier and Gershenfeld, 1987).

As some members reveal more of their thoughts and feelings, others become more aware of these members as people who are present with them. If members value the interpersonal learning that begins to occur, they can help each other to explore individual's experiences and concerns and the meanings of ongoing interactions. Mutual assistance in exploration requires members to become sensitive to the issue of imposition of values and directions. As members learn how they can facilitate each other's exploration of self and experience, they also learn to be aware of each other's defenses and vulnerabilities. This awareness can help them to move towards just norms to regulate exploration and revelation and towards an acceptance of the various ways that individuals define and maintain interpersonal boundaries.

The interpersonal dynamics of love, power, and justice evolve toward integration in an escalating manner. As one member risks exposing a vulnerable area and is heard and accepted, other members often spontaneously begin to do the same. Members' desires to move toward more personal levels of relationship are 'triggered' by one member who shares at a personal level at the right time in a group's process. The timing is right for this triggering if other members have sensed that they would benefit from sharing personal feelings and problems, but have not yet acted on these intuitions.

The interpersonal dynamics that assist integration can also be sidetracked or can dissipate due to a lack of involvement of the leader or members (Gemmill and Wynkoop, 1991). Interruptions and other shifts away from a meaningful focus can occur if interpersonal events have been experienced as unusually intense, demanding, or chaotic. These shifts may provide a method to avoid a challenge or growing conflict but can also serve to regulate interactions so that members maintain a comfortable sense of distance and safety. When members discuss especially intense personal issues, such as family problems, interruptions can also provide a way of allowing the participants to take a break from what is being discussed and to return to the discussion later when they are ready. Interruptions can occur in the form of humor, abrupt shifts in topics, or assertions of self that ignore the current interpersonal process.

Members' assertion of who they are in the group can be viewed as an expression of personal power. Power can be asserted within the context of awareness of interpersonal process or with a lack of awareness. During the phase of exploration, members learn how their assertions of self can facilitate learning or can interrupt it. Members are also likely to encounter their wishes to be approved of and understood during this phase. Their motivation toward love influences the level of closeness that participants seek with each other, and their fears of closeness affect how much they are willing to disclose and express. Members learn that they must find a workable balance between a need for safety and a motivation to take interpersonal risks. If interpersonal safety occurs that allows risk-taking, individuals are likely to experience excitement rather than boredom (Perls, Hefferline and Goodman, 1951/1980).

At times, the influence of the group atmosphere that encourages the mutual sharing of problems can have a noticeable impact on individual members. A member may suddenly share a problem or concern that she or he has not confided in others outside the group. Members may have the experience of disclosing at a level of intimacy that is unusual and unexpected for them. For example, in a therapy group conducted by one of the authors with prison inmates, a member disclosed obviously deep and uncomfortable feelings of rage at his father, who had sexually abused his sister. This individual had not intended to share these feelings when he joined the group and did not appear to have been consciously aware of how deep and disturbing they were. Because there was a level of mutual acceptance and concern established in the group, these feelings spontaneously 'came to the surface'. The unconscious desire of this member for reunification, his need to assert his own perceptions, and the current level of creative justice in the group were all contributing elements. In turn, this member's self-exploration and disclosure led to the same from another member who was dealing with similar problems.

As support and mutuality begin to develop between members, the scope of personal disclosures tends to increase. Participants express aspects of who they are aware of being, who they are aware of having been, who they see themselves becoming, and their problems or concerns. Members may experience their ongoing relationships with each other as increasingly meaningful. They discover both their similarities and differences. Their similarities are likely to include shared emotions, such as love, sorrow, or fear; perspectives; and life experiences. Members may find that they have similar problems in dealing with relationships, self-assertion, and anger, in developing self-esteem, in coping with depression, or in dealing with issues of loss or death. Differences that may surface can be related to individuals' backgrounds and living environments, to socioeconomic and class distinctions, to unique ways of perceiving events, or to idiosyncratic patterns in relationships.

Although various levels of sympathy and empathy can develop around members' shared concerns and feelings, members may not fully encourage each other's actualization of self if support is limited to those aspects of others' experiencing that is similar to one's own. Self-actualization involves acceptance and development of unique aspects of being-in-the-world, as well as universal and shared aspects. The phase of exploration and self-revelation inevitably increases members' awareness of their differences as well as their similarities. Although people generally feel comfortable approving of those who seem similar, their developing awareness of differences creates important opportunities to move toward integrated and open relationship dynamics. The integration of love, power, and justice develops as members respond to the challenge of accepting and caring about others while respecting and acknowledging those aspects of others' lives and selves that are different from their own.

Conversely, if group members overemphasize similarities in beliefs and experiences, they can avoid the difficult work of exploration in an atmosphere of freedom. Group members can collude to maintain an artificial atmosphere of homogeneity (a distorted form of love), may adopt limiting norms (a restrictive form of justice), and may create subtle or overt penalties for those whose perceptions or experiences are too divergent (a misuse of power). During this phase of a group, a group's leader can assist the development of integrated relationships by supporting those who question norms, by assisting those who wish to express what they are experiencing and observing, and by encouraging those who may feel unsupported or rejected.

Besides creating directions that facilitate exploration, members can respond to self-disclosures by providing comments that demonstrate caring and facilitate learning. Empathic responses and absence of pressure, particularly as members reveal their vulnerabilities, are valuable contributions to an atmosphere of safety (Korda and Pancrazio, 1989). These kinds of responses help participants to reveal themselves fully and to receive feedback that might be uncomfortable or disturbing to their defined images of self.

During the phase of exploration, some members are likely to experience a contradiction between their desire to belong and their wish to demonstrate their uniqueness. Members may also experience a conflict between their desires to conform to obviously acceptable areas for exploration and their desires to test the boundaries that have developed. This kind of dilemma is likely to develop for an individual who has a pressing need to work on a problem or who enjoys the stimulation of emotional openness. Following the phase of ambivalence towards authority, members often feel free to explore differences and investigate conflicting needs or attitudes.

Creative cohesion can increase when members deal with an emotional conflict between members. Such a conflict may arise if a member presents a problem or mode of relationship that challenges the stereotypes or expectations held by others. For example, members may have difficulty accepting feelings or opinions voiced by someone who is in some sense in the minority. Some minorities may be more acceptable in a given group than others. In a group of well-educated college students, for instance, expressions of values associated with African-Americans or lesbians may be more acceptable than those associated with drug-addicts or racists. For some members, problems associated with the experience of sexual abuse from an alcoholic parent could be unfamiliar and difficult to hear. Creative cohesion can be created in these situations if members learn that their group can grow by demonstrating that members can acknowledge and accept differing perspectives, backgrounds, life experiences and controversial issues that arise among the members.

As members explore and reveal themselves to each other in an unstructured group, one or more themes will usually be developed as the basis for their ongoing interaction. During this phase, themes are oriented to more personal concerns of members and grow out of their need to make sense of their interactions, their desire to communicate meaningfully, and their maintenance of cohesion in the process of discourse. Themes are structures created by members that allow them to relate themselves to each other.

Themes can be categorized in many ways, and a nearly infinite number of potential themes exist. Some questions, however, are typical during this phase. What does it mean to care about another person? What is the meaning of my anger? What is the connection between hurt and anger? How can I express myself so that you'll understand? Participants may also state, 'Relationships are vital to my life', 'I feel hurt when you say "no"', 'Change is possible but scary', 'Life is unfair', 'Love is developed through giving', or 'Coping with loss is terribly difficult'. A continuing interaction between two or more members can also form a theme around which other members orient their interactions. Other participants may learn from processing their observations about these interactions between specific members and may refer to this knowledge throughout a group.

Group phases are formed by the themes with which members concern themselves. As we stated earlier in this chapter, these themes can develop in slightly different forms across separate group phases. For example, the theme of questioning authorities may arise during the socialization phase, direct questioning of the leader may occur during the phase of ambivalence, and disclosure of hurt suffered with parents may occur during the phase of exploration. Awareness of patterns developed to deal with feelings of hurt may be understood in terms of ongoing group relationships during the phase of mutuality. These themes develop as members find areas where they have shared problems or concerns.

Structured therapy groups usually provide a predetermined thematic focus, and members of these may work on knowledge and skills that relate to that particular focus. Unstructured therapy groups encourage members to create their own foci. Therefore, members of unstructured groups may need to cope with ambiguity to learn how to assume responsibility for focusing on themes. During the phase of exploration, members begin to develop themes that allow them to deepen their awareness of each other's personality and life experience.

Certain interpersonal skills can be enhanced through the process of participating in an unstructured therapy group. Essentially, these are relationship skills associated with the acceptance of differences, the willingness to listen and to share, and a decision to engage in open and authentic communication. These skills are not taught but are learned through a process of participation. As members explore issues with each other, their interest is usually directed to learning about each other's experience, rather than to learning relationship skills. Therefore, unstructured groups facilitate the development of these skills by encouraging the development of relationships. As members become willing to reveal who they are to others, they facilitate the potential development of interpersonal relatedness.

As members explore their feelings, experiences, personal problems, and goals, they may feel relief and may become more aware of freedom. This awareness grows as they find that they are able to be honest with others about who they are and what they want. Members frequently seek and receive feedback from others that can lead to new approaches to situations and relationships both within and outside the group or to increased acceptance of themselves and others. They may encourage each other to explore new patterns of relating to others, or to take risks in forming directions or expressing themselves. In the process, a new level of mutuality and involvement is achieved. Transactions that lead to I-Thou relationship begin to emerge as possibilities for members who are willing to contact each other openly and fully.

## PATTERNS OF MUTUAL RELATIONSHIP

A person can open to another, can allow self to be influenced, and can resonate with others' experiences. Yet human beings are limited in the degree to which they can share themselves with others. The ability to share experientially is constrained by time limitations, physical limitations and inadequacies of language and nonverbal forms of communication. An individual's interpretation of another persons' experiencing is inevitably influenced by the individual's ability to be aware, focus of attention, and perceptual map. No one can know the experience of another the way that the other knows it. In spite of these limitations, people attempt to share important aspects of themselves and hope to feel understood and accepted by others for who they are.

As we have already seen, group participants may hold back aspects of themselves and their experience that they believe to be fear-provoking or undesirable. Other members may have convinced themselves that they are not interesting or worth knowing. Individuals frequently judge themselves more harshly than others do. The phase of mutuality tends to present a challenge to members. During this phase, members can allow boundaries within self and between themselves to become more permeable to emotionally meaningful issues and aspects of awareness (Gemmill, 1989; Gemmill and Wynkoop, 1991).

Besides safeguarding the comfort achieved with adherence to social roles, people may also keep part of themselves hidden from others (and from themselves) out of fear of discovering who they really are or might become. During the phase of mutuality, members can experience the quality of interpersonal acceptance that can facilitate work to reclaim these hidden aspects. Individually, this kind of work involves the owning of negative emotions that individuals have previously only seen in others. Mutuality in relationships facilitates this work to own negative feelings because participants perceive that their vulnerability won't be used against them.

Anxiety about increasing awareness of 'negative' aspects of self can form a therapeutic impasse frequently associated with feelings of shame and self-blame. An impasse for an individual represents an inability of this person to recognize or let others recognize something about himself or herself that remains hidden and that is a source of shame or guilt. An impasse for a group often represents a crisis that occurs when members are unable or unwilling to deal with or resolve crises that occur in the group; these crises can arise because of the impasses that individuals are experiencing that affect the group. The phase of mutuality is the time in a group's life when members, individually and collectively, are most likely to confront impasses that they have previously ignored or avoided.

An impasse generally requires prolonged work in awareness and often cannot be resolved in a single meeting (see Perls, 1992). Therefore, awareness of an individual or collective impasse should not lead to attempts to manufacture a breakthrough but to attempts to grow through honest self-examination and confrontation. Participants in therapy grow if their struggle with an impasse results in increased energy, awareness, and willingness to live life more fully (Korb, Gorrell and Van De Riet, 1989).

During the phase of mutuality, members can address individual and collective aspects of such an impasse. They can examine individual splits in awareness, splits between subgroups, and ways that the group as a whole has avoided dealing with conflicts or negativity (Agazarian, 1992). Members can also choose to avoid awareness of an impasse and thus avoid anxiety about openness and interdependence. A group can choose to stagnate within the phase of mutuality by having a meandering, unfocused discussion. Additionally, members can undermine trust by voicing judgments of others based on stereotypical views or by ignoring aspects of others' communication that question individual or collective expectations. Members can move from the beginnings of mutuality to a phase of superficiality in communication.

The risk that is involved in exposing one's being to another is that one will be misunderstood, harshly evaluated, rejected, or imposed upon. There is also the risk of exposing one's being in areas in which one perceives oneself to be vulnerable. In addition, there is uncertainty in revealing longings for love and justice that have previously been denied or shut out of awareness. By reconnecting with these longings, members allow themselves the opportunity to experience reunification with others. Individuals subjectively experience certain aspects of their lives and selves as more central to their process of being than other aspects (Combs and Snygg, 1959; Mahoney, 1990). Certain aspects of experience and self are more intimately associated with being because they reflect vulnerabilities, needs, desires, and hopes. These aspects of experience are more likely to emerge as central themes during the phase of mutuality.

Mutuality that develops in a therapy group intensifies the group principle: that what goes around comes around. Members may respond quickly and spontaneously to those who are perceived as subverting movement toward mutual awareness. For example, members who unduly criticize or label others are likely to receive feedback from others about the effects of these actions. Members move toward mutuality by confronting self-created interpersonal barriers to intimacy and freedom. As members move towards increasing intimacy, they also learn about their own resistance to it.

Participants are more likely to confront what they perceive as each other's self-deceptions, games, anxieties, and self-defeating strategies as they become more comfortable with honest expressions in their group (Berne, 1964; Rogers, 1970). They may give feedback that is subtly blaming or may give responses that are clear and direct. Members may also respond in ways that are imaginative and emotional. Members who feel that others in the group have attempted to impose on them or to manipulate them may learn that they are accepted even if they express perceptions of unjust treatment. If participants have been harboring unexpressed frustrations about their group or about specific members, they are likely to express these during the development of mutuality in relationships.

Members tend to become relatively relaxed and open in their interactions during the mutuality phase. Participants are likely then to decrease reliance on their leader for cues on how to create their interpersonal process. As they place less dependence on a leader, members demonstrate a movement from tributive justice (that confers status on those who are powerful) toward creative justice. Participants question the imposition of values and do not respect or honor conformity for its own sake. If members express negative feelings during this phase, some of these may represent dissatisfaction with interactions that lack creative justice. For example, members may express dissatisfaction with themselves or others if they perceive responses as highly predictable, inflexible, or incomplete. Participants increasingly display intuitive, spontaneous and uncensored responses during this phase.

During the phase of mutuality, listening, giving, and accepting are likely to become noticeably and actively employed in members' interactions. Participants have gained experiential learning during the course of their group concerning how to disclose their perceptions of self and others and how to use these disclosures to create interactions in which mutual involvement is enhanced. At times, the experience of interpersonal acceptance may deepen to the point that members express loving feelings toward others and show that they feel sincerely cared for. The *agape* form of love may become evident in the group as a deep level of interpersonal acceptance and mutual respect. The *philia* aspect of love also plays an important role in the life of the group during the phase of mutuality as members are increasingly able to acknowledge how specific others in the group have contributed to their experience and understanding.

A majority of group members may sometimes be relating on the level of mutuality while one or two other members are resisting this way of relating. The dynamic element of reuniting love is often expressed by members who reach out to those who have distanced themselves, have withdrawn, or have disengaged from contacts that seemed intense or perhaps threatening. Reuniting love is not expressed as a demand or imposition upon reluctant group members; the possibility of acceptance is generally extended to those who seem to feel that they have not been included. Members commonly can accept differences in each other's need for distance and desire to communicate during this group phase.

A crisis can occur for the group if a member is so threatened by the growing intimacy in the group that he or she begins to act out this discomfort in ways that interfere with communication. Acting out in a group therapy context involves behaviors that subvert the growing closeness of members (for example, through unjust accusations or through dramatic expressions of feeling that serve to interrupt communication or that distract attention from developing relationships). Yalom (1995) defines acting out in group therapy as a type of resistance where the patient refuses either to examine his or her own behavior or to allow others to do so.

Nonverbal expressions of disinterest or boredom, indirectly expressed hostility, withholding of feelings after beginning a confrontation, or resentment expressed toward members who seem to be enjoying acceptance from others may be part of such acting out. Additionally, a member may insist on keeping the group's attention for a prolonged time while she or he discusses an issue with very little focus on feelings. This long discussion may serve to interrupt patterns of mutuality that were previously being expressed and worked on.

Members often learn about themselves by working together to resolve interpersonal crises that occur in the group. They can gain insight by receiving feedback about how their own behavior and unfinished business have contributed to a crisis occurring. If the crisis is successfully resolved, the members can additionally learn about how to establish new relationship styles with one another that are more helpful in promoting effective communication. As the members learn how to deal with crises in the group, they learn facilitative approaches of dealing with interpersonal conflict that can help them to improve the quality of their relationships outside of the group.

While acting out can be a problem for the group to deal with, so can the ways that participants defensively define which member attitudes or behaviors are undesirable or unacceptable. For example, members' images of a worthwhile group can function similarly to self-images that define desirable feelings and behaviors and exclude undesirable ones. Just as effective unstructured group therapy challenges self-images that restrict individual growth, this therapy can challenge images that restrict growth for the group as a whole. The member who confronts the group by taking a deviant stance may therefore actually be allowing other participants to bring into awareness a conflict in the overall group dynamics of love, power, and justice.

Members become willing to try to understand and work with the deviant thoughts and actions of others during the phase of mutuality. They become willing to discuss how their own attitudes have shaped the ways they have reacted in the group to members who are perceived as threatening or different. Sometimes participants can have a strong emotional reaction to an individual they see as being deviant. They may attack this individual as a scapegoat rather than recognize their own needs for group cohesion. By coming to terms with their own strong feelings, they can extend acceptance towards a member whom they previously wanted to reject.

During the phase of full mutuality, members develop awareness of a shared and interdependent context for their communications. This context is an optimal environment for the development of I-Thou relations between members. Although members are likely to move towards this form of relationship, they may not fully experience it; after all, it is an ideal state.

Group participants often find that they more easily establish genuine I-Thou relatedness with other members than with the leader (Yalom, 1995). If members are able to accept and affirm each other's uniqueness, they are likely to feel that this affirmation is fully genuine. Affirmation from a leader may be experienced as genuine but also as conditioned by the role of leadership. Similarly, members are likely to believe that they can more fully give to other participants than to their leader. They are likely to perceive that these others may need something from them, and these people are less restricted than the leader in personally asking for something from them.

The members additionally may believe that the leader will feel successful if they are able to find ways to generate interpersonal healing and to experience growth. Of course, if members concern themselves with meeting the leader's wants, they may distort their own directions for growth. Therefore, effective leaders cultivate a willingness to allow mistakes and failures in areas they might think are important. The less that a leader needs to feel successful, the more she or he can contribute to the atmosphere of freedom that promotes healing and growth.

During the phase of mutuality, the leader is more likely to reveal himself or herself as a person with hopes, needs, and wants than during other phases. This self-revelation should not be made in order to receive therapy from others; attempting to do so can detract from the personal growth of the members. However, appropriate use of self as a more fully interactive participant can serve as a leader's acknowledgment of mutuality and can assist movement toward creative justice.

As interactions move towards mutuality, members tend to mirror each other's growing openness and are likely to see themselves as altered by those who have allowed themselves to be altered. This mirroring effect occurs in individual

140

relationships as well but can be greatly enhanced by the nature of collective participation in an unstructured therapeutic group. One person's affirmation of personal power opens the way for others to assert their power. Potentially, a network of I-Thou relatedness can evolve through this process.

Typically, members share most about who they are during the phase when relationships move toward mutuality and begin to withdraw as they deal with termination of the group (Vander Kolk, 1985). The termination phase represents the ending of the life of the group or the participation of a particular member. Recognition of the therapeutic power of the termination stage of a therapy group arises from our recognition that dealing with endings is an often difficult and meaningful aspect of interpersonal relationships.

## ENDING

A person who is able to accept and integrate the meaning of loss is more likely to risk the openness and caring that characterizes intimacy and mutuality. People frequently hold back from the possibilities for I-Thou relationship because they fear the likelihood of losing what they have worked to develop. Additionally, many people have unfinished business related to previous losses they have experienced. They may refuse intimacy to avoid experiencing again painful feelings that they have not accepted and integrated. The phase of ending is potentially therapeutic in part because members may become more open to integrating experiences of loss.

Members, of course, have some awareness that their group will end from its inception. They may have addressed some termination issues during previous phases of group process. These interactions may have involved certain members' threats to leave the group or members actually leaving. These may have also involved expressions of sadness that one will have to let go of relationships that are developing.

If a participant leaves an ongoing group or if it ends, members are likely to experience ending differently than they would if they were terminating a one-day group or a weekend group. One difference is that an ongoing group oftentimes comes to represent a stable and continuing source of support and understanding, whereas participants in a one-time group do not develop the same kind of expectations. If a member leaves an ongoing group, he or she may need to deal with the loss of ongoing support and concern from the other members. Those who remain must deal with the experience of losing someone whose presence and participation have lent a unique quality to their group. Issues of abandonment may arise for some members who remain in the group, and abandonment issues and fears of independence may arise for the one who leaves.

Elizabeth Kübler-Ross (1975), who worked extensively with dying patients, views death as 'the final stage of growth'. She writes 'when it is the evening of our life we will hopefully have a chance to look back and say: "It was worthwhile because I have really lived"' (p. 126). This hope is also our wish for how participants will experience the termination stage of a therapy group. We hope that members will feel that the group has been a place where they have really lived. Unstructured group therapy will have proven to be effective if the members have moved towards an integrated relationship dynamic through the process of opening themselves to others. If members have used their experience to move toward an integrated process of relationship that can be renewed and recreated in ongoing encounters, then the ending phase is a transition that can lead to continued growth in awareness that is self-directed and self-organized.

Kübler-Ross (1975) also writes that death is avoided as an issue because it 'reminds us of our human vulnerability' (p. 5). Similarly, members may be reluctant to address termination as an issue. Members in addition differ in how they deal with the termination of a group. Some participants may want to review past events, others may want to talk about their future, and still others may want to deal with their present feelings about leaving other members. Whereas members during the phase of mutuality tend to give clear signals about their emotional reactions to events, clear communication may be less evident in the termination phase. The participants frequently experience feelings of isolation, aloneness, or loss but may have difficulty expressing these feelings directly. Members can help each other if they are able to say goodbye and can openly discuss their feelings of sadness and loss.

Sometimes the members will spontaneously discuss feelings of sadness they have about their group ending but at other times they will avoid this topic. If the leader believes that the members need help in discussing the end of their group, she or he may decide to ask the members directly how they feel about this upcoming event. Sufficient group time needs to be allowed for this to occur. It is also in the main not helpful for the leader to encourage the members to make plans for a future meeting where they can renew their former group relationships. This is often an unrealistic goal and making such plans can sometimes allow the members and leader to avoid dealing with difficult issues related to the ending of the group. There may, however, be some situations where having such reunions is feasible although planning for these events should not prevent the members and leader from dealing with termination issues in a complete manner.

Although members may want to continue their contact and sharing with others, they may also be aware that separating from others creates distance. Participants may experience ambivalence between feelings of being connected and separateness. If members have had ambivalence about ending past relationships, an echo of these ambivalent feelings can arise for them as they terminate with their group. Some members may again experience feelings of abandonment. They may try to cling to others or may react by acting aloof and unconcerned. Participants may be maintaining a pattern of dealing with termination that is continued from past relationships.

Ending sometimes brings unfinished business to the surface, particularly if someone has been 'sitting on their feelings' about previous incidents and interactions.

# Development of Therapeutic Process

At times it is appropriate for members to deal with their unfinished business during this group stage. This may especially be the case if members have unfinished business with one another that can be discussed and resolved at this stage of the group. Unfinished business, on the other hand, can at other times provide a way for participants to hold on to the group at a time when letting go is most appropriate. The leader usually will choose not to encourage members to bring up new, emotionally charged personal problems at this stage because there is generally not enough time for them to gain closure on what is discussed. Most participants will hesitate to bring up emotionally charged personal issues at the time of termination.

A difficulty that some members may have with accepting the end of their group is that losses can cause setbacks for people. Members may have experienced deaths or significant losses in the past that contribute to them having difficulties during this stage. Sometimes the leader may need to assist the group in devoting time to these members to help them express their feelings or what they are experiencing. If a participant is experiencing unusual levels of anxiety, resentment, depression, or guilt, the leader or others can assist this individual by providing encouragement and possibly references to pursue additional therapy.

It is to be expected that most participants will have difficulty gaining full closure on their experience of ending. Whether a participant will be able to accept lack of closure comfortably is likely to be related to this person's capacity to accept incompleteness as an unavoidable aspect of life experience. Acceptance of incompleteness is a healthy response to termination insofar as all loose ends cannot be tied up, all possibilities cannot be explored, and movement toward the future opens up unknown territory.

Most theorists who describe the developmental process of unstructured therapy present the most therapeutic time in a group as the phase of mutuality (for example, Rogers, 1970; Yalom, 1995). Theorists rightly view the establishment of trust and development of potential I-Thou relatedness as a central healing dynamic that unstructured therapy has to offer. Because members tend to create interpersonal distance during the ending phase, it can be construed as less than optimal. As we have seen, participants generally disengage with each other, and their interpersonal communication generally becomes less intense and personal. Members may not feel the same quality of contact and being understood by others at this time, and may feel confused about their own feelings.

Nonetheless, though Rogers (1970) for one does not address growth during termination, it can assist therapy. The benefit comes not necessarily through contact or empathic understanding that others express but through the meaning gained because of experiencing the process of ending. The participants can gain in confidence that they have the strength to cope with the ending of relationships and personal loss. As we have indicated, this confidence is important to obtain because loss is an inevitable aspect of human existence. The members can also learn that distance allows space for them to figure out how and when they wish to create new connections with others. Termination is a letting go of the experience of being connected, but this letting go can be part of a process through which members learn that ending creates freedom to form new connections.

As participants become able to express how they are feeling about the end of their group, those who are experiencing sorrow, regrets, or hurt at the ending of significant relationships are likely to realize that they are not alone. If members express painful or regretful feelings, others in the group are likely to hear this pain as a reaction that reveals a universal aspect to loss within human experience. By acknowledging that something is being lost, members simultaneously recognize that something worthwhile has been shared. If participants are able to mourn together, they may constructively manage and express the anxiety or sadness that ending relationships can bring.

Along with expressing feelings related to loss, members frequently discuss the plans that they are making to deal with problems that they have addressed in the group and that remain concerns. Members may also spend some time reviewing certain meaningful aspects of their group or what they have learned from their group participation. As they review events, members often express awareness of their involvement with others and their feelings about their shared experience. Individuals may discuss their plans for establishing new relationships or for working on existing relationships. They may also discuss whether or not they think they need further therapy or referrals to therapy once their group ends.

Members whose awareness is present-centered may respond to termination without any apparent need or desire to review experiences, gain closure, or formulate plans for the future. These individuals are likely to feel content simply to participate with others in the process of ending their group. There is no one 'correct' response to the ending of a group; it is merely hoped that members will feel free to express their reactions in a manner that is congruent with their own experience of events.

# CHAPTER 7

# RESPONSIBILITIES
# AND GROUP MEMBERSHIP

We learned in Chapter 4 that participants move towards the assumption of responsibility in a group as they explore personal problems, examine their splits or blocks in awareness, and investigate the patterns that they bring into their relationships with one another. Especially during the phases of exploration and mutuality, participants may challenge themselves and others to assume responsibility for what occurs in their group. However, members' responsibilities influence each phase of a group.

Responsibility is also a central element of constructive leadership within therapeutic groups as well as other social groups. Leaders in various social groups evidence irresponsibility when they deceive others (and often themselves) about the nature of their actions and motivations, blame others as a result of their perfectionism or as a way to increase power, maintain or manufacture polarities in relationships, and attempt to control the awareness of others. Responsible leaders are honest with themselves and others, and accept their own and others' mistakes as evidence of humanness and as opportunities for learning.

An effective group leader also recognizes that the growth of individuals and the group as a whole is facilitated as the members recognize their own abilities to be authorities within group process (Foulkes, 1975; Page, 1983b; Page, Weiss and Lietaer, 2002; Rogers, 1970). Each participant is an authority on his or her own experience and awareness of events and relationships. Leadership is therefore not a separate role from membership in a therapeutic group. As dynamics shift during therapeutic interactions, a group's leader may temporarily behave more as a co-participant while another member may function in a more influential and assertive manner. Thus, the dynamics of unstructured therapeutic encounters, in both individual and group therapy settings, encourage participants to move toward recognition of themselves as responsible and aware beings.

The role of the group leader has a *difference* in quality from the roles of other members insofar as the group leader is understood to be the organizer of the group and is expected to assist others to work on personal problems rather than using the group to work on his or her own concerns. The role of the group leader also has a *similarity* in quality to the roles of other members in that the group leader is co-responsible with others for what the group becomes and for the modes of communication that develop there. Since successful therapy helps participants to recognize themselves as co-creators of the process of their group, a successful leader finds ways to use his or her difference and similarity to others as means to facilitate co-construction of directions in process.

## INTERBEING

As group members move from self-protection to more open sharing of self within immediate experience, they move from a position of psychological distance from one another to psychological connectedness. Members become less concerned with finding safe topics for discussion and more interested in learning how they can create meaning through being with one another (Bozarth, 1981, 1998; Foulkes, 1948, 1975; Rogers, 1970). This shift in perspectives can be considered as the formation of an ontological focus for group process. This shift represents movement away from expectations that learning will be conferred or provided, towards an understanding that learning can be created together. Members then form a basis for responsible co-authorship of group experience. This all-important shift in the focus of members' awareness is related to an ontological consciousness that occurs if members are willing to use their process of being together to open themselves to their current experience and to increase their awareness of the meaning of relationship. It is as if members recognize nonverbally that 'I am responsible for the being and becoming of this group, by and with which I am co-affected'.

*Interbeing* is a present-centered focusing and basis for interrelating. This kind of centering involves awareness of one's own present and ongoing experience as interconnected with the present and ongoing experience of others. Interconnection is established through interactions and transactions that involve shared aspects of experience and perception, emotional resonance, and communication of empathic understanding.

Interbeing occurs as a nonlinear and relatively unpredictable process through which members simultaneously affect one another across boundaries. For example, a communication between two members may go on through an exchange of empathic understanding to an impasse. This impasse may reveal differences in perspectives that participants accept and value because they are attuned to each other's emotional responses and world-views. However, if one member perceives aspects of this difference as threatening or unfair, relationship may be diminished rather than enhanced. The development of an encounter between participants can also be altered by any number of variables: members' personal histories, emotional states, perceptions of meaning, and spontaneous and intuitive reactions to events.

If members experience congruence between their own dynamics and those of others, there is a natural sense of involvement and connection and ontological awareness or interbeing has the potential to operate within ongoing group process. Being with others may then become in itself therapeutic, and the roles that members play in their group become secondary to their ongoing process of relationship. Members' roles become flexible and participants become willing to relate to each other without imposing their definitions and expectations on each other or on their group.

The experience of interbeing does not negate autonomy or individuality, but rather enhances individuality. Individuality is a form of personhood that is created through the activity of encountering and expressing one's uniqueness and universality. Members' awareness of interbeing occurs as they recognize responsibilities that link their own process of self-actualization with the actualization of others. Participants will then sense that fulfillment of their own being occurs within a context that includes others who also wish for fulfillment.

For example, a college student named 'John', who participated in an unstructured therapy group, consistently discounted his own impulses towards more risk-taking in relationships. He also minimized the importance of his occasionally expressed wishes to 'feel that life could be worth living'. However, John frequently assisted others with self-exploration, and could be counted on to give feedback that facilitated others' awareness of positive aspects of themselves and their lives. As John observed and participated in the growth of others in the group, he seemed to gain recognition of and confidence in his own wishes to increase self-actualization. At a time near the ending of the year-long group, John stated, 'At first I didn't feel like I could gain anything from a group like this. It didn't seem to offer much. But now I feel that I did accomplish something important, although it's hard to say exactly what that is. I know I feel better about myself, and part of that is the way we were able to work together here. I know I've tried some new things in my life, although I'm not sure how much of that is because of group work and how much is because of me.'

Therapy is created in a process that involves meeting, touching, communicating, and transacting. Personalities interact and co-create. Therefore, members must learn to function therapeutically for one another to realize the healing potential of their group. They do not need to learn therapeutic strategies as much as they need to learn how to draw on their own potential to create a balanced interpersonal dynamic. To do this, they must tap their own abilities to facilitate each other's growth toward integration. Effective unstructured group therapy requires the active and responsible co-creation of healing dynamics by aware participants.

Interbeing links observation, participation, and mutual influence within an ongoing dynamic. Interbeing often functions as the primary healing influence in unstructured group therapy; a particular therapeutic approach or device cannot serve as a substitute for the awareness of interbeing. A group leader with a relatively integrated personal dynamic of love, power, and justice will use an approach and strategies that reflect and express this integrated dynamic. However, no activity of the group leader can create the recognition of interbeing for participants in a therapeutic process.

As members become aware of interbeing, the connectedness that they establish can enhance their individual power of being. They tend to confront their barriers to intimacy and authenticity as they move toward an understanding of this process that intertwines self and others. Members generally require time, patience, and practice to become comfortable with the experience of interbeing. They need to learn to trust that the interaction of divergent personalities can promote the health and well-being of participants. This trust will develop only if members perceive each other as willing and able to assume responsibility for a healing process. Mutually responsible participation and willingness to move toward integration are necessary for developing a shared awareness of interbeing.

## TRANSFERRING LEADERSHIP

Participants who join therapy groups may wish for the leader or the group itself to provide an answer for their problems, relief from their unhappiness, and success for them in their lives. In spite of this longing for a magical solution, they generally recognize that waiting for magical interventions does not facilitate productive work. Members are often aware at an intuitive level that what they really need from their group is to find a working relationship with others that can help them to discover and create their own answers and paths to fulfillment. Perhaps their group cannot make pain go away, but it can help them to bear their pain and to explore their options for change. Their group can provide an experience of acceptance that helps them to learn who they are and what goals they want to set.

As we have already noted, a therapist is in an influential leadership position during the initial phase of an unstructured group. At the same time, an effective therapist helps members perceive themselves as leaders and initiators within their own group (Page, 1983a; Page, Weiss and Lietaer, 2002; Rogers, 1970). Group leadership therefore requires having an ability to meld the dynamics inherent in the social role of being a leader with those that move a group toward more integrated love, power, and justice. A leader needs to maintain enough of his or her role to mediate both legally and ethically between a therapy group and society while simultaneously assisting the members to assume responsibility in their group.

## WU-WEI AND THE ART OF GROUP MEMBERSHIP

Leadership of unstructured therapy groups can be described as the art of leading *without* leading. A group leader who focuses on facilitating a therapeutic process is likely to place less emphasis on her or his overt role as an authority figure. A group leader who desists from overt acts of leadership at appropriate times can allow others to experience leadership capabilities. Members are able to assist each other in working on emergent themes as they learn to encourage each other without attempting to dominate. Leading without dominating helps integrate the dynamics of love, power, and justice.

The Chinese Taoists developed a concept called *wu-wei*, action that is simultaneously nonaction (Chang, 1963). In application to therapy process, *wu-wei* suggests that individuals heal and grow as they recognize and trust an inherent ordering process that does not need to be controlled or forced and that integrates self and experience with ease and unselfconscious simplicity (Suler, 1991). This idea is also useful in assisting us to understand how leadership in an unstructured group can be highly effective at times when none of the participants feel that they are being led.

Certain theorists believe that they have developed their knowledge about healthy functioning and effective therapy by learning about principles that have traditionally been investigated in Eastern philosophy. For example, Meador and Rogers (1984) write, 'It is doubtful that there would be any precursors of person-centered therapy. However, to set the person-centered point of view in historical perspective, person-centered therapy could probably best be traced to some Oriental thinkers' (p. 147). Shostrom's (1976) view of therapy incorporates a Taoist perspective that polarities can function in a unified manner and persons can grow when they cease struggling against their own natures. Jung (1964) was also influenced by Eastern thought about the human potential to integrate polarities in awareness. Fromm, Suzuki, and DeMartino (1960) and Perls (Shepard, 1975) were influenced by Zen Buddhism, a philosophy that emphasizes the centrality of awareness and the power of present experience.

Meador and Rogers (1984) thought that Zen Buddhism corresponded with some of their views, particularly the 'Zen tradition of insisting that the person can find the answers within himself' (p. 147). They also mentioned the importance of *wu-wei*, described as a 'Taoist virtue', one basic to 'the person that the person-centered therapist would like to become' (p. 147). Buber's (1957) explanation of the nature of *wu-wei* influenced the perspectives of Meador and Rogers (1984). Buber describes *wu-wei* as the belief that 'to interfere with the life of things means to harm both them and one's self. He who imposes himself has the small, manifest might; he who does not impose himself has the great secret might ... The perfected man does not interfere in the life of beings, he does not impose himself on them, but he helps all beings to their freedom' (pp. 54–5).

Attempts to impose directions and values in psychotherapy can interfere with the therapeutic work of assisting participants to reach values based on their own perceptions and interpretations of events (Korda and Pancrazio, 1989). Of course, therapists are not value-free beings. Attempts to maintain a value-free presence may impair therapeutic effectiveness if clients lack a sense of contact with the therapist as a fully present human being (Cain, 1989). The highest quality therapeutic assistance is likely to come from individuals who can recognize and clarify their own values, can demonstrate the development of values from experience, can assist others in this work if appropriate, and can accept and respect divergence in experiences and values. A person is least likely to impose values if others are respected as creative beings capable of constructing directions within their own experiential, perceptual, and cultural worlds.

The parallels between the direction of some Western psychotherapists and that of some Taoist philosophers can be clarified by examining the value of assisting people to accept and learn within their own experiential process. The idea of noninterference that is associated with *wu-wei* should not be misinterpreted as nonparticipation or noninvolvement in the context of therapy. Therapists are more likely to be able to help people learn from within their own experience if they can establish contact, co-participation, and presence. Therefore, valuing *wu-wei* does not lead to maintenance of an inactive or inert presence in a group, limitation of responses to clarifications and reflections, or failure to acknowledge personal directions and values. Nonimposition does not mean discounting one's ability to influence persons. A person's attempt to deny her or his influence will itself influence relationship dynamics, often by distorting this person's ability to be actively present. Nonimposition requires an understanding of how one can most respectfully, coherently, and usefully influence interpersonal situations and address options within them (Cain, 1989).

If presence is itself influential, *nonimposition* means learning to be as fully present as possible but in a manner that does not interfere with others' abilities to participate. One's presence in itself may encourage and stimulate others to make their presence known. Willingness to support others in this way reflects an openness to the being and choices of others, and does not reflect a presumption that a person knows how others should choose to be present.

The principle of *wu wei* has traditionally been applied to martial arts such as T'ai Chi Ch'uan (Cheng and Smith, 1967). Cheng and Smith (1967), in writing of the application of T'ai Chi to martial arts, relate the practice of *wu-wei* to an ability to empty oneself of fear and psychological resistance to pain. Applying the principle of *wu-wei* to group therapy should therefore enable a therapist to proceed without resistance into whatever emotions, tensions, or painful conflicts that may arise.

Cheng and Smith (1967) state that the T'ai Chi Ch'uan classics have advised: 'In resting, be still as a mountain; in moving go like the current of a great river' (p. 110). *Wu-wei* can be used as a basis for martial arts because it involves the awareness of knowing when and how to move and when and how to be still. *Wu-wei* is simultaneously nonaction and 'effortlessness' (p. 2). The noninterference of *wu-wei* is a noninterference with Tao—the essential nature of things, or the movement of Nature (Watts, 1961). To practice *wu-wei* therefore requires sufficient awareness to grasp the nature of present events and persons from a position fully with and within them, as opposed to a position that is separate from them or uninvolved.

A group leader who is able to practice *wu-wei* serves as a model for other participants of how they can interact spontaneously and with awareness. Yet the group leader serves as more than a model because the integrity of her or his being with others influences them. If group members are able to practice *wu-wei*, their nonimposition on each other occurs, not as a matter of moral principle, but as a natural consequence of their grasp of each other's essential nature and needs. This understanding of each other's nature comes through co-participation in a mutually shared activity, not from an analysis undertaken from a position of separation.

A person whose awareness is clear and integrated is capable of being fully silent if silence is necessary, and can move with great energy if movement is necessary. Applied to group therapy, *wu-wei* does not lead to imposition upon the nature of others, but it often does create spontaneous interactions, high levels of interest and energy, and intuitive understanding that supplements cognitive understanding. Chang (1963) observes that the noninterference of *wu-wei* includes not interfering with one's ordinary mind. Whereas *yu-wei* involves cultivating the mind, *wu-wei* is non-cultivation of the mind. Thus, a leader or group member who practices *wu-wei* does not attempt to make others conform to her or his expectations, nor to deny his or her feelings and intuitions. Rather, this individual comes to feel increasingly free to express his or her everyday thoughts, feelings, concerns, and honest observations of occurrences in the group and outside his group.

Noncultivation allows the emergence of *tzu jan* or 'self-so-ness' (Chang, 1963). In self-so-ness, all things are revealed as unique, spontaneous and natural. The leader and other participants do not see others in terms of how they can help them to improve themselves but in terms of their self-so-ness—their uniqueness and ability to contribute spontaneously. A therapist who values self-so-ness does not check his or her responses against an internalized picture of an 'ideal' therapist, and members who learn to appreciate the potential for self-so-ness in their group do not strive to be 'ideal' participants. Uncultivated honesty and openness can then be incorporated into the group atmosphere as healing factors.

*Wu-wei* is a concept that derives from Taoists' belief that the human experience of freedom arises from the experiential awareness that nature itself is intrinsically free. *Wu-wei* reflects the awareness that freedom is found through learning from and cooperating with nature. The principle of freedom within nature represents a 'playful freedom beyond human, or even humane, bounds' (Girardot, 1983: 269). This freedom is the simultaneously ordered and chaotic movement of nature, of life, and of the universe—a movement that ultimately cannot be constrained by human thought, morals, or imposed values. The group leader who values *wu-wei* believes that members will gain from experiencing themselves precisely as they are and by meeting life exactly as it is. A group therapy experience is not meant to be contrived; it is one that often tests the ability to remain aware as members increasingly come in contact with the reality of who others are.

The sage figure of early Taoism was humorously pictured as muddled, chaotic, confused, and even useless to the world of society (Girardot, 1983). The sage was a leader who did not contend with others and who was not invested in demonstrating power or superiority (Chang and Page, 1991). People might not be aware of the leadership that the sage was actually demonstrating because the actions of the sage did not necessarily meet social expectations for charisma and authority. If a group leader is practicing *wu-wei*, she or he is likely to affect a group constructively without necessarily being seen as imposing or even leading. If he or she is able to be present and aware within the flux of interactions in an unstructured group, his or her presence itself will affect the process of the group and the quality of communication there. Members will then be likely to notice that their presence also influences their group's process.

## LEARNING FROM DIFFERENCES

At some point in their group process, often during the phase of mutuality, members tend to realize that they have created norms that influence the quality and direction of their communication. If members desire to create a shared and meaningful experience, they will need to learn how to work with each other to meet each other's needs and desires. Because members have different assumptions, they can help each other to examine their reactions from different perspectives. If members draw on the resources available in their group, they often find that rich learning is possible due to the variety of life experiences and perspectives that members bring. As members learn from each other's perceptions and modes of relationship, they become involved in encounters that influence each other in ways that would have been difficult to predict. By reacting to the unexpected, members can learn about aspects of themselves that were previously hidden or unknown.

For example, during a workshop that was conducted by one of the authors with university students, a woman named 'Janet' revealed that she had had an affair with someone who was not her husband; she had not told her husband or anyone else about having this affair. She discussed her affair at length during this group and the reasons that it had occurred. Janet expressed her guilt about what had happened and explored different ways she might deal with what had occurred. When Janet discussed her affair, several of the other group members were able to empathize with Janet even though they initially expressed strong disapproval about what had occurred. These members were able to become more tolerant toward people who have had an affair because they sympathized with Janet's specific situation.

## FRIENDSHIPS AND ROMANTIC INVOLVEMENTS

Through empathic engagement with others, members develop connections that may deepen into caring and friendship. In ongoing unstructured therapy groups, members may decide to extend the intimacy and contact of their relationship by meeting together outside the group. They may then face certain dilemmas that affect the group since participation with others *in* their group may be influenced by relationships with certain members *outside* the group.

Some theorists have taken the position that members should not have relationships with each other outside of their group (Bion, 1959; Yalom, 1995). Other theorists, such as Perls (Shepard, 1975) and Rogers (1970), do not discourage these because feelings of closeness and bonding can often arise naturally and can often be a source of growth for clients. Members of ongoing therapy groups may decide to meet each other outside of their group to extend their ability to provide friendship and mutual support. This decision is sometimes an indication that members have moved from experiencing themselves as observers to experiencing themselves as authentic participants in each other's lives. This form of meeting can be a way to extend the development of relationships that begin when they are together within a group.

At other times, these relationships may represent expressions of anxiety about initiating involvement with 'strangers'. If a group's cohesion leads members to perceive outsiders as untrustworthy or unapproachable, members meeting together outside the group may be fostering an unhealthy form of dependency. Their involvement outside their group may then additionally negatively affect their relationships with others in their group. They may form a separate subgroup that interrupts or distracts from the development of contact between others. Members can grow by exploring their feelings of anxiety and mistrust and by accepting responsibility for learning how to bring into their group aspects of an external relationship that is affecting other members.

Another drawback of these kinds of relationships can be that certain members can feel excluded. A member who becomes aware that certain others meet for coffee or a movie may feel inadequate or hurt because he or she has been left out. Excluded members are likely to feel uncomfortable about bringing up these kinds of issues in their group because they hesitate to trust others with their feelings of isolation, loneliness, and rejection. Members may also be concerned that others will feel pity or will extend themselves simply to appear 'fair'. Participants may also want to avoid disrupting an illusion of togetherness that has become a shared assumption.

The issues of freedom and responsibility are likely to become a focus for a group that is dealing with subgroups. Members may question whether their freedom should mean that they are free to focus attention on those about whom they care the most and to spend less time and attention on those in whom they are not interested. If participants are willing to address these issues, they may learn something new about the feelings of those who experience themselves as separated observers. Dealing with such issues exposes members' awareness of the operation of love, power, and justice in their group. Members can then address whether each person is simply responsible for self and his or her own participation or whether each is responsible to extend opportunities to those who feel they have been separated. People can move from thinking of responsibility as a function of isolated and autonomous selves to perceiving themselves as having interconnected responsibilities (McClure, 1990; O'Hara, 1984).

Additionally, those who feel separated from others can be helped to look at how they have influenced others and contributed to events. They may be able to see that they have in some instances moved toward a distanced perspective through choices that altered their responses and interaction. Members who have formed subgroups can be helped to look at how their choices to form exclusive groupings have affected others.

Members are often able to maintain supportive relationships outside their group that do not impinge negatively on their group. To suggest that they avoid all such relationships would separate the integration of love, power, and justice within the group from relational dynamics outside of it. Learning can be more comprehensive if members recognize that no separation exists between relational processes they explore in their group and those in life outside the group.

By and large, members do not choose to pursue friendships outside the group with other participants because they value a chance to explore feelings and awareness with individuals who do not play other roles in their lives. If friendly supportive relationships grow between certain members, other members usually understand their value and can learn from their growth. Members involved in friendships outside their group are likely to communicate in a way that does not exclude others. Of course, some participants may feel annoyed if two members frequently use group time to discuss issues that have arisen between them outside the group. This kind of conflict can be explored like any other conflict involving subgroups and can lead to enhanced learning about love, power, and justice.

Members of unstructured therapy groups sometimes become romantically involved. This involvement can develop from a sexual or romantic attraction experienced in the group or from a friendship outside the group that becomes a sexual or romantic relationship. A romantic linking between members can raise concerns about subgroups that are similar to those surrounding the development of an external friendship. However, with sexual and romantic involvement, the emotionalism associated with these concerns is often intensified. As other members become aware of this sexual activity or romantic involvement, interactions are likely to be altered. If some participants experience their group as a family, they may experience feelings related to incestuous themes in their family of origin. Other members may be jealous. Still other participants may have questions about the relationship dynamics displayed between these two people. If a romantic dyad becomes the center of emotion and attention in a group, some members may feel left out. A romantically linked couple that has problems may want to use their group to help them work these out. Other participants may feel that this use of the resources of the group is not fair to those who want to explore their own issues and problems.

Although a group's leader will probably find it impossible to prevent romantic and sexual involvement by members with each other, he or she would obviously be making a mistake to promote the development of such relationships or to encourage the extended work on such relationships in the group. The leader can assist her or his group by facilitating discussions about how a romantically involved couple is influencing the group, if an impact is observed. Members can grow by assuming responsibility for working through the various emotions and misgivings that may be stirred up by the development of a romance between members. Although such romances or sexual liaisons can be disruptive for a group, these situations also can provide a focus for learning about interpersonal justice. Any aspect of individual and relational experience can be grist for the mill of awareness if participants use their group as a vehicle to enhance learning.

## THE EXTENSION OF NEW LEARNING

Members of unstructured therapy groups learn vicariously and through direct experience. As an ongoing therapy group develops and when members terminate their involvement, they are faced with the question of how to apply what they have learned. If participants have experienced a new integration of the dynamics of love, power, and justice, this learning may be perceived as potentially altering their process of being with others. If members have moved toward enhanced responsibility, increased empowerment, and a more integrated mode of relationship, we might even assume that a dramatic change in a person's life should be observable as a direct result of his or her participation in a therapeutic group.

Dramatic observable changes in outside relationships, however, are not always appropriate criteria for evaluating the significance of a group experience. Freedom as a grounding for life experience and for the creation of relationships would be negated by proposing that members *should* have improved relationships, or *should be expected* to experience certain predictable life changes. The specification of changes identified as beneficial for members or the suggestion that these are causally produced by participation in a therapeutic group would undermine members' own awareness, responsibility, and potential for creative justice. Participants can determine directions for growth that are meaningful for them, directions that are appropriate to changing circumstances within their unique life circumstances. The manner in which new knowledge is extended is a personal choice made by a member within that person's experience of unpredictable life events and encounters.

Some members benefit from therapy groups by developing an enhanced willingness to initiate and experience change whereas others profit from their greater acceptance of themselves and others as they are. Some participants learn that they have the courage to create changes in situations that they perceive as having existed far too long in a static form. They may make decisions to develop new interests, initiate new relationships, work on their physical well-being, pursue risks in careers, or develop talents that were unused. Others may learn that they were in a rush to alter something because they were unwilling to accept what they were experiencing. For example, a person who has been sexually abused may work in a therapeutic group to acknowledge this reality and accept associated feelings and perceptions. She or he may then learn that being preoccupied with perfectionistic attempts to change self has served as a way of denying feelings of anger and hurt. By doing less to change self, this member may experience greater happiness and fulfillment.

Persons' abilities to identify directions, make choices, define self, and construct forms for relationship are directly a function of being aware. Although enhancement of awareness is a major source of growth that can arise from participation in unstructured therapy groups, it can lead to new struggles and anxiety as well as new confidence and initiative. Awareness is analogous in some ways to eyesight. We use vision as a metaphor for awareness in statements such as 'I see what you mean' or 'I had a sudden insight'. Vision can bring either joy or pain and can reveal beauty or ugliness. Members in a group may enthusiastically extend new knowledge about strengths and abilities. However, they may experience anxiety as they continue to deal with new perceptions of their limitations or blind spots. They may have gained new awareness of self-actualizing, but they may also have encountered unattractive aspects of their experience that they had previously been successful in denying.

Hence the fruits of new awareness may be immediately apparent through decisions and actions, or new awareness may take time to process and be enacted. A person may become more effective personally and interpersonally by becoming more aware. At the same time, becoming more aware may bring a loss of certain illusions and beliefs that were comforting and reassuring even though these same beliefs may also have prevented a person from feeling satisfied with himself or herself or feeling fulfilled when relating to others. Individuals tend to perceive their losses of illusions of security as irrevocable. New options may appear but the very perception of these may destroy former perceptions of certainty.

Members are most likely to generalize changes in relationship dynamics that they have established in their group if these changes have led to an experience that is perceived as rich, and communication that is viewed as involving. Experiences of fulfillment, meaningfulness, and beauty serve as reinforcers that induce people to maintain newly established patterns of love, power, and justice, and to extend these to other situations and relationships. The ideal situation in group therapy is therefore for members to have a shared experience that is fulfilling.

There can be, or course, no guarantee that members will have such an experience. Self-conscious attempts to generate fulfillment are likely (paradoxically) to destroy the possibility that it will occur because such a happening usually arises spontaneously at times when attention is not focused on oneself (Frankl, 1969; Maslow, 1962, 1964; Yalom, 1980). Additionally, aiming towards one's own happiness decreases the ability simply to listen to others with openness. This kind of listening is necessary as a prerequisite for experiences of genuine interpersonal communion. Therapy groups can aim towards relationship dynamics that make possible such experiences.

These groups can also assist people to experience meaning in sharing feelings of hurt and sorrow or joy and happiness. The experience of sharing difficult or painful experiences with people who hear and are accepting has its own kind of beauty. The sharing of happy feelings can have an important effect on the participants as well. Members can extend this learning by allowing themselves to be more fully present with others, regardless of the kinds of feelings being expressed.

## ETHICS AND RESPONSIBILITY

If unstructured therapy groups address and promote responsibility, awareness, freedom, creativity, power, justice, and love, they also reflect ethical considerations. These groups promote an ethic that encourages perceptions of freedom and personal power; that recognizes individuals as unique and as potentially just and responsible; and that values the ability of human beings to create beauty and love in their interactions with others.

The ethics that underlie unstructured therapy groups cannot be fully actualized unless members identify with at least some of the ethical values listed in the preceding paragraph. Of course, the leader of an unstructured therapy group does not attempt orally to instruct members in the appropriate ethics for human interactions in groups. The leader should embody these ethics in her or his interpersonal behaviors in the group and can hope to impart them in this way.

Therapy develops through the power of the group process to draw from members their abilities to create just forms of relationship and to learn from each other as movement toward integrated relationships occurs. The leader may often voice a perspective on what is occurring in the group's process or may ask others to notice what is occurring. This emphasis on interpersonal process represents a kind of faith that if people become aware of what is transpiring between them, they can then move toward creatively just modes of interaction. Without at least some faith in the creative potential of individuals, there would be no purpose in conducting unstructured therapy groups.

Every human group makes ethical decisions concerning the value that is given to self-determination or conformity, the merit of a judgmental atmosphere versus a more accepting atmosphere, and the value of trusting and accepting oneself and one's feelings versus mistrusting oneself and accepting the group's right to dictate. Each therapist and each group member who intends to behave therapeutically would benefit from clarifying her or his awareness of values that relate to freedom, autonomy, interdependence, and issues of individual and collective responsibility. These values are implied in the very enterprise of group therapy and their form is inevitably communicated and constructed during therapy.

The purpose of unstructured therapy groups is not to eliminate any pressure toward conformity but to allow the members sufficient freedom to experiment creatively within group norms and to participate in the construction of these. The group leader's initial attitudes about the desirability of conformity influence the development of a group's interpersonal process. For example, if a leader verbally or nonverbally strongly communicates the importance of establishing overly rigid norms, members may agree to this demand because of their social conditioning. If, however, they have a strong negative reaction to their leader, they may act in ways that contradict the leader's norms. In either case, members will not feel encouraged by their leader to develop their own norms creatively.

The unstructured group therapist who values the integration of love, power, and justice is likely to view coercion and an ardent emphasis on conformity as generally counterproductive forms of interaction. Nonetheless, as has been indicated, a certain degree of conformity is necessary and desirable. The sought-after norms of unstructured group therapy can be defined in terms of the balanced operation of love, power, and justice during group process. The group as a whole and the individual always influence each other's norms and always maintain some degree of tension due to the testing that occurs between one perspective and the other.

## THERAPIST RESPONSIBILITY AND ETHICAL GUIDELINES

Ethical guidelines have been established by professional associations in many different countries that are applicable to the fields of counseling, psychology, social work, marriage and family therapy, and psychiatry. All of these indicate the essential importance of valuing clients as persons and understanding what will benefit and harm them. Although guidelines attempt to prescribe and proscribe certain actions in well-defined situations, they cannot successfully serve as a substitute for a therapist's own judgments and awareness of contexts within which actions are taken.

As indicated by these guidelines, therapists should beware of potentials for misuse of power to manipulate clients, who can be hurt or disillusioned or whose self-esteem can be damaged. Clients are often suffering because of the long-term effect of imbalanced love, power, and justice in relationships. If a therapist uses a position of power to manipulate clients, she or he may be confirming the clients' worst expectations about the nature of human relationships. In a worst-case scenario, clients may give up any hope of reaching a harmonious integration of love, power, and justice in human relationships. Such people may drop out of therapy permanently, may judge themselves unworthy of a caring relationship, or may be harmed in other ways.

# Responsibilities and Group Membership

Clients who have adjusted to imbalanced love, power, and justice in relationships are likely to reinstate these dynamics by attempting to manipulate their therapist (or other members) or may unconsciously encourage the therapist (or others) to manipulate them. This enactment of imbalanced ontological dynamics can occur through actions that are controlling, self-deprecating, domineering, antagonistic, demeaning, or seductive. Members may also pose as more weak and helpless than they really feel to get others to play the role of helper and caretaker. The efficacious group leader will recognize such games and avoid repeating the distorted forms of relationship that may have previously harmed clients.

No code or guideline can guard against all the subtle ways in which a position of power can be misused (Kitchener and Harding, 1990). At the same time, if a therapist (or other participant) becomes too cautious and careful about using power and influence, she or he may repress those spontaneous responses to situations that are most valuable therapeutically (Polster and Polster, 1973). This kind of over-concern can also lead to a constrained approach to relationships in which therapists withhold themselves from others and are unable to model freedom (Cain, 1989).

The experience of caring about and respecting others is basic to genuinely ethical behavior. Without this experience, no guidelines will suffice to direct a therapist toward effective group leadership, nor will members learn what it means to interact with others helpfully. If a group leader is capable of care and respect, he or she will be more likely to be able to deal with interpersonal conflicts that arise during a group, even if their solution cannot be clearly defined by the broad recommendations of codes and guidelines.

A fine line sometimes seems to separate constructive and destructive aspects of human relationships. For example, therapists or members may sometimes be unclear whether an interaction represents a personal attack that is unnecessarily hurtful or whether the pain of this confrontation can lead to empowerment and increased awareness for the parties involved. A group leader may be called on to assess whether members are using personal power to undermine the confidence or self-belief of those who are weaker (Gans, 1989). A person who is in tune empathically with others in a group is generally in the best position to assess the integration (or lack thereof) of the elements of love, power, and justice.

Assessment of the dynamics of relationships is essential for dealing effectively with members involved in potential or present ethical problems, such as how to deal with those who breach confidentiality. Although guidelines generally address the issue of confidentiality, in some situations during group therapy, no clearly defined standards pertain. Therapists also often vary in their responses to ethical dilemmas. Evidence suggests that individual awareness, perceptions of threat, settings for group practice, and theoretical training all influence therapists' responses to confidentiality dilemmas (Roback, Purdon, Ochoa and Bloch, 1992).

In most cases, members respect each other's integrity and are able to concur early in the group process on the ethical standards that they will agree to uphold. A leader may assist participants to develop a consensus agreement on ethical ground rules as part of their group's process and may also promote an ethic that allows members' flexibility as interpersonal situations change. The leader's responsibility for behaving and communicating ethically can be clarified if ethics are viewed as values based on awareness of and respect for each member's full humanity and potential for wholeness. Leaders and members share responsibility for supporting an atmosphere that encourages ethical interactions. The role of leader obviously involves social and professional expectations for ethical behavior. What is just as important, the leader's commitment to an ethical process of therapy will be reflected in his or her support and enhancement of the element of justice throughout interactions with members.

## CREATIVE JUSTICE AND ETHICAL RELATIONSHIPS

Creative justice uses awareness within the experience of freedom as the basis for ethical choices in ongoing interactions. Members who voluntarily choose to participate in an unstructured therapy group, and who are informed about the goals of these groups, are likely to place some intuitive value on the ethical implications of creative justice. These include valuing personal responsibility, individual awareness, and freedom.

The unstructured group therapist is well advised, whenever possible, to conduct groups wherein participation is voluntary. Clients are more likely to engage in productive and meaningful work if participation is voluntary (Page, Weiss and Lietaer, 2002; Patterson, 1985). If members have the option of participating or not participating, a therapist's advocacy of an ethic based on personal responsibility will support the group's initial organization and ground rules. Group members whose participation is voluntary are also more likely to adhere to confidentiality than those who are forced to attend. It is also difficult for members who attend a group on a voluntary basis to justify acting out in a group by saying the reason they are doing it is because they did not want to attend the group in the first place.

A therapist's perception of responsibility based on an ethic of creative justice can sometimes place him or her in a confrontational position with respect to other group members. This kind of challenge can occur if a group leader decides to bring to members' attention his or her perceptions and feelings about dynamics in the group, particularly if unjust attitudes are regulating an encounter. For example, members may decide that they want to expel a participant who has broken confidentiality for the first time. If the leader reviews events and points out the value of extending acceptance, members may change their decision. A group leader might also insist on the importance of allowing participants to learn from mistakes. Of course, if a member repeatedly breaks confidentiality, the member's intention to participate on an equal basis with others can be questioned.

# Responsibilities and Group Membership

As we have already indicated, there are various ways that therapists can act in unjust ways in groups. Therapists who lack awareness of themselves in relation to clients may allow themselves to be manipulated into a relationship that blurs boundaries between therapy and romance or other forms of intense interpersonal attraction. Both clients and therapists may use therapy to express seductiveness or destructive manipulations that were the basis of hurtful previous relationships. Clients cannot be expected to avoid I-It forms of relationship, because these forms of relationship are often the reason that they seek therapy and counseling. However, a therapist can be expected not to exacerbate I-It relationship patterns by reinforcing and extending them.

The implicit power dynamics involved in the role of therapist can be misused to promote one-sided forms of confrontation. These dynamics can also be misused if therapists favor or single out certain group members over others. For example, a group leader may speak in a more supportive way, may take on a seductive demeanor, or may communicate in subtly demeaning or critical ways to particular members. Cultural stereotypes about gender roles or ethnic groups may also play a part in unfair communication patterns.

These unjust patterns of communication are often not conscious; therapists generally want to think of themselves as fair-minded and helpful. A participant who notices unjust interpersonal patterns in a therapist's relations with members may hesitate to bring this subject to the group's attention. If the member perceives imbalanced interpersonal dynamics, he or she may appropriately fear being rebuffed, discredited, or even attacked by others.

Members tend to experience their therapist as a presence whose impact on group dynamics is noticeable. They therefore usually want to be liked and supported by their leader and tend to be less direct when confronting a therapist than when challenging other members (Napier and Gershenfeld, 1987). A group leader who values creative justice will encourage honesty and open disclosure. If members notice specific patterns of attraction or antagonism between certain participants, including the therapist, this awareness can be used productively if the therapist helps to create an atmosphere where members can express what they are seeing and feeling.

As members move towards openness in their interactions, they increasingly experience the freedom to examine the dynamics that influence justice in relationships. In therapeutic group settings, members usually reveal how issues of justice affect them on emotional or intuitive levels of experience. The members often focus on interpersonal events in their group that have to do with observing when someone was treated unfairly or learning how to treat someone more fairly (for example, moving toward mutual respect and consideration).

The most powerful impact of a therapy group can occur: (1) if the ethical foundation established and promoted by the leader is congruent with that person's own pattern of relationship in therapy, (2) if this ethical basis for interaction encourages members to assume responsibility for affecting the development of their group, (3) if such a framework is consistent with ethical standards in counseling, psychology, and other associated professions, and (4) if these ethics consistently support and encourage those group dynamics that serve to promote the movement of members towards new learning, enhanced awareness, constructive interpersonal relationships, and the possibility of greater fulfillment in life. Ethics based on creative justice can create a foundation for increasing group members' awareness of differences as well as similarities, experiential learning of responsibility, and growth in an atmosphere of freedom that they construct.

# CHAPTER 8

# APPLICATION OF THEORY

The theory of group therapy that we have presented in this book is intended to provide a basis for conceptualizing and directing therapeutic work. The ideas that we have investigated are applicable in therapeutic group work, and indeed to any situation that requires an understanding of relationship dynamics.

## DIMENSIONS OF A VIABLE GROUP THEORY

In an influential article Liberman, Lakin and Whitaker (1969) assert that a viable theory of group therapy should meet seven criteria. These can be used to review the theoretical constructs presented in this text. The first of these criteria is that the psychology of group membership needs to be presented from the perspective of the group member.

The psychological aspects of group membership that we have presented as influencing and being affected by members' perceptions include: (1) presentation of and work on personal problems, (2) the giving and receiving of feedback related to relationships with others who are present, (3) self-actualization within an interpersonal field, (4) choices to move towards awareness of freedom and responsibility, and (5) participation in the dynamics of love, power, and justice in group relationships. The perspectives of group members affect and are affected by an interpersonal atmosphere that influences who participants become within their relationships with one another. Members' expectations are the basis for creating directions for interpersonal exploration and development. Members' perceptions of themselves being with others can be used to promote recognition of interbeing and interdependence.

The second criterion for a viable group theory, according to Liberman, Lakin and Whitaker (1969), is the provision of an explanation for the function and significance of the therapist's role. We have described the therapist's role in an unstructured setting as influenced by his or her organization and presentation of the group, by his or her theoretical understanding and concerns, by personally and socially influenced ethical responsibilities, by expectations that are held by members, by the institution (if any) that provides the therapeutic setting, and by the larger society and culture. Leadership functions of the therapist are involved in the setting of time limits, selection of members, and establishment of fundamental ethical ground rules. We have shown that this role needs to be integrated with nonrole requirements of group participation. These requirements are ontological in nature and derive from being with other persons, constructing a dialogue, and extending self to include others. The effective therapist can integrate requirements of a role with personal openness and interpersonal presence.

The third criterion proposed by Liberman, Lakin and Whitaker (1969) is that the major regulatory factors that affect members—that is, the norms and standards of the group—need to be explained. We have described how group members develop norms and how this development can be influenced by members' perceptions of the values and expectations of the leader and by their own hopes, demands, values, and expectations. If members recognize their mutual responsibility to create norms that express awareness of relationship, they can move from restrictive norms to norms that are based on creative justice.

Norms can support or inhibit members' movements toward creative justice. This understanding of norms permits us to address the fourth criterion of Liberman, Lakin and Whitaker: an explanation of how a group develops into a therapeutic rather than a nontherapeutic force. The norms and interpersonal dynamics of a therapeutic group extend acceptance to those who are estranged, enable members to experience their own power and responsibility more and more, and increasingly facilitate members' growth through explorations of self being with others. Participants in an effective therapeutic group recognize and encourage each other's choices to move towards more open and comprehensive awareness of self and others. Members use awareness to integrate ongoing dynamics of love, power, and justice if they recognize their mutual responsibility to create themes and meaningful directions. Members can be increasingly open to and can integrate affective, cognitive, behavioral, and intuitive aspects of being. The development of an integrated ontological dynamic requires the leader along with other members to be able to listen and hear, to accept, to be aware, to form directions, to respond honestly and appropriately, and to interact spontaneously.

The fifth criterion for a viable theory of group therapy is an examination of changes that occur because of members' participation (Liberman, Lakin and Whitaker, 1969). We have indicated that although many potential benefits can be associated with participation in an unstructured therapy group, the therapy process tends to frustrate efforts to predict exactly what form these will take. Additionally, as a group progresses, personal and interpersonal awareness changes. Thus, during various phases, members may alter their perceptions of needs or wants.

Members' unique and changing perspectives influence their use of group interactions, their interpretations of interactions, and their integration of experiences. The positive changes that members experience derive from participation in a mutually created healing dynamic. This dynamic is based on interactions wherein members experience love without sacrificing personal power and wherein a form of justice is created through which participants can express awareness and creative abilities. Additionally, therapeutic changes generally involve increased recognition of responsibility and increased acceptance of self and others. Changes in a nontherapeutic direction can result from group interactions wherein values and perspectives are imposed on others, members move towards estrangement from their perceptions and interactions, and conformity is rewarded and interpersonal differences are disrespected. Nontherapeutic interactions usually stifle open exploration of experience and form barriers to the enhancement of intensity and extensity of awareness.

The sixth criterion for a viable theory is that it must account for how members generalize what they have learned from participation in a group to their lives outside the group (Liberman, Lakin and Whitaker, 1969). We have portrayed members as being responsible for deciding when and how to implement any new learning that may have occurred. Assumptions that members will or should have learned some type of predictable skill or perspective are inherently limited. Similarly, we have recommended caution about predicting how members will typically apply their learning to outside situations. Although participants in effective groups often report that they have changed the qualities of existing relationships or formed new relationships, they usually do not perceive their group as having imposed expectations upon them that they 'should' change in specific ways (Korda and Pancrazio, 1989). In our view, therapeutic groups are most beneficial if members perceive that their own perceptions and evaluations of situations form the basis for their decisions to change circumstances or accept circumstances or explore new circumstances.

Lastly, Liberman, Lakin and Whitaker (1969) have stated that group therapy needs to be compared with other forms of treatment, such as behavior modification. We have not spent much time or space dwelling on comparisons with other forms of treatment because we believe that the reader will be able to make comparisons and draw her or his own conclusions from the observations and arguments we have presented. Different assumptions and goals are involved in treatments that attempt to provide solutions to clients' problems (such as some behavioral and strategic approaches) as compared to treatments that focus on clients' abilities to enhance awareness and construct their own solutions. Moreover, the resources available, and the process developed in a group setting create an atmosphere for therapy that differs from individual therapy. A major difference in emphasis occurs from the multiple perspectives and objectives that influence interpersonal process in group therapy. A similarity between these treatment settings is that both can assist recognition of responsibility.

## LEARNING FOR LEADERSHIP

We have emphasized the experiential aspects of learning that are important for participants in a therapy group. This experiential emphasis is consistent with a recommendation that potential group leaders also experience group membership. A viable theory of unstructured group therapy does not substitute for experience but guides the initiation and assimilation of experience. Firsthand experience and observation are a necessary basis for understanding how unstructured groups operate and what they can mean for participants. Conclusions developed from actual experience will be more convincing to practitioners than those developed from afar.

Prospective leaders can, of course, benefit from gaining familiarity with the theoretical issues and concerns that influence the organization and interpersonal process of therapeutic groups. However, these persons also need to develop clear awareness of their own experience with interpersonal process in unstructured groups. Similarly, experienced group leaders can benefit by examination of their own life as a member and leader. Supervision can help therapists to learn how to notice the themes that evolve for members and for the group as a whole in the unstructured therapy situation. Prospective or practicing group leaders can enhance their effectiveness by becoming more fully aware of how they are affecting the openness, content, and direction of other members' participation. Experienced therapists may seek consultation, supervision, and training on an ongoing basis to avoid complacency or stagnation. Supervision and training can stimulate self-observation, which helps to develop greater centeredness and responsibility. Observation by a competent peer, supervisor, or workshop leader tends to intensify self-observation and can provide new information about the effects of one's feelings and attitudes on group process (Korda and Pancrazio, 1989).

The relationship between a group leader and an effective consultant or supervisor is characterized by sufficiently integrated love, power, and justice to promote trust and self-exploration. Trust encourages self-disclosure, openness to constructive criticism, and willingness to risk new behaviors and approaches. A supervisor can create a double-binding situation for a therapist-trainee by instituting an unjust relationship pattern with the trainee while encouraging the trainee to develop integrated relationships with clients. The quality of a relationship between supervisor and trainee is as important to the learning of the trainee as any of the verbal observations about a group process that are imparted by the supervisor.

## THE APPLICATION OF UNSTRUCTURED GROUP THEORY IN VARIOUS SETTINGS

The training received by a prospective leader of unstructured therapy groups can be applied to diverse settings. Such groups are commonly appropriate because many settings seek to promote experiential learning about responsibility and balanced relationships. The nature of unstructured therapy varies in different environments because the central concerns of clients may change according to their backgrounds and problems, but the ontological processes of these groups retain a great deal of similarity. This similarity is evident in the universality of persons' wishes for acceptance, desires for personal power and efficacy, and hopes for just relationships.

Over time, the leader of unstructured groups in a particular setting may become familiar with the concerns that members tend to bring to groups. For example, disabled clients in a rehabilitation setting will usually have themes that are distinct from the concerns of emotionally disturbed adolescents. If the leader becomes familiar with certain themes, this familiarity is likely to facilitate his or her ability to notice and focus on specific issues. However, familiarity can also lead to false presuppositions about these themes. Therefore, an effective therapist can gather knowledge and expertise with a specific population but must maintain sufficient openness to recognize the uniqueness of each client's concerns.

Some therapists, due to personality characteristics or individual communication styles, may function more effectively in one setting than in another. Therapists may gravitate towards environments in which they are most comfortable or towards clients with whom they believe they work most effectively. However, therapists' personal and professional growth can be limited by restriction to a specific setting in which particular types of clients (for example diagnostically or culturally similar clients) are treated in a similar manner. Therapists can challenge their own growth in awareness by seeking a degree of diversity in their work. Workshop or seminar activities can be used to augment learning for a therapist who feels financially or emotionally bound to a particular setting.

Common concerns of members that can be addressed and changed through unstructured group therapy are awareness of responsibility, recognition of patterns of relationship, movement from estrangement to acceptance of self and others, self-expression in social situations, and desire to enhance interpersonal effectiveness and perceptions of personal power. Unstructured therapy groups are environments wherein members can experience interpersonal acceptance leading to personal integration and to integration of self with others. Alienation is reduced by acceptance. Members may grow from experiencing trust or by coping with mistrust. Perceptions of personal power are enhanced through members' acknowledgment and working through of uncomfortable or unsettling experiences and of their anxiety in interpersonal relationships.

These generic problems that members commonly address in unstructured therapy groups never occur in the abstract and are always expressed as particular dynamics of relationships and self-perceptions. Thus, specific personal and interpersonal events form a context in which these generic kinds of problems take on specific configurations. Certain settings that provide unstructured therapy groups also contribute a context in which problems are expressed and relationships are formed. Settings may be oriented towards a certain population or certain types of presenting problems.

Adolescents and elderly people are two groups that may receive unstructured group therapy in settings specifically oriented towards them (for example, see Kwiatkowski, 1987; Leszcz, 1990). The generic problems that we have discussed are likely to be linked to particular behavioral and social concerns that are typical of a given population. An adolescent's problem with responsibility and sense of alienation is likely to be linked specifically to a family environment and peers. These group participants' lack of a sense of personal power is associated with their lack of social and financial autonomy and status. They may be concerned with formation of attitudes towards authority and sexuality and may test these attitudes on a group leader (Kwiatkowski, 1987). Unstructured therapy groups for elderly clients tend to address ways in which perceptions of self have been damaged due to social or physical problems associated with aging (Kapur and Pearce, 1987). Many of these clients suffer from feelings of depression and age-related losses of close relationships (Kapur and Pearce, 1987). Members of these groups can provide mutual support and opportunities to invest in emotional connections. Leszcz (1990) asserts that generally the most successful approach to group therapy is an open one that allows members to draw what they need from their group.

Other specific populations to engage in this form of therapy include sex offenders (Aubrey and Dougher, 1990), other offenders (Zimpfer, 1992), and chemically dependent clients (Matano and Yalom, 1991; Page, Weiss and Lietaer, 2002). Each of these groups may receive treatment as a unique population for many reasons, including placement in institutional settings, legal and ethical obligations, and attraction of participants to particular groups.

Unstructured therapy groups may be conducted in college or university settings at counseling centers, mental health centers, or as experiential workshops for students who plan to work as therapists. If such groups are part of a university counseling center's services, these groups can be used to provide peer encouragement and support during times when students encounter problems with relationships, school, drugs or alcohol, or self-esteem. If unstructured groups are offered as workshops or seminars for students of counseling or other helping professions, members may discuss universal themes such as desires for support and encouragement or development of personal power. Themes that are distinctly of interest to counseling students as a group, or to particular individuals, are also likely to arise.

One of the authors has conducted numerous therapy groups in a university setting. These groups are constrained by the semester system, which leads to a specific time that groups must begin and end, although members may rejoin the next semester. As a result, these groups meet for about ten to thirteen sessions before terminating. Themes such as dealing with emotions and moods, relationships, identifying wants and needs, and sense of identity in general are typically addressed. The group leader often suggests a 'check-in' period at the beginning of each group

168

meeting. This 'check-in' allows each group member to briefly speak about the concerns or experiences that have been relevant during the past week. Each member is heard from, and members then can decide where to place attention and energy.

While a structuring is involved in the 'check-in' format, an unstructured approach is involved in the evolution of dialogue from that beginning. Group interactions proceed from more structure to less structure (in terms of the roles and expectations involved). Thus, application of the theory of unstructured group therapy is not against the use of any structure and is adaptable to different settings and demands.

In a prison setting, members of unstructured groups frequently address issues of self-esteem, emotional self-expression, and relatedness to others (Page, 1979; Page, Campbell and Wilder, 1994; Page, Richmond and DeLaSerna, 1987; Page, Weiss and Lietaer, 2002). As participants develop themes in their interactions, they may emphasize such concerns as dealing with anger and coping with the violence that usually plays a significant role in prison life. Two issues that concern group leaders in a prison setting are whether participation should be voluntary and unrelated to institutional inducements and whether inmates who make incriminating disclosures in their groups should be protected by confidentiality. Although some authors (for example Patterson and Eisenberg, 1975) have advocated forced or rewarded participation in unstructured groups for inmates, we believe that this kind of participation generally undermines the principle of freedom and autonomy that is basic to effectiveness in these groups. Page (1980, 1981, 1983a, 1985) has conducted unstructured groups with inmates of correctional institutions; these groups were voluntary and involved no incentives (such as favorable reports to probation or parole boards). The advantages of voluntary participation are evident in the participants' degree of involvement and willingness to form nonmanipulative relationships and to reveal themselves. Voluntary participation can also become an issue for clients in mental health centers or drug rehabilitation programs if a court system is involved in the referral process.

Unstructured therapy groups can be useful in rehabilitation hospital settings to give clients opportunities to discuss their feelings and concerns, those either related or unrelated to their disability (Page, 1978). Psychological difficulties that often accompany physical disabilities are related to unexpected limitations, coping with pain, changes in self-image and body image, and needs for emotional support. These individuals may also experience difficulties coping with institutionally generated stress, and with attitudes of family members. Unstructured groups in these settings may be useful as short-term therapy, but they can also be conducted on a long-term basis that allows extended exploration of feelings, relationships, and themes (Page, 1978). Successful unstructured therapy groups met weekly in a rehabilitation setting for as long as two years; participants were thus able to work on relationship issues that developed and changed over relatively long periods of time (Page, 1978).

169

Terminally ill patients may learn in these groups that they can form empathic and supportive interpersonal relationships that are mutually empowering (Leszcz, 1990). They may also come to terms with their awareness of aging and death as inevitable processes. Unstructured therapy can be used to reach closure on unfinished business and to share present experiences. Human contact that is open, honest, and direct can be a deeply meaningful experience for these clients.

If a therapist forms an unstructured therapy group in a private practice setting, he or she has control over who will be admitted. Therapists can then form groups with members of diverse backgrounds and with somewhat different personal problems. Diversity can help members to avoid certain potential pitfalls of group therapy, such as the development of assumptions of sameness, feelings of being special, and exclusivity (Wolf and Schwartz, 1962).

Therapists who are comfortable conducting unstructured groups (whether in community mental health settings, hospital settings, educational settings, or other settings) find that they are able to meet the needs of many more clients than would be the case if they restricted themselves to individual therapy. These groups can be effective in encouraging awareness of responsibility and in experientially validating and enhancing relationship skills and awareness. Unstructured groups can be useful for dealing with problems associated with self-acceptance, self-esteem, and relatedness to others. Members also can create opportunities for examination of lifestyles that are unnecessarily self-limiting and/or self-destructive.

## INTERNAL AND EXTERNAL FRAMES OF REFERENCE

An institution in which a therapist practices may support a frame of reference that is external to the needs of clients or that may actually undermine or invalidate the value system that underlies unstructured group therapy. An advantage for a group conducted in a private practice setting is that the therapist is not influenced by the agenda or frame of reference of a larger institution. Institutions may believe that certain other (perhaps contrasting) agendas are important to the functioning of the institution.

For example, institutions often wish to encourage conformity and predictability in the behavior and attitudes of a population and therefore find that various forms of pressure and coercion are necessary. This use of pressure reflects an ethical system based on tributive justice, which can be the rule rather than the exception in some institutional settings. Group leaders who work in settings that stress the control or conformity of behavior of the population they are serving need to be able to adhere to the values inherent in doing unstructured group therapy (such as client confidentiality) while at the same time abiding by the rules of an institution or agency. This may make doing group therapy in certain settings difficult or perhaps impossible. Oftentimes the people who have power in institutional or agency settings can permit therapists to conduct unstructured therapy groups without compromising the rules of their particular locale. One set of rules can apply to what goes on in a group and the outside milieu can have its own set of rules and policies. Often the group leader may have to negotiate with authorities concerning how the unstructured group can operate within certain settings and still maintain the integrity of its focus.

This kind of negotiation may be necessary in a penal institution, where the administrators may believe that inmates have lost their rights to autonomy, self-determination, and choice. A group leader may attempt to conduct an unstructured therapy group in an institution where members are not given many opportunities to assume responsibility. To function as a therapist in such an institution requires an ability to reconcile a therapeutic frame of reference with a relatively authoritarian one. This reconciliation requires an awareness of interacting social systems and an ability to work with administrators to set up an unstructured therapy group that meets the needs of inmates and that does not compromise the values and ethical principles inherent in doing effective group therapy (see Page, 1981).

As they apply their theory, group therapy practitioners often need to learn how their frame of reference can be integrated with the frames of reference of other professionals. For instance, a therapist who advocates the promotion of awareness and responsibility may have to accommodate others in an institution who believe that clients' problems are biologically based and thus outside the realm of personal responsibility (Matano and Yalom, 1991). While genetic heritage may influence an individual's behavior and psychological problems, genetic influences do not preclude an individual's movement towards integration in awareness and relationships. Awareness and responsibility function interdependently with physical systems because a person exists as a meaningful whole. The concerns of an unstructured group therapist do not necessarily have to conflict with concerns of professionals who investigate specifically biological aspects of functioning.

## POLITICAL IMPLICATIONS OF THERAPEUTIC PRACTICE

As we have stated, the integrated system that is a person includes chemistry, biology, perception, affect, cognition, action, and interactions in social systems and ecological systems. The person is more than the sum of these subsystems. A person's unique individuality can only be partly known by understanding the contexts and systems within which the person forms an identity and contributes behaviorally. Besides systems and subsystems, individuals are formed by their decisions, perceptions, values, and self-definitions.

We have seen how unstructured therapy groups can encourage the exploration of experience rather than necessarily submitting to others' ideas about who a person is or can become. The idea that group members are capable of creatively authoring their own lives may conflict with the teachings of their religions or the patterns of relationship in their families. Institutions, organizations, and families may have an

171

investment in maintaining people in positions where they do not have personal power, do not perceive themselves as potentially powerful, and do not recognize their abilities for creativity and self-determination. Thus, the application of a theory of unstructured group therapy inevitably has political overtones.

For example, unstructured therapy groups are unlikely to be sponsored or recommended by a religious institution that encourages its members to view people as sinners, that expects members to unquestioningly accept religious injunctions as a matter of faith, and that reacts with suspicion toward individuals' desires to be self-responsible beings. Similarly, an addictions treatment facility will generally not use unstructured therapy if that facility views addicts as people who need to be forced to conform or to be brainwashed into changing deviant lifestyles or behavior (Yablonsky, 1965).

The process of unstructured group therapy is not congruent with the process of authoritarian family structures or totalitarian political systems. The process by which members reach decisions and the rules for expressing feelings and ideas differ because the need for authoritarian leadership is questioned by the very format of unstructured therapy. Members of authoritarian families, political parties, or cultural subgroups can sometimes benefit from participation in unstructured groups but they should realize that their group experience will probably take place in a different political and ethical environment than they experience in their ordinary lives.

The application of unstructured therapy theory to actual situations must account for the possibility that participants live in an environment that will resist their recognition of responsibility and the development of a personally valid frame of reference for evaluating experiences. Members may need to use their group as a source of support for reconciliation between what they are learning about themselves in their group in comparison with what they need to do to survive outside. Members can often help each other to learn about how to conduct themselves successfully within external social systems by providing useful feedback to one another that assists the formation of constructive directions outside of a therapy group.

## UNSTRUCTURED GROUP THERAPY IN CROSS-CULTURAL SETTINGS

The concept that human existence involves ontological dynamics inherent in any individual's process of being suggests that unstructured therapy can be useful across cultures. Person-centered theory, which stresses certain core conditions involved in individuals' ways of being, has led to the formation of unstructured groups in Japan (Murayama, Nojima and Abe, 1988), South Africa (Hill-Hain and Rogers, 1988), South America (Wood, 1982) and various countries in Europe (Lietaer, 1994; McIlduff and Coghlan, 1989). Research on the attitude changes associated with an unstructured training group among psychology students in Ireland has shown the effectiveness of these groups (Page and O'Leary, 1992). One of the authors has also led several unstructured therapy groups in Finland that contained psychology student members from many different European countries who were being trained to use these groups; the participants evaluated their group experiences positively after the groups were completed. The dialogues created in these unstructured groups demonstrate that persons can participate in meaningful interactions that reveal differences and universalities within and across cultures. This learning is not independent of culture, but it potentially applies within any culture constructed by human beings (Page, 1983a; Page, Weiss and Lietaer, 2002).

When members from different cultures meet in an unstructured group, they can learn about each other's world-views and cultures (see McIlduff and Coghlan, 1989). If members are willing to learn about and from others with different cultural backgrounds, then unstructured therapy groups can promote the increased cross-cultural awareness of the participants. Members can learn that abilities to care and understand are not limited to the members of certain cultures and that they can gain awareness about themselves and their own culture by interacting with people who are culturally different. They can also learn that certain basic human concerns (such as relationship problems or adjusting to the death of a loved one) exist regardless of one's culture.

No single culture or subculture has the final word about the meaning of human life and human relationships. Individuals can use a group made up of culturally different members to question their own or others' cultures, or to explore what their culture means to them and others. In unstructured groups, participants often learn that their assumptions and stereotypes about people who live in other cultures are not useful for predicting the reactions of their specific representatives. The uniqueness of individuals, as well as the influence of cultures, tends to be expressed during group interactions. Even when participants are all from the same background or culture and assume that everyone in their group shares the same values, this assumption is usually shown to be incorrect if members develop enough trust to share their true feelings about different life situations.

## IMPLICATIONS OF UNSTRUCTURED GROUP THEORY FOR SOCIAL DYNAMICS

The dynamics of unstructured group therapy, as they have been discussed in this book, have implications for patterns of interpersonal relationships in the larger society. The ontological elements of love, power, and justice operate in families, business corporations, schools, international organizations, and in all other social institutions, human groups, and relationships. The discussion of how the members of a therapy group can grow toward integrated interpersonal and intrapersonal dynamics has implications for how relationships in other settings can develop toward creative justice and mutual acceptance and empowerment.

We are all aware that the current historical epoch is a time of rapid change. Some of these changes include the increasing importance of information-processing technologies, a more globally integrated economic structure, and worldwide political changes that are increasingly emphasizing the importance of individuals and various aspects of freedom (Naisbett and Aburdene, 1990). Human relationships are currently in transition within and across cultures in ways that are effecting rapid changes in political structures, vocational and economic structures, family structures, and ideas of personhood. Unfortunately, some of these changes are also exacerbating conflicts between different cultures and countries as evidenced by the current unstable situation in the Middle East and other parts of the world and by the global effects of terrorism and the war against terrorism. It should be remembered, however, that in spite of these conflicts, some global changes are tending to associate more power and responsibility with individuals and less power with traditional structures and traditional authorities.

Thus, traditional roles for women are changing; minorities are questioning cultural stereotypes that have prevailed in the past; democratic decision-making has grown in importance for many families and societies; and some corporations now attempt to allow workers' viewpoints to be included in decision-making processes. At the same time, of course, many families and societies adhere to rigid roles, many businesses are run autocratically, and many religions and cultures continue to rely on traditional models based on a central authority figure. Although the current epoch involves transition and questioning for many people, many others wish to resist the uncertainty of change and the ambiguity of transition.

The model that we have proposed for unstructured group therapy is one that values the principle of change and accepts uncertainty and ambiguity as part of the process. Predetermined outcomes or goals are viewed as less important than is integration within ongoing process. Constructive change can occur according to this model in ways that people experience as unexpected, spontaneous, or serendipitous; it can also occur through interactive and self-reflective processes. Recognition of individual responsibility for creating change and determining goals occurs as members support each other's abilities to function responsibly.

This perspective can be extended to the dynamics of families, businesses, and social institutions. In principle, maximal development of individual potentials and integration of diverse human elements will occur if people in various settings recognize themselves and others as responsible and nonexpendable. The principle that individuals are nonexpendable means that effective social systems accept and encourage the potential ability of each member of the system to contribute constructively. Social systems are most adequate when they provide members with opportunities to exercise their abilities to learn from experience in an atmosphere of freedom and to have some responsibility for determining what occurs within the system.

## IMPLICATIONS OF UNSTRUCTURED GROUP THEORY
## FOR FAMILIES

Family relationships provide a symbolic and emotional foundation for people's later learning about the dynamics of love, power, and justice. For example, the form of justice learned in a family context can later be used by individuals to regulate their conceptualizations of others and their responses to perceived emotional demands made in close relationships. Similar learning occurs about needs, wishes, and expressions of love and power. Some of the problems that members work on in unstructured therapy groups involve recognizing and changing patterns of love, power, and justice that were first experienced in their families. Unstructured therapy groups can challenge members to use their growing awareness of past dynamics to experiment with new roles and dynamics.

Within a given family all the members are not likely to have equal power or to express love equivalently or to employ the same mode of justice. For instance, children and adults often have unequal power and assert themselves differently within a family. Nonetheless, each family member has an influence on the total gestalt of love, power, and justice within ongoing relations. The impact of this gestalt will have a continuing effect on each of the family's members and can influence how they unconsciously and consciously create future relationships. Members in therapeutic groups often experience growth if they are able to acknowledge decisions they have made to create splits in awareness or to identify with negative self-images. They are more likely to acknowledge their roles within painful family dynamics if they feel emotionally supported by others in their group.

## CREATIVELY JUST SOCIAL SYSTEMS

Businesses, religious organizations, and political parties operate according to principles that can acknowledge, distort, or deny interbeing. The structures that people create within organizations reflect their decisions concerning how responsible and interconnected individuals will be allowed to be within these milieus. Individuals create power hierarchies that contribute to determining the form of justice that regulates interaction in different settings. Love may be permissible as an expression only in particular situations and following specific limits and guidelines.

Decision making in organizations often is designed to occur in a strictly 'top-down' fashion. Those who are at the bottom of a social hierarchy frequently have little or no decision-making power and regularly are expected to abide by the decisions of others. Responsibility may only be associated with those at the top of the hierarchy. Systems that allow input from those who have less power within the organization generally function as more open structures with more flexible forms of justice. If 'ground-up' decision making is acknowledged as valuable in a family or business, the social structure will allow for a greater awareness of mutual responsibility.

Both families and businesses generally require some kind of power hierarchy based on divisions of labor, access to resources, and abilities to influence events. The power hierarchy is always associated with the form of justice being employed. One means to gain awareness of the form of justice used by a family or business is to examine how influential decisions are made and how key policies are determined and implemented. If coercion and threats are commonly used to implement decisions, a 'disintegrated' system is evidenced, and love then functions separately from power. If people who are affected by decisions are involved in making them, love is more likely to function in alignment with power.

Integration of love, power, and justice involves understanding the unique needs of all of the individuals within a social system and accommodating those needs in as equitable a manner as possible. If social systems function according to the perception that the welfare of an organization is associated with increasing the potential empowerment and awareness of each member, then they move towards creative justice. Such systems function to make the most of existing possibilities for learning and growth. Members within such systems are expected to contribute constructively to others, not out of fear, but out of awareness of mutual benefit and responsibility. Love is assumed to be as important as power in creatively just systems.

As it moves towards creative justice, a social system becomes increasingly able to accommodate and respond to the changing needs and goals of members and subgroups. Novel challenges are addressed creatively in an atmosphere that fosters full and open communication and an assessment of resources. A creatively just system is not designed to perpetuate itself beyond its usefulness or to maintain its norms by avoiding or repressing evidence that does not fit its definitions of reality.

At the time of this writing, the creatively just society represents a goal toward which we can move, rather than a reality that we have established. Many world events are working against rather than for the establishment of creatively just societies in different countries. It is beyond the scope of this book to examine the specific social and cultural events that have marked movement toward or away from creative justice. For the present, we can simply observe that individuals and nations have struggled historically with themes of fragmentation and reunification, empowerment of certain groups and the disempowerment of others, and changes in the forms of justice that regulate decision making and the allocation of resources.

The theory of unstructured group therapy is an attempt to describe a pattern of relationship that can be utilized in therapy settings but which can also potentially be employed at a societal or international level. Members of therapy groups often are able to create an environment wherein people can learn from each other without imposing their values on one another. In this kind of situation, participants can learn to acknowledge and express conflict constructively and can recognize their mutual responsibility to assist each other's mutual empowerment. Members of therapeutic groups can learn to be their own authorities for determining directions and values.

# Application of Theory

Throughout the world, millions of people are crying out for justice in a variety of contexts. Individuals who enter therapy are not different in quality from these millions, and each client brings an inimitable life and a unique demand for justice. The struggle of those who participate in unstructured therapy groups does not represent an attempt to change the world. This form of therapy, however, does offer the possibility that people can change themselves and then can help others change by using their newly found abilities to listen, offer what is needed, and accept what is given.

Individuals who participate in these groups may have observed members face up to and change past patterns of relationship. Other members may have realized that it is possible to accept and to be accepted by others. If members have experienced a degree of healing or a rejuvenation of hope, they may extend these changes to other relationships in their lives. The unstructured therapy group can provide a psychological environment wherein faith in the possibilities of human existence and interpersonal interaction can be reaffirmed. If a group is effective, members can take small steps (and even large ones) in the direction of personal and collective integration.

# REFERENCES

Adler, A (1969) *The Practice and Theory of Individual Psychology*. Paterson, NJ: Littlefield.

Adler, A (1972) *The Neurotic Constitution*. Freeport, NY: Books for Libraries Press.

Agazarian, YM (1992) Contemporary theories of group therapy: A systems approach to the group-as-a-whole. *International Journal of Group Psychotherapy, 42*, 177–294.

Alexander, F (1961) *The Scope of Psychoanalysis*. New York: Basic Books.

Applbaum, RL, Bodaken, EM, Sereno, K and Anatol, KW (1974) *The Process of Group Communication*. Chicago, IL: Science Research Associates.

Arnett, RC (1989) What is dialogic communication? *Person-Centered Review, 4*, 42–60.

Aubrey, M and Dougher, MJ (1990) Ethical issues in outpatient group therapy with sex offenders. *The Journal for Specialists in Group Work, 15*, 75–82.

Bacal, HA (1985) Object-relations in the group from the perspective of self psychology. *International Journal of Group Psychotherapy, 35*, 483–501.

Bach, GR (1957) Observations on transference and object relations in the light of group dynamics. *International Journal of Group Psychotherapy, 7*, 64–76.

Barrett-Lennard, G (1985) The helping relationship: Crisis and advance in theory and research. *Counseling Psychologist, 13*, 279–94.

Bateson, G, Jackson, DD, Haley, J and Weakland, JH (1956) Toward a theory of schizophrenia. *Behavior Science, 1*, 251–64.

Becker, E (1973) *The Denial of Death*. New York: The Free Press.

Berkow, D and Page, RC (2000) Asian psychological approaches and Western therapy. In M MacLachlan (ed), *Cultivating Health: Cultural perspectives on promoting health*. (pp 91–113). London, England: John Wiley and Sons.

Berne, E (1961) *Transactional Analysis in Psychotherapy*. New York: Grove Press.

Berne, E (1964) *Games People Play*. New York: Grove Press.

Berne, E (1966) *Principles of Group Treatment*. New York: Oxford University Press.

Berry, CE (1991) Self psychology and its relationship to the practice of group psychotherapy. *International Journal of Group Psychotherapy, 41*, 523–32.

Bion, WR (1959) *Experiences in Groups*. New York: Ballantine Books.

Bonney, WC (1974) The maturation of groups. *Small Group Behavior, 5*, 445–61.

Bozarth, JD (1981) The person-centered approach in the large community group. In GM Gazda (ed), *Innovations to Group Psychotherapy* (2nd ed, pp 100–33). Springfield, IL: Charles C Thomas.

Bozarth, JD (1984) Beyond reflection: Emergent modes of empathy. In RF Levant and JM Schlien (eds), *Client-Centered Therapy and the Person-Centered Approach* (pp 59–75). New York: Praeger.

Bozarth, J (1986) The basic encounter group: An alternative view. *Journal for Specialists in Group Work, 11*, 228–32.

Bozarth, J (1998) *Person-Centered Therapy: A revolutionary paradigm*. Ross-on-Wye, UK: PCCS Books.

Bozarth, JD, Zimring, FN and Tausch, R (2002) Client-Centered Therapy: The evolution of a revolution. In DJ Cain and J Seeman, (eds), *Humanistic Psychotherapies: Handbook of research and practice* (pp 147–88). American Psychological Association: Washington, DC.

Buber, M (1957) *Pointing the Way*. New York: Harper and Row.

Buber, M (1970) *I and Thou* (W Kaufmann, trans). New York: Charles Scribner and Sons.

Bugental, JFT (1978) *Psychotherapy and Process: The fundamentals of an existential-humanistic approach*. Menlo Park, CA: Addison-Wesley.

Burnand, G (1990) Group development phases as working through six fundamental human problems. *Small Group Research, 21*, 255–73.

Cain, D (1989) The paradox of non-directiveness in the person-centered approach. *Person-Centered Review, 4*, 123–31.

Chang, C (1963) *Creativity and Taoism*. New York: Julian Press.

Chang, R and Page, RC (1991) The characteristics of the self actualized person: Visions from the East and West. *Counseling and Values, 36*, 2–10.

Cheng, M and Smith, RW (1967) *T'ai Chi*. Rutland, VT: Charles E Tuttle.

Cohen, AM and Smith, RD (1976) *The Critical Incident in Growth Groups: Theory and technique*. La Jolla, CA: University Associates, Inc.

Combs, AW and Snygg, D (1959) *Individual Behavior: A perceptual approach*. New York: Harper and Row.

Corey, G (1990) *Theory and Practice of Group Counseling* (3rd ed). Pacific Grove, CA: Brooks/Cole.

Corey, G (1991) *Theory and Practice of Counseling and Psychotherapy*. Pacific Grove, CA: Brooks/Cole.

Corey, G and Corey, MS (1987) *Groups: Process and practice*. (3rd ed). Pacific Grove, CA: Brooks/Cole.

Cushman, P (1989) Iron fists/velvet gloves: A study of a mass marathon psychology training. *Psychotherapy, 26*, 23–39.

Daniels, M (1988) The myth of self-actualization. *Journal of Humanistic Psychology, 28*, 7–38.

# References

Egan, G (1970) *Encounter: Group processes for interpersonal growth*. Belmont, CA: Brooks/Cole.

Foulkes, SH (1948) *Introduction to Group-Analytic Psychotherapy*. London: W Heinemann.

Foulkes, SH (1951) Concerning leadership in group-analytic psychotherapy. *International Journal of Group Psychotherapy, 1,* 319–29.

Foulkes, SH (1953) Some similarities between psychoanalytic principles and group analytic principles. *British Journal of Medical Psychology, 26,* 30–5.

Foulkes, SH (1957) Group-analytic dynamics with specific reference to psychoanalytic concepts. *International Journal of Group Psychotherapy, 7,* 40–52.

Foulkes, SH (1975) *Group Analytic Psychotherapy*. Paris, France: Interfare Books.

Foulkes, SH and Lewis, E (1944) Group analysis: A study in the treatment of groups on psycho-analytic lines. *British Journal of Medical Psychology, 20,* 175–84.

Frank, J (1963) *Persuasion and Healing: A comparative study of psychotherapy*. New York: Schocken Books.

Frankl, V (1963) *Man's Search for Meaning*. New York: Washington Square Press.

Frankl, V (1965) *The Doctor and the Soul*. New York: Bantam Books.

Frankl, V (1966) Self-transcendence as a human phenomenon. *Journal of Humanistic Psychology, 6,* 97–107.

Frankl, V (1969) *The Will to Meaning: Foundations and applications of logotherapy*. New York: New American Library.

Freud, S (1948) *Group Psychology and the Analysis of the Ego*. London: Hogarth Press. (Original work published 1921).

Freud, S (1953a) Inhibitions, symptoms and anxiety. In J Strachey (ed), *The Standard Edition of the Complete Psychological Works*. London: Hogarth Press. (Original work published 1926).

Freud, S (1953b) Instincts and their vicissitudes. In J Strachey (ed), *The Standard Edition of the Complete Psychological Works*. London: Hogarth Press. (Original work published 1934).

Freud, S (1955) Beyond the pleasure principle. In J Strachey (ed), *The Standard Edition of the Complete Psychological Works*. London: Hogarth Press. (Original work published 1920).

Freud, S (1961) Civilization and its discontents. In J Strachey (ed), *The Standard Edition of the Complete Psychological Works*. London: Hogarth Press. (Original work published 1930).

Freud, S (1962) *The Ego and the Id*. New York: Norton. (Original work published 1923).

Freud, S (1964) An outline of psychoanalysis. In J Strachey (ed), *The Standard Edition of the Complete Psychological Works*. London: Hogarth Press. (Original work published 1940).

Frick, WB (1990) The symbolic growth experience: A heuristic inquiry and a quest for synthesis. *Journal of Humanistic Psychology, 30*, 64–80.

Friedman, M (1963) Dialogue and the 'essential we'—the basis of values in the philosophy of Martin Buber. In M Rosenbaum and M Berger (eds), *Group Psychotherapy and Group Function* (pp 604–13). New York: Basic Books.

Friedman, M (1986) Carl Rogers and Martin Buber: Self-actualization and dialogue. *Person-Centered Review, 1*, 409–35.

Friedman, M (1992) *Dialogue and the Human Image: Beyond humanistic psychology.* Newbury Park, CA: Sage.

Fromm, E (1956) *The Art of Loving.* New York: Harper.

Fromm, E (1964) *Escape from Freedom.* New York: Avon Books.

Fromm, E, Suzuki, DT and DeMartino, R (1960) *Zen Buddhism and Psychoanalysis.* New York: Harper and Row.

Fung, YL (1948) *A Short History of Chinese Philosophy.* New York: Macmillan.

Gans, JS (1989) Hostility in group psychotherapy. *International Journal of Group Psychotherapy, 39*, 499–516.

Ganzarain, R (1992) Introduction to object relations group psychotherapy. *International Journal of Group Psychotherapy, 42*, 205–23.

Garfield, SL and Bergin, AE (eds) (1986) *Handbook of Psychotherapy and Behavior Change* (3rd ed). New York: Wiley.

Geller, L (1984) Another look at self-actualization. *Journal of Humanistic Psychology, 24*, 93–106.

Gemmill, G (1986) The dynamics of the group shadow in intergroup relations. *Small Group Behavior, 17*, 229–40.

Gemmill, G (1989) The dynamics of scapegoating in small groups. *Small Group Behavior, 20*, 406–18.

Gemmill, G and Wynkoop, C (1991) The psychodynamics of small group transformation. *Small Group Research, 22*, 4–23.

George, RL (1990) *Counseling the Chemically Dependent: Theory and practice.* Englewood Cliffs, NJ: Prentice-Hall.

Girardot, NJ (1983) *Myth and Meaning in Early Taoism.* Berkeley, CA: University of California Press.

Goble, F (1971) *The Third Force.* New York: Pocket Books.

Greenson, RR (1967) *The Technique and Practice of Psychoanalysis.* New York: International Universities Press.

Hawkins, PJ (1997) Psychodynamic psychotherapy. In OJ Hawkins and JN Nestoros (eds), *Psychotherapy: New perspectives on theory, practice, and research* (pp 97–130). Athens, Greece: Ellinika Grammata Publications.

Hill, WF (1965) *HIM: Hill Interaction Matrix.* Los Angeles, CA: University of Southern California.

Hill, WF (1969) *Hill Interaction Matrix Supplement.* Pomona, CA: California State Polytechnic Institute.

# References

Hill-Hain, A and Rogers, CR (1988) A dialogue with Carl Rogers: Cross-cultural challenges of facilitating person-centered groups in South Africa. *Journal for Specialists in Group Work, 13*, 62–9.

Janis, IL (1982) *Groupthink: Psychological studies of policy decisions and fiascoes.* Boston: Houghton Mifflin.

Johnson, JA (1963) *Group Therapy: A practical approach.* New York: McGraw-Hill.

Jourard, SM (1971) *The Transparent Self.* New York: Van Nostrand Reinhold.

Jung, CG (1916) *Analytical Psychology.* New York: Moffat, Yard.

Jung, CG (1933) *Modern Man in Search of a Soul.* New York: Harcourt, Brace and World.

Jung, CG (1956) *Two Essays on Analytical Psychology.* New York: Meridian Books.

Jung, CG (1958) Psychology and religion. In *Collected Works (Vol 11)*. Princeton, NJ: Princeton University Press.

Jung, CG (1964) *Man and His Symbols.* New York: Doubleday.

Jung, CG (1968) The archetypes and the collective unconscious. *Collected Works (Vol 91)*. Princeton, New Jersey: Princeton University Press. (Original work published 1936).

Kaplan, RE (1985) Some hidden elements of control in group facilitation: Appreciating the bounded and binding aspects of openness. *Small Group Behavior, 16*, 462–76.

Kapur, R and Pearce, M (1987) Group psychotherapy with the elderly. *British Journal of Psychotherapy, 3*, 289–96.

Kitchener, KS and Harding, SD (1990) Dual role relationships. In B Herlihy and LB Golden (eds) *Ethical Standards Casebook* (pp 146–54). Alexandria, VA: American Association for Counseling and Development.

Kohut, H (1971) *The Analysis of the Self.* New York: International Universities Press.

Kohut, H (1977) *The Restoration of the Self.* New York: International Universities Press.

Kohut, H and Wolf, ES (1978) The disorders of the self and their treatment: An outline. *International Journal of Psychoanalysis, 59*, 413–25.

Korb, M, Gorrell, J and Van De Riet, V (1989) *Gestalt Therapy: An introduction.* New York: Pergamon Press.

Korda, LJ and Pancrazio, JL (1989) Limiting negative outcome in group practice. *Journal for Specialists in Group Work, 14*, 112–20.

Kübler-Ross, E (1975) *Death: The final stage of growth.* Englewood Cliff, NJ: Prentice-Hall.

Kwiatkowski, RM (1987) The psychotic adolescent in the group. *British Journal of Psychotherapy, 4*, 23–9.

Lao Tzu (1963) Tao-te Ching. In WT Chan (ed and trans), *A Source Book in Chinese Philosophy* (pp 139–76). Princeton, NJ: Princeton University Press. (Original work published in 600 BC).

Leszcz, M (1990) Towards an integrated model of group psychotherapy with the elderly. *International Journal of Group Psychotherapy, 40,* 379–99.

Leszcz, M (1992) The interpersonal approach to group psychotherapy. *International Journal of Group Psychotherapy, 42,* 37–62.

Lethbridge, D (1986) A Marxist theory of self-actualization. *Journal of Humanistic Psychology, 26,* 84–103.

Lewis, JA, Dana, RQ and Blevins, GA (1988) *Substance Abuse Counseling: An individualized approach.* Pacific Grove, CA: Brooks/Cole.

Lieberman, MA, Lakin, M and Whitaker, DS (1969) Problems and potential of psychoanalytic and group-dynamic theories for group psychotherapy. *International Journal of Group Psychotherapy, 19,* 131–41.

Lietaer, G (1994) Authenticity, congruence and transparency. In D Brazier (ed), *Beyond Carl Rogers* (pp 17–46). London: Constable.

Maddi, SR (1985) Existential psychotherapy. In SJ Lynn and JP Garske (eds), *Contemporary Psychotherapies* (pp 191–220). Columbus, OH: Charles E Merrill.

Mahler, M (1968) *On Human Symbiosis and the Vicissitudes of Individuation.* New York: International Universities Press.

Mahoney, MJ (1990) *Human Change Processes: The scientific foundations of psychotherapy.* New York: Basic Books.

Maslow, AH (1962) *Toward a Psychology of Being.* New York: Van Nostrand.

Maslow, AH (1964) *Religions, Values and Peak Experiences.* Columbus, OH: Ohio State University Press.

Matano, RA and Yalom, ID (1991) Approaches to chemical dependency: Chemical dependency and interactive group therapy—a synthesis. *International Journal of Group Psychotherapy, 41,* 269–93.

May, R (1969) *Love and Will.* New York: Norton.

May, R (1972) *Power and Innocence.* New York: Norton.

May, R (1977) *The Meaning of Anxiety* (revised ed). New York: Norton.

May, R (1981) *Freedom and Destiny.* New York: Norton.

May, R and Yalom, ID (1984) Existential psychotherapy. In RJ Corsini (ed), *Current Psychotherapies* (3rd ed) (pp 354–91). Itasca, IL: FE Peacock.

McClure, BA (1987) Metaphoric illumination in groups. *Small Group Behavior, 18,* 179–87.

McClure, BA (1990) The group mind: Generative and regressive groups. *Journal for Specialists in Group Work, 15,* 159–70.

McIlduff, E and Coghlan, D (1989) Process and facilitation in a cross-cultural communication workshop. *Person-Centered Review, 4,* 77–98.

Meador, BD and Rogers, CR (1984) Person-centered therapy. In RJ Corsini (ed), *Current Psychotherapies* (3rd ed) (pp 142–95). Itasca, IL: FE Peacock.

Moreno, JL (1947) *Theatre of Spontaneity: An introduction to psychodrama.* Beacon, NY: Beacon House.

Moreno, JL (1964) *Psychodrama: Volume 1* (3rd ed). New York: Beacon House.

Moreno, ZT (1965) Psychodrama rules, techniques, and adjunctive methods. *Group*

*Psychotherapy, 18,* 73–86.

Mosak, HH (1984) Adlerian psychotherapy. In RJ Corsini (ed), *Current Psychotherapies,* (3rd ed) (pp 56–107). Itasca, IL: FE Peacock.

Murayama, S, Nojima, K and Abe, T (1988) Person-centered groups in Japan: A selective review of the literature. *Person-Centered Review, 3,* 479–92.

Naisbett, J and Aburdene, P (1990) *Megatrends 2000: Ten new directions for the 1990s.* New York: Morrow.

Napier, RW and Gershenfeld, MK (1987) *Groups: Theory and Experience* (4th ed). Boston: Houghton Mifflin.

O'Hara, MM (1984) Person-centered gestalt: Toward a holistic synthesis. In RF Levant and JM Schlien (eds), *Client-Centered Therapy and the Person-Centered Approach* (pp 203–21). New York: Praeger.

O'Hara, MM and Wood, JK (1983) Patterns of awareness: Consciousness and the group mind. *The Gestalt Journal, 2,* 103–16.

O'Leary, E (1992) *Gestalt Therapy: Theory, practice and research.* London: Chapman and Hall.

O'Leary, E and Keane, N (1997) Person-centered therapy. In OJ Hawkins and JN Nestoros (eds), *Psychotherapy: New perspectives on theory, practice, and research* (pp 131–46). Athens, Greece: Ellinika Grammata Publications.

O'Leary, E and O'Connor, K (1997) Gestalt therapy. In OJ Hawkins and JN Nestoros (eds), *Psychotherapy: New perspectives on theory, practice, and research* (pp 147–70). Athens, Greece: Ellinika Grammata Publications.

Page, RC (1978) The social learning process of severely disabled group counseling participants. *Psychosocial Rehabilitation Journal, 2,* 28–36.

Page, RC (1979) Developmental stages of unstructured groups with prisoners. *Small Group Behavior, 10,* 271–9.

Page, RC (1980) Marathon groups: Counseling the imprisoned drug abuser. *International Journal of the Addictions, 15,* 765–70.

Page, RC (1981) Client rights and agency demands: The ethical tightrope of the offender counselor. *Counseling and Values, 26,* 55–62.

Page, RC (1982) Marathon group therapy with users of illicit drugs: Dimensions of social learning. *International Journal of the Addictions, 17,* 1107–15.

Page, RC (1983a) Marathon group counseling with illicit drug abusers: A study of the effects of two groups for one month. *Journal for Specialists in Group Work, 8,* 114–25.

Page, RC (1983b) The cross cultural implications of unstructured group therapy. *Counsellor, 1,* 20–30.

Page, RC (1984) Unstructured group therapy. In Raymond Corsini (ed), *Wiley Encyclopedia of Psychology, Vol 3,* (pp 451–2). New York: John Wiley and Sons.

Page, RC (1985) The effects of marathon groups on the ways illicit drug users perceive counseling. *International Journal of the Addictions, 20,* 1683–92.

Page, RC and Berkow, D (1991) Concepts of the self: Western and Eastern perspectives. *Journal of Multicultural Counseling and Development, 19*, 83–93.

Page, RC and Bridges, N (1983) The interpersonal relationship styles of illicit drug users participating in marathon group therapy. *Small Group Behavior, 14*, 253–9.

Page, RC and Chang, R (1989) A comparison of Gestalt therapy and Zen Buddhist concepts of awareness. *Psychologia, 32*, 33–9.

Page, RC and O'Leary, E (1992) A pilot study on the effects of a training group on Irish counseling students. *Journal of Multicultural Counseling and Development, 20*, 23–34.

Page, RC and Wills, J (1983) Marathon group counseling with illicit drug users: Analysis of content. *Journal for Specialists in Group Work, 8*, 67–76.

Page, RC, Campbell, L, and Wilder, DC (1994) Role of the leader in therapy groups conducted with illicit drug abusers: How directive does the leader have to be? *Journal of Addictions and Offender Counseling, 14*, 57–66.

Page, RC, Davis, KC, Berkow, DN and O'Leary, E (1989) Analysis of group process in marathon group therapy with users of illicit drugs. *Small Group Behavior, 29*, 220–7.

Page, RC, Richmond, BO and DeLaSerna, M (1987) Marathon group counseling with illicit drug abusers: Effects on self perceptions. *Small Group Behavior, 18*, 483–97.

Page, RC, Weiss, JF and Lietaer, G (2002) Humanistic group psychotherapy. In DJ Cain and J Seeman, (eds), *Humanistic Psychotherapies: Handbook of research and practice.* (pp 339–68). American Psychological Association: Washington, DC.

Page, RC, Weiss, JF, Stowers Wright, L, McAuliffe, E, Ugyan, J and MacLachlan, M (1998) Self-awareness of participants in a long-term Tibetan retreat. *Journal of Transpersonal Psychology, 29*, 85–98.

Patterson, CH (1980) *Theories of Counseling and Psychotherapy.* New York: Harper and Row.

Patterson, CH (1985) *The Therapeutic Relationship: Foundations for an eclectic psychotherapy.* Belmont, CA: Brooks/Cole.

Patterson, LE and Eisenberg, S (1975) *The Counseling Process.* Boston: Houghton Mifflin.

Perls, F (1969) *Gestalt Therapy Verbatim.* Lafayette, CA: Real People Press.

Perls, F (1971) *In and Out of the Garbage Pail.* New York: Bantam Books.

Perls, F (1973) *The Gestalt Approach and Eyewitness to Therapy.* New York: Bantam Books.

Perls, F, Hefferline, R and Goodman, P (1980) *Gestalt Therapy: Excitement and growth in the human personality.* New York: Bantam Books. (Original work published 1951).

Perls, L (1992) Concepts and misconceptions of gestalt therapy. *Journal of Humanistic Psychology, 32*, 50–6.

# References

Polster, E and Polster, M (1973) *Gestalt Therapy Integrated*. New York: Vintage Books.

Rank, O (1945) *Will Therapy and Truth and Reality*. New York: Alfred A Knopf.

Roback, HB, Purdon, SE, Ochoa, E and Bloch, F (1992). Confidentiality dilemmas in group psychotherapy. *Small Group Research, 23*, 169–84.

Rogers, CR (1951) *Client-Centered Therapy*. Boston: Houghton Mifflin.

Rogers, CR (1961) *On Becoming a Person*. Boston: Houghton Mifflin.

Rogers, CR (1967a) Some learnings from a study of psychotherapy with schizophrenics. In CR Rogers, B Stevens, T Gendlin, JM Shlein and W Van Dusen (eds), *Person to Person: The problem of being human* (pp 181–92). Lafayette, CA: Real People Press.

Rogers, CR (1967b) The interpersonal relationship: The core of guidance. In CR Rogers, B Stevens, T Gendlin, JM Shlein and W Van Dusen (eds), *Person to Person: The problem of being human* (pp 89–103) Lafayette, CA: Real People Press.

Rogers, CR (1970) *On Encounter Groups*. New York: Harper and Row.

Rogers, CR (1977) *On Personal Power*. New York: Delacorte Press.

Rogers, CR (1980) *A Way of Being*. Boston: Houghton Mifflin.

Rogers, CR (1983) *Freedom to Learn for the 80s*. Columbus, OH: Charles E Merrill.

Rogers, CR (1987) The underlying theory: Drawn from experience with individuals and groups. *Counseling and Values, 32*, 38–46.

Roller, B (1989) Having fun in groups. *Small Group Behavior, 20*, 97–100.

Rossel, RD (1981) Word play: Metaphor and humor in the small group. *Small Group Behavior, 12*, 116–36.

Rubin, TI (1969) *The Angry Book*. New York: Collier Books.

Sartre, JP (1956) *Being and Nothingness*. New York: Philosophical Library.

Scheidlinger, S (1980a) Freud's group psychology. In S Scheidlinger (ed), *Psychoanalytic Group Dynamics: Basic readings* (pp 5–13). New York: International Universities Press.

Scheidlinger, S (1980b) Current psychoanalytic group theory. In S Scheidlinger (ed), *Psychoanalytic Group Dynamics: Basic readings* (pp 285–99). New York: International Universities Press.

Schneider, K (1990) *The Paradoxical Self: Toward an understanding of our contradictory nature*. New York: Insight Books/Plenum Press.

Shepard, M (1975) *Fritz*. New York: EP Dutton and Co.

Shostrom, EL (1976) *Actualizing Therapy*. San Diego, CA: Edits.

Simkin, JS (1976) *Gestalt Therapy Mini-lectures*. Millbrae, CA: Celestial Arts.

Slavson, SR (1951) The dynamics of analytic group psychotherapy. *International Journal of Group Psychotherapy, 1*, 208–17.

Slavson, SR (1953) Common sources of error and confusion in group psychotherapy. *International Journal of Group Psychotherapy, 3*, 3–28.

Slavson, SR (1957) Are there group dynamics in therapy groups? *International Journal of Group Psychotherapy, 7,* 131–54.

Smith, B (1973) On self-actualization: A transambivalent examination of a focal theme in Maslow's psychology. *Journal of Humanistic Psychology, 13,* 17–33.

Strumpfel, U and Goldman, R (2002) Contacting Gestalt therapy. In DJ Cain and J Seeman, (eds), *Humanistic Psychotherapies: Handbook of research and practice.* (pp 189–220). Washington, DC: American Psychological Association.

Suler, JR (1991) The T'ai Chi images: A Taoist model of psychotherapeutic change. *Psychologia, 34,* 18–27.

Szasz, TS (1961) *The Myth of Mental Illness: Foundations of a theory of personal conduct.* New York: Harper and Row.

Tillich, P (1952) *The Courage to Be.* New Haven, CT: Yale University Press.

Tillich, P (1954) *Love, Power, and Justice.* New York: Oxford University Press.

Tillich, P (1955) *The New Being.* New York: Charles Scribner and Sons.

Travis, C (1982) *Anger: The misunderstood emotion.* New York: Simon and Schuster.

Unger, R (1990) Conflict management in group psychotherapy. *Small Group Research, 21,* 349–59.

Vander Kolk, CJ (1985) *Introduction to Group Counseling and Psychotherapy.* Columbus, OH: Charles E Merrill.

Van De Riet, V, Korb, M and Gorrell, J (1980) *Gestalt Therapy: An introduction.* New York: Pergamon Press.

Vaughan, F (1986) *The Inward Arc: Healing and wholeness in psychotherapy and spirituality.* Boston: Shambhala/New Science Library.

Vaughan, F (1991) Spiritual issues in psychotherapy. *The Journal of Transpersonal Psychology, 23,* 105–19.

Walsh, RA and McElwain, B (2002) Existential psychotherapies. In DJ Cain and J Seeman, (eds), *Humanistic Psychotherapies: Handbook of research and practice.* (pp 253–78). Washington, DC: American Psychological Association.

Watts, A (1961) *Psychotherapy East and West.* New York: Pantheon Books.

Watzlawick, P (1990) *Münchausen's Pigtail, or Psychotherapy and 'Reality'.* New York: WW Norton.

Wilber, K (1980) *The Atman Project.* Wheaton, IL: Quest.

Wilson, SR (1988) The 'real self' controversy: Toward an integration of humanistic and interactionist theory. *Journal of Humanistic Psychology, 28,* 39–65.

Winnicott DW (1958) *The Maturational Processes and the Facilitating Environment.* New York: International Universities Press.

Wolf, A and Schwartz, EK (1962) *Psychoanalysis in Groups.* New York: Grune and Stratton.

Wood, JK (1982) Person-centered group therapy. In GM Gazda (ed), *Basic Approaches to Group Psychotherapy and Group Counseling* (3rd ed) (pp 235–75). Springfield, IL: Charles C Thomas.

Yablonsky, L (1965) *Synanon: The tunnel back.* Baltimore, MD: Pelican Books.

Yalom, ID (1980) *Existential Psychotherapy.* New York: Basic Books.

# References

Yalom, ID (1995) *The Theory and Practice of Group Psychotherapy* (2nd ed). New York: Basic Books.

Zimpfer, DG (1992) Group work with adult offenders: An overview. *Journal for Specialists in Group Work, 17*, 54–61.

# INDEX

# Index

# Index

# PCCS Books

The largest list of person-centred titles in the world

www.pccs-books.co.uk

• browse by subject and author •

• pre-publication offers •

• discounts on all orders •

• free p&p in the UK •

• low cost shipping worldwide •